Elementary
School
Science

Elementary
School
Science
why and how

Kenneth D. George
University of Pennsylvania

Maureen A. Dietz
University of Maryland

Eugene C. Abraham
Temple University

Miles A. Nelson
University of Wisconsin

D.C. Heath and Company
Lexington, Massachusetts   Toronto   London

7-18-74

Published simultaneously in Canada.

Printed in the United States of America.

International Standard Book Number: 0-669-83162-X

Library of Congress Catalog Card Number: 73-7670

PREFACE

Before teaching a science lesson, you will have to make three decisions: the objectives to be attained, the methods of attaining those objectives, and the methods of evaluating what is attained.

The first decision is curricular; it requires you to have an understanding of (1) the nature of the learner, (2) the science program, and (3) the relation of the learner to the science program. Objectives are analyzed in Section I of the text.

The second decision is instructional. Sections II and III describe practical teaching tactics and strategies designed to help you attain your objectives. These tactics and strategies should arouse children's curiosity about observations in their environment and help them to make their own "discoveries" about these observations.

Evaluation, the third decision, is the subject of Section IV. Student and teacher performance, as well as the quality of the science program itself, require careful and continuous evaluation by you.

Each section is divided into chapters containing concise topics. Each topic opens with clearly stated objectives and is later followed by a list of activities to help you in achieving the objectives; and resource materials are given to supplement the material in the text.

We hope you will enjoy this book, as well as the companion text, *Science Investigations for Elementary School Teachers.* We believe they will both help you to be an outstanding teacher of science.

CONTENTS

Elementary
School
Science

Objectives of an Elementary School SECTION
Science Program

A basic assumption of the educational enterprise is that what the individual learns in it will be of use to him in his personal, social, and natural environments, now and in the future. The educational institutions must help students to develop content, skills, attitudes, appreciations, and interests that are transferable to other situations and resistant to forgetting.

The world in which we live is always changing. Ideas that were valid yesterday may not seem as valid today or tomorrow. As Ellsworth Obourn says, "Never was the life of man more serious, more precarious, or more challenging. The entire world is having its knowledge, its way of life, its power, and its resources tested. In every nation the wisdom of the common man as well as that of the intellectual leader is challenged to solve day-to-day problems."[1]

During the period after Sputnik I, there was great discontent over school curricula in the United States. Much progress had been made in science and technology, but these advances were not evident in the curricula of the schools. Children were not learning the new science content or being equipped with the necessary skills of a scientific world.

Since that time, the school science programs have been critically examined, especially their objectives and the teaching methods used to attain these objectives. One finding of this examination was that science textbooks were organized around a body of content. Another was that the programs expected students to read these texts, memorize the content, and repeat it on examinations. Still another finding was that teachers thought their role was to present the content of the textbooks through lectures or class discussions, and their major objective was to complete the textbook during the school year. The conclusion of this scrutiny was that the schools were teaching science as if it were only a body of content.

Educators and scientists could not accept this view of science. They reasoned that science is not just content; science also includes the *methods used to generate, organize, and evaluate that content.* Therefore, curricula and textbooks based only on the content of science, and teaching methods stressing the importance of memorizing this content, could not be justified. Programs needed to be developed and teachers had to learn how to present science so that it was not just a body of content, but also the methods used to generate, organize, and evaluate that content.

How can science in the elementary school help the child today, tomorrow, and in the future? Why should science be taught in the elementary school? Why not wait until the child reaches high school, where the teachers are better prepared to teach science? More time and money, it is argued, could then be spent on the elementary school's reading and mathematics programs. But research in developmental psychology and science education has given us a fundamental reason why science should be a part of the child's elementary school program: science can provide the child with some of the experiences necessary for the attainment of *formal thought,* a topic that has been the subject of research of one of the world's leading psychologists, Jean Piaget. That is, science can provide

[1] Ellsworth S. Obourn, "Science as a Way of Life," in *Readings in Science Education for the Elementary Schools,* ed. Edward Victor and Marjorie S. Lerner (New York: The Macmillan Co., 1967), p. 5.

FIGURE I-1
Jean Piaget.

experiences in analyzing a problem, isolating major variables, systematically exploring possible solutions, testing possible solutions, and reflecting upon the solution arrived at.

Formal thought is a mental activity requiring the ability to think about abstract ideas without relying upon concrete, empirical materials. This mental activity may include theorizing, manipulating abstract statements, and deriving conclusions. Formal thought goes beyond the given data as well as formulating many interpretations of these data.

Formal thought is not normally attained by the elementary-school child; however, the elementary school can provide the child with experiences that will help him attain formal thought. The attainment of formal thought is a *goal of education;* this goal must permeate the entire elementary school program, including the science program. The relationship of formal thought to the elementary school science program can be seen from the works of Jean Piaget and others.

Piaget has shown that children proceed through stages of development from early childhood to adolescence. There are indications that when certain experiences are lacking during the child's development, the development of formal thought may be hindered.[2] Gagnè, another psychologist, has also shown that

[2] David E. Berelyn, "Recent Developments in Piaget's Work," in *The Cognitive Processes,* ed. R. J. C. Harper et al. (Englewood Cliffs: Prentice-Hall, 1964), pp. 311-323.

FIGURE I-2
Physical Manipulations Are Important. (Courtesy of The University of Kansas.)

early experiences affect the later performance of an individual.[3] Thus, in order
for the child to achieve formal thought, it is important for him to have certain
experiences in the early years of his life. As Karplus, a physicist who has been
involved in elementary school science curriculum development, puts it: "The
elementary school acquires a particularly deep responsibility, because the child's
thinking is especially sensitive to experiences as it undergoes a gradual transition
from the concrete to the abstract in the age range from six to fourteen years."[4]

In his writings, Piaget asserts that children should be allowed to do their own
learning. Good teaching, according to Piaget, involves placing a child in a situation
where he physically manipulates objects and observes the results of this manipulation. During this manipulation, the child may ask questions that the teacher
needs to answer. But the child will learn more from doing things himself than
he will from being told what he should learn by either a book or the teacher.
These physical manipulations are especially important in the child's development
towards formal thought.[5]

[3] Robert Gagnè, "The Learning Requirements for Enquiry," *Journal of Research in Science Teaching* 1 (1963): 144-153.
[4] Robert Karplus, *Theoretical Backgrounds of the Science Curriculum Improvement Study* (Berkeley: Science Curriculum Improvement Study, 1964), p. 6.
[5] Jean Piaget, "Cognitive Development in Children: The Piaget Papers," in *Piaget Rediscovered: A Report of the Conference on Cognitive Studies and Curriculum Development,* ed. R. E. Ripple and V. N. Rockcastle (Ithaca: Cornell University, School of Education, 1964), pp. 6-20.

The Nature of the Learner 1

The work of Jean Piaget has greatly influenced most elementary school science programs during the past decade. Piaget has identified four stages of child development, the final stage being formal thought (or formal operations). In order for the child to attain formal thought, he must proceed sequentially through the prior stages of development. Each stage is essential to the subsequent stage of development. Stages cannot be skipped or eliminated, since each is integrated into the next. For teaching, you need to understand these stages, as the child's particular stage of development will affect what and how you will teach and evaluate. The four stages of development identified by Piaget are

1. Sensory-motor.
2. Preoperational.
3. Concrete operations.
4. Formal operations (or formal thought).

It is important that a specific stage of development not be identified with a specific chronological age, as some children reach a specific stage earlier or later than other children. The most important principle is that *not every child achieves the final stage of development—formal thought.* The child will not reach this final stage if he lacks some experiences of an earlier stage of development. The science curriculum is, therefore, an important part of the elementary school program, because it can provide the child with experiences essential for the attainment of formal thought.

Sensory-Motor Stage of Development

Objective

To identify the characteristics of a child in the sensory-motor stage of development.

The sensory-motor stage of life is the period before the acquisition of verbal language, when the child is dependent upon his body for communication and self-expression. For the sensory-motor child, there is no other time than the present and no other place than where he is.

This stage begins with the child using his reflexes. With experience, these reflexes develop into controlled responses. The child learns through his bodily movements and his senses to deal with external objects and events. However, the child's world is directly related to his desires for physical satisfaction.

During the sensory-motor stage, the child develops certain behaviors not present at birth:

1. The child begins to understand that objects still exist even when they can no longer be seen or touched.
2. The child begins to develop verbal language.
3. Observing an object, the child can move his body in a coordinated manner in the direction of the object.
4. The child can observe an object and manipulate it at the same time.
5. He can repeat an event, such as moving his hand back and forth to touch an object.

However, in spite of these changes, the child is mainly directed by outside stimuli, because he cannot think about an act before carrying it out.

Activities

1. Observe a young child that you have identified as being in the sensory-motor stage of development.
2. Record the reactions of a sensory-motor child to your placing behind your back a toy he has been playing with.

Resource Material

Bearley, Molly, and Hitchfield, Elizabeth. *A Teacher's Guide to Reading Piaget.* London: Routledge and Keagan Paul, 1966.

Bybee, Rodger, and McCormack, Alan. "Applying Piaget's Theory." *Science and Children* 8 (December 1970): 14-17.

Chittenden, Edward A. "Piaget and Elementary Science." *Science and Children* 8 (December 1970): 9-14.

Duckworth, Eleanor. "Piaget Rediscovered." *Journal of Research in Science Teaching* 2 (September 1964): 172-175.

Flavell, John H. *The Developmental Psychology of Jean Piaget.* Princeton: D. Van Nostrand Co., 1963.

Furth, Hans G. *Piaget and Knowledge: Theoretical Foundations.* Englewood Cliffs: Prentice-Hall, 1969.

Ginsburg, Herbert, and Opper, Sylvia. *Piaget's Theory of Intellectual Development: An Introduction.* Englewood Cliffs: Prentice-Hall, 1969.

Inhelder, Barbel, and Piaget, Jean. *The Growth of Logical Thinking from Childhood to Adolescence.* New York: Basic Books, 1958.

Renner, John W. et al. "Piaget Is Practical." *Science and Children* 9 (October 1971): 23-26.

Preoperational Stage of Development

Objectives

1. To identify the characteristics of a child in the pre-operational stage of development.
2. To compare the characteristics of a sensory-motor child and a preoperational child.
3. To define operational thought and preoperational thought.

The preoperational stage of development is the child's greatest period of language development; that is when he acquires an understanding of words and concepts. These words and concepts now begin to dominate the child's mental life; he can now describe the outside world as well as his own thoughts and feelings.

But this child has not yet developed operational thought. Operational thought means that the child can perform mentally what a preoperational child must do through physical manipulations. For example, suppose you present the preoperational child with two identical drinking glasses and have him put exactly the same amount of water into each glass. After the child is satisfied that the two glasses contain the same amount of water, pour the water from one of the glasses into another glass of a different shape. Ask the child if there is still the same amount of water in this different glass. If the different glass is taller and thinner, the child will usually indicate that there is more water in this glass (probably because the water level is higher). If the second glass is shorter and wider, the child will usually indicate that there is less water in this glass (probably because the water level is lower). If the water is poured into several smaller glasses, the child will usually indicate that the little glasses together have more water in them (probably because there are more of these glasses). The child cannot mentally grasp the "operations" that were involved when the water was poured into different-sized containers.

When the child can indicate that the water is the same amount when it is poured into different-shaped containers, his stage of development may now be operational rather than preoperational. This is a very important change, because the child does not physically have to pour water from one glass to another glass; he can now mentally perform these operations. He knows that the water amount will remain the same, even though it is poured into different-sized containers.

During the beginning years of the preoperational stage of development, the child is constantly investigating. As he explores his environment, he learns words to communicate with himself and others. These words, however, are the child's own words for objects, and may be different from the general meaning held by adults. Therefore, even though an adult and a child may use the same words, they do not necessarily have the same meaning for each. For example, a child may call a small furry animal a "cat." When the child sees other small animals, cats or not, he may make a "meow" sound.

The preoperational child is aware of the world only through his own experiences. He believes that everyone sees things as he does and, therefore, will understand what he is saying and doing. This self-reference is predominant in the child's thoughts, communications, and actions.

FIGURE 1-1
Children Become Aware of the World Through Experiences.
(Courtesy of the University of Kansas.)

There are certain behaviors characteristic of the child in the preoperational stage of development:

1. The child cannot take the role of another person (he is egocentric).
2. The child focuses attention on a single property of an object. Therefore, he does not see that an object can have more than one property.
3. The child's explanations may be magical or animistic.
4. His actions are frequently dependent upon trial and error.
5. The child cannot follow a series of operations or changes and then reverse the direction back to where the series started (irreversibility).

During this stage, the child does develop a widening interest in the world about him. Experiences with the world tend to reduce egocentricity as the child reaches the end of this stage; however, at the time he enters school he is still largely egocentric. This may cause problems with adults, because his observations and interpretations are largely personal. When he enters school, he can only think of one idea and observe one property out of many that a given object may possess, such as shape, texture, size, or color. He will have trouble with cause-and-effect relationships, with measuring, and with number and quantity concepts.

Following are some other examples of observations that indicate that the child is in the preoperational stage of development:

1. Present the child with six or eight blue discs (such as buttons) aligned with small spaces between them. Ask him to pick out the same number of red discs from a pile near him.
   (a) At four to five years, on the average, the child will line up the red discs so that they are exactly the same length as the blue discs, but

without bothering about the number or that each red disc corresponds to each blue disc.

(b) Between five and six years, the child matches a red disc with each blue disc and therefore concludes the equality of both discs. However, if you move out the red discs at each end so that they are no longer exactly underneath the blue discs but a little to each side, the child believes the numbers of blue and red discs are no longer the same and concludes that there are more red discs.[6]

2. Present the child with three different colored balls, A, B, and C, which are strung on a wire. Then pass the balls through a tube. The child will see the balls start in the order A, B, C and expect to see them at the other end of the tube in the same order A, B, C—which is a correct assumption. However, when the tube is rotated 180^0, the preoperational child will not expect the order C, B, A and, if asked, will indicate the colors to be in the original order.[7]

Activities

1. Have different children between the ages of four and seven perform each of the various activities just explained:
   (a) With two identical glasses of water.
   (b) With the blue and red discs.
   (c) With different-colored balls.
2. Compare the behavior of these children during each of the activities and write a report to explain the differences that you observed.

Resource Material

See resource material listed under "Sensory-Motor Stage of Development."

Concrete Operations Stage of Development

Objectives

1. To identify the characteristics of a child in the concrete operations stage of development.
2. To compare the characteristics of a preoperational child and a concrete operational child.
3. To define the term "conservation."

During the stage of concrete operations, the child internalizes actions so that he can perform mentally what previously he had to do through physical actions. However, even though the child no longer has to manipulate the actual objects in order to understand their relationships, his mental operations are limited to

---

[6] Jean Piaget, *Six Psychological Studies,* trans. Anita Tenzor and David Elking (New York: Random House, Inc., 1967), pp. 30-31.

[7] Ibid, p. 31.

his direct (concrete) experiences. If the child has had no direct experience of a phenomenon, he reasons by analogy to some previous experience.

The thinking of the child becomes operational, as compared with preoperational, when he can remember the properties of an object that is undergoing a change. For example, when a long piece of clay is rolled into a ball, the concrete operational child indicates that the clay still contains the same amount as before it was rolled into a ball.

The important characteristic of the child in the concrete operations stage of development is that he can now carry out an operation mentally. He can also reverse the operation mentally (reversibility). In the example of the clay, this means the child mentally can change the shape of the clay back into its original shape by reversing the operation. Moreover, he will understand that the amount of clay will then still be the same as it was in the beginning.

When a child is aware that the amount is not changed when an object is broken into subgroups, he has attained the concept of *conservation.* The child must be able to conserve before he can attain formal thought. However, the ability to conserve is not something that the child acquires all of a sudden. It is a gradual process that usually begins when the child is about seven or eight years old. At this age, he has usually attained the concept of conservation of quantity. As the child develops, he begins to understand more fully the concept of conservation, including the concepts of conservation of mass, length, weight, area, volume, and displacement of volume (explained on pages 10-13).

Many primary-school children believe that the weight of an object will change if it is squeezed; for example, children will squeeze a piece of clay to make it "heavier." An awareness of conservation of weight does not begin to develop until the child is about nine or ten years old. The child begins to develop the concept of displacement of volume much later than this, usually when he is about twelve years old. Prior to understanding this concept, children believe that objects with different weights will displace different amounts of water. They cannot predict that objects of different weights, but of the same volume, will displace the same amount of water.

It is important to know that these concepts develop at different ages. Some do not develop until the end of the elementary school years—for example, the concept of displacement of water. How many of you have seen the concept of buoyancy ("Why do ships float?") in the elementary school science curriculum? Imagine how frustrating this must be for the child. He has no concept of displacement, but yet is expected to understand why ships float.

Following are some activities that indicate whether or not the child is in the concrete operations stage of development:

1. Conservation of quantity: Present a child with a ball of clay (See Figure 1-2). Ask the child to observe it. Then roll the clay into a long cylinder. Ask, "Does the snake have less, more, or the same amount of clay as the ball?" (If the child is confused, say, "Was the ball bigger, smaller, or the same size as the snake?") Justification—ask the child, "Why do you think the snake was bigger? or smaller, or the same."

Clay ball   Clay rolled

FIGURE 1-2
Conservation of Quantity.

2. Conservation of length: Use a complete and a sectioned straw. Start with
    both straws lined up parallel. (See Figure 1-3a.) Note with the child that
    both straws are the same length. Move the straws to the position shown
    in Figure 1-3b. Ask, "Would two ants starting a hike at this end (point
    to one end) and walking at the same speed both finish the hike at this
    point (point to other end of straws) at the same time?" If the child is
    confused, ask, "Would they both travel the same distance?" Justification—
    repeat the question. "Would they both travel the same distance? Why do
    you think so?" Now move the straws into the position shown in Figure
    1-3c. Repeat the question, "Would the ants both travel the same dis-
    tance?" Justification—"Why do you think so?"

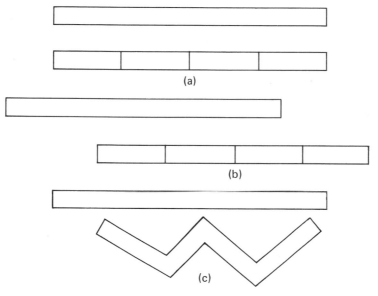

FIGURE 1-3
Conservation of Length.

3. Conservation of area: Present the child with two identical pieces of green
    construction paper. Tell him these represent fields or pastures. Place one
    toy animal on each piece of paper. Ask the child to compare the fields.
    Note they are the same size. Comment that since the fields are the same,
    each animal will have the same amount of grass to eat. Tell the child you

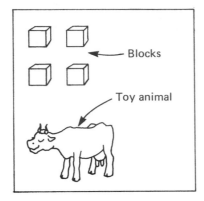 

FIGURE 1-4
Conservation of Area.

are going to use blocks to represent barns. Place four barns on each field as shown in Figure 1-4. (Leave the animal on the field.) Ask, "Now which animal will have the most grass to eat—or will the amount of grass be the same?" Justification—"Why do you think this is true?" Continue adding equal numbers of barns to each field. Each time repeat the question, "Which animal will have the most grass to eat?"

4. Conservation of volume: Use two jars (a baby food jar and a tall cylinder) and enough colored water to fill the tall jar (see Figure 1-5). Present the jars with the water in the short jar. Ask, "What will happen if I pour the water into the tall jar? Will I have more, less, or the same amount of water?" Pour the water into the second container. "Is there less, more, or the same amount of water?" Justification—ask the child, "Why do you think the amount of water was (more, less, the same)?"

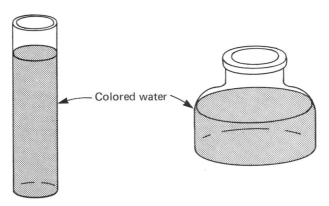

FIGURE 1-5
Conservation of Volume.

5. Displacement of volume: Use a tall cylinder three-quarters (3/4) full of colored water and two metal blocks of the same size (volume) but different weights (see Figure 1-6). Tell the child to compare the weights of the two blocks. Hand him the blocks and ask, "Which is heavier?" Say,

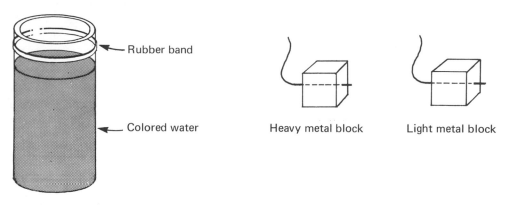

FIGURE 1-6
Displacement of Volume.

"If I take the lightweight block and lower it into the water, what will happen to the level of the water?" Tell the child, "Place the rubber band around the cylinder at the level you think the water will move to." You may wish to aid the child in holding the cylinder or helping with the rubber band. Gently lower the lighter block into the water and observe. If necessary, move the rubber band to the level of the water at this point. Then remove the block. Ask the child, "Where do you think the level of the water will be when the heavier block is lowered into the cylinder? Will the water level for the heavier block be lower, higher, or the same as the water level for the lighter block?" Justification—ask, "Why do you think this will happen?" Lower the heavier block into the cylinder and observe. Record the child's comments about the result.[8]

The behaviors characteristic of the child in the concrete operations stage of development are that he

1. Mentally plans a series of events or actions relevant to some goal.
2. Can mentally reverse actions by returning to the starting point of a series of actions (reversibility). In other words, he can think an action through from its beginning to its end or from its end to its beginning.
3. Realizes that objects do not change their weight or volume when their shape has been changed (conservation).
4. Realizes that the parts of a whole are related; therefore, he can classify and order objects.
5. Understands geographical space and historical time.

Activities

1. Have different children between the ages of seven and eleven perform each conservation task:
   (a) Quantity.
   (b) Length.

[8]The examples are quoted from Rodger Bybee and Alan McCormack, "Applying Piaget's Theory," *Science and Children* 8 (December 1970): 14-17.

   (c)   Area.
   (d)   Volume.
   (e)   Displacement of volume.
2. From the above activity, prepare a chart which will help you to compare conservers with nonconservers. Include each child's age. After examining the chart, give the approximate ages for mastery of each conservation task.

Resource Material

See resource material listed under "Sensory-Motor Stage of Development."

Carlson, Jerry S. "Effects of Instruction on the Concept of Conservation of Substance." *Science Education* 51 (March 1967): 138-145.

Verizzo, Quid. "Conceptions of Conservation and Reversibility in Children of Very Superior Intelligence." *School Science and Mathematics* 70 (January 1970): 31-36.

Formal Operations Stage of Development

Objectives

1. To identify the characteristics of a child in the formal operations stage of development.
2. To compare the characteristics of a concrete operational child and a formal operational child.

Formal operations (or formal thought) is the stage at which a child can think beyond his own world and his own beliefs. He can handle abstractions and deal with things he has never experienced.

   The thinking of a person who has achieved formal thought (or formal operations) is different from the person who has not, because the person in formal thought can imagine many of the possibilities in a given situation. Unlike the concrete operational child, a child who uses formal thought can mentally go beyond the immediate to the future. Before acting on a problem, he analyzes it and attempts to develop hypotheses regarding its solution. The hypotheses are many and complex, because he takes into account the possible variables or combination of variables. As he proceeds in testing his hypotheses, the child designs experiments that disprove some hypotheses and support others. He can accurately collect data from the experiments and then draw conclusions based on these data. He can interpret his conclusions and apply these conclusions to new situations.

   Following are some activities that indicate whether or not the child is in the formal operations stage of development:

1. Ask the child to answer the following question: "Edith has darker hair than Lily. Edith's hair is lighter than Susan's. Which of the three has the darkest hair?" Usually children not in the formal operations stage of

development will reply that since Edith and Lily are dark-haired and Edith and Susan are light-haired, Lily is the darkest, Susan the lightest, and Edith is in between. Children who are capable of formal thinking realize that the fictional people in the above example are presented in the abstract as pure hypotheses. Their thinking involves reasoning about these hypotheses drawing conclusions from the hypotheses.[9]

2. Tests similar to those presented in the part of this chapter on concrete operations (to determine if the child has acquired the concept of conservation) can be constructed to determine if the child is in the stage of formal operations. However, the tasks must be in spoken or written form, without the use of concrete objects.

The characteristics of the child who has acquired formal thought are that

1. He can think in abstract terms.
2. He systematically analyzes a problem and considers many possible solutions.
3. He can isolate variables in a given problem and control for them, which is true scientific reasoning.
4. He can formulate and test hypotheses and interpret their effects.
5. He can analyze and critically evaluate the process used to solve a problem.

In summary, the thought process of formal operations is characterized by the tendency of the child to analyze a problem, isolate the variables, systematically explore possible hypotheses, test these hypotheses, and reflect upon the solution of the problem. Formal operations are, therefore, similar to the process that a scientist uses in analyzing a problem. He has a plan for analyzing and solving the problem. In contrast, children in the sensory-motor and preoperational stages of development will have no plan. Although children in the concrete operations stage have a plan—they identify the various variables and test for them—they do not see all of the possible combinations of variables, as do children in the formal operations stage. Appendix A is an activity you can do with children that will help you to understand how children in different stages of development approach a problem.

Activity

Repeat the conservation tasks with children who are between ten and fifteen years of age, but instead of using the actual materials, use only the spoken word.

Resource Material

See resource material listed under "Sensory-Motor Stage of Development."

[9] Piaget, *Six Psychological Studies,* pp. 62-63.

The Nature of the Learning Process

Objectives

1. To identify factors that affect the learning process and the age at which a specific stage of development is reached.
2. To distinguish between the processes of assimilation and accommodation.
3. To describe the learning process.

In order for you to develop an understanding of the learning process, a few terms should be introduced.

1. *Concept* in science: the simplest form of understanding the environment. It is a generalization about related observations.
2. *Principle* of science: the simplest collection of concepts that explain the events and objects in our environment.
3. *Conceptual scheme:* the relationship that exists between principles.
4. *Conceptual framework:* the total structure of the concepts, principles, and conceptual schemes that we have related in our own minds. The conceptual framework gives meaning to what we observe in the environment.

Perhaps an example will help you to understand these terms. The principle of science, *sunlight is needed by plants in order to make food,* consists of a number of concepts that must be understood prior to understanding the principle itself. These concepts are *sunlight, plants,* and *food.* If you understand these concepts, you will probably understand the principle itself. The statement *plants are the only living organisms that can make food* also consists of a number of concepts, namely, *plants, living, organisms,* and *food.* As you develop an understanding of these two principles, you may organize them into a much larger structure, the conceptual scheme. These two principles might be organized around the conceptual scheme, *matter and energy interact between living organisms and their environment.* These concepts and principles, and the conceptual scheme, as well as all other concepts, principles, and conceptual schemes that help you to understand the environment are a part of your conceptual framework.

Learning is a process of adding observations, concepts, and principles to the conceptual schemes that make up our present conceptual framework; learning also involves the restructuring of the conceptual framework. According to Piaget, the learning process and the age at which the child attains a certain stage of development is dependent upon the following factors:

1. *Maturation:* an older child can physically and mentally do things that a younger child cannot.
2. *Experience:* the more direct experiences the child has, the more observations he puts into his conceptual framework.
3. *Social transmission:* this involves contacts with other people, television, books, and, more specifically, education.
4. *Equilibration:* the child maintains the balance of his conceptual frame-

work by either assimilating or accommodating observations.

(a) *Assimilation:*[10] the child incorporates into his conceptual framework observations from the environment. These observations are consistent with what the child believes should be happening; his conceptual framework helps him to understand what he observed.

(b) *Accommodation:*[11] the child's conceptual framework is changed because an observation did not fit into it. In other words, something the child observes is different from the way he thought it should be. Until the child has accommodated this observation, he is no longer in a state of equilibration.

The learning process is dependent upon observations, which are the necessary components of concepts and principles, and consists of assimilation and accommodation of these observations. The young child is dependent on the actual manipulation of materials prior to assimilation and accommodation. However, as the child matures, he can mentally assimilate and accommodate independent of the actual materials.

An observation that fits the child's conceptual framework is assimilated into the framework. Related observations form concepts, which are needed to make order out of the observations. When an observation is not consistent with the child's conceptual framework, this observation must be accommodated before the child is again in a state of equilibration.

For example, for a five- or six-year-old child, a sugar cube no longer exists after it dissolves and disappears in a glass of water. As the child observes the sugar cube in the glass of water, he assimilates his observation (the sugar cube disappearing). He concludes that the sugar cube no longer exists. For him, this observation and interpretation is consistent with his conceptual framework. This child cannot comprehend that the sugar still exists in the glass of water, because in his conceptual framework, when an object disappears, it is gone. If the teacher tells the child that the sugar is still in the water, the child may repeat this information for the teacher. However, placed in a situation where he must use this information, the child will again state or demonstrate by his behavior that he believes the sugar is gone.

As the child changes from the preoperational stage to the concrete operational stage of development, he begins to realize that there is something wrong with his "knowledge" that the sugar is gone. There is an inconsistency between this "knowledge" and his observation that the water tastes sweet after the sugar cube has disappeared. This observation can no longer be assimilated into his present conceptual framework; the inconsistent observation must be accommodated. However, until the child realizes that there is something inconsistent about his

---

[10] Schwab calls this *stable enquiry* (Joseph J. Schwab, *The Teaching of Science as Enquiry* [Cambridge: Harvard University Press, 1964], pp. 15-21); Shulman and Keislan call it *minor discovery* (Lee S. Shulman and Evan R. Keislan, *Learning by Discovery: A Critical Appraisal* [Chicago: Rand McNally and Co., 1966], pp. 29-30.)

[11] Schwab calls this *fluid enquiry* (Schwab, *The Teaching of Science as Enquiry*); Shulman and Keislan call it a *major discovery* or *conceptual invention* (Shulman and Keislan, *Learning by Discovery*).

FIGURE 1-7
Young Children Are Dependent upon Materials. (Courtesy of the
University of Kansas.)

observation, he will assimilate this observation and use it to support what he believes to be true. "The sugar is gone"; however, the sweetness of the water is not perceived by the child as being related to the vanished sugar. This example may help you to understand why some children have difficulty understanding some of the science topics of the primary grades.

It is important that the science lesson not be organized around the verbal name of the concept to be investigated (such as *dissolve* in the previous example). After the child has had experiences that illustrate the concept, the verbal name can then be given. Subsequently, he can demonstrate his understanding by using the concept in situations different from the situation in which he learned it.

If the name of the concept is given to the children in a classroom before they understand what is meant by the term, the elementary school science program becomes a series of lessons in vocabulary, with the major objective to have the children learn as many words as possible. In this type of teaching, the teacher usually writes the science word on the chalkboard and then defines the word for the child (or has the child look the word up in his science book). Words become the end products of science.

But the best learning situation is one where the child can manipulate materials and make observations. From these manipulations and observations, the learning process begins. The child must then assimilate and accommodate these observations for himself—you cannot do it for him. However, you can provide the child with the opportunity to manipulate objects and to make observations that he can then assimilate and accommodate. Then you can give a verbal name to the concept that the child discovered.

Activities

1. Have a five- or six-year-old child explain to you his observations of what happens to a lump of sugar placed in a glass of water.
2. Observe the child manipulating materials. Record his verbal observations. Identify what the child is assimilating and note any inconsistent observations.

Resource Material

Almy, Millie (with Edward Chittenden and Paula Miller). *Young Children's Thinking.* New York: Teacher's College Press, Columbia University, 1966.

Heffernan, Helen. "Concept Development in Science." *Science and Children* 4 (September 1966): 25-28.

Kuhn, D. J. "Science Teaching, Concept Formation, and Learning Theory." *Science Education* 56 (1962): 189-196.

Labinowich, Edward P. " Psychological Controversies Revisited." *The Science Teacher* 36 (February 1969): 12-14.

Mascolo, Richard. "Performance in Conceptualizing: Relationship Between Conceptual Framework and Skills of Inquiry." *Journal of Research in Science Teaching* 2 (1964): 176-186.

Shulman, Lee S. "Psychological Controversies in the Teaching of Science and Mathematics." *The Science Teacher* 35 (September 1968): 34-38, 89-90.

2 Inquiry–Collecting and Processing Information

When a child observes some event, he can either assimilate or accommodate it. If the observation is consistent with what the child believes should have happened, he can assimilate it into his conceptual framework. If the observation of the event doesn't fit into what the child believes should have happened, the observation is then an inconsistent observation.

These inconsistent observations may cause the children to ask questions, which are an important part of the science program. Children must be encouraged to ask questions and then encouraged to pursue answers. *Inquiry* is the term used for the process whereby a child tries to solve his problem.

In order to solve problems, the child needs certain skills and attitudes, as well as some information. Though it may be defined in many ways, we have defined inquiry as the *mode of learning whereby perceived inconsistent observations are resolved through collecting and processing information.* Inquiry helps children find answers to problems arising in their lives, just as they arise in the explorations of scientists. Children will not always be students in a classroom, but they will be living in a world with many problems, which each person must answer in his own way.

The Inconsistent Observation

Objectives

1. To identify the situation necessary for the child to have an inconsistent observation.
2. To develop guidelines for encouraging children to inquire.

When the child sees some phenomena that confuse him, the inquiry process begins. This confusion is caused by an inconsistency in what the child perceives as happening and what he believes should be happening. In order to perceive an inconsistency and to inquire, the child must manipulate materials and make observations. The very young child must manipulate the actual materials, while the older child can manipulate mental concepts. The child in the concrete operations stage of development can use mental materials; however, he must have manipulated the actual materials at one time. The child capable of formal thought can work with the abstract and is not limited to the actual material or the mental processing of materials that he has manipulated at one time. These ideas of Piaget can help you in planning your classroom lessons around the stage of development of the child.

The previous experiences of the child, as well as his stage of development, will determine whether or not he perceives an inconsistency in some event. For example, present a child with a picture showing two thermometers in two glasses of liquids. One thermometer reads "hot," in spite of the fact the glass of liquid is in the snow. The second thermometer reads "cold," and its glass of liquid is in the sun. The child might give any of the following three responses:

1. He recognizes no inconsistency, because he has had little or no experience with thermometers, snow, or hot and cold liquids.
2. He identifies inconsistency: a thermometer should not read "hot" if it is in a glass containing a liquid, and that glass is in the snow.
3. He recognizes no inconsistency, because his conceptual framework assimilates the observation as consistent.

Not all children will identify the same inconsistency. As the child observes the picture below, he may or may not perceive an inconsistency, depending upon his conceptual framework. What he observes may be as he believes it should have occurred. On the other hand, different children may perceive different inconsistencies. For example, in the above situation, some children will perceive the inconsistency that the thermometer reads "hot" when they believe it should read "cold." Others will perceive that the snow around the glass with the thermometer reading "hot" has not melted. Therefore, in your class will be some children who see no problem, while others may see several different problems, depending upon

FIGURE 2-1
An Inconsistent Observation.

their perceived inconsistency. These inconsistencies are important in designing instructional programs, since they are the beginning of inquiry.

To construct situations likely to produce an inconsistency, the following guidelines should be followed:

1. Materials must be present in order for the children to have something to manipulate.
2. Inquiry into all inconsistencies must be encouraged, even those that you did not expect to be perceived by the children.
3. Provide only information requested by the child, and only information that cannot be obtained through the child's own inquiry process.
4. Withhold any explanation for his perceived inconsistency; the child will quickly learn that he must inquire on his own.

Activities

1. Show the picture of two thermometers to a few primary-grade children. Record their observations. Identify any observations that seemed inconsistent to the children and note the questions they ask.
2. Plan an activity that encourages children to make inconsistent observations. Try the activity with a group of children. Record any inconsistencies that were perceived by the children, any you expected that were not perceived, and any the children perceived that you had not planned.

Resource Material

Brandwein, Paul F. "Elements in a Strategy for Teaching Science in the Elementary School." *The Teaching of Science.* Cambridge: Harvard University Press, 1962, pp. 107-144.

Lehman, Robert H. "The Effects of Creativity and Intelligence on Pupils' Questions in Science." *Science Education* 56 (1972): 103-121.

Schwab, Joseph J. "The Teaching of Science as Enquiry." *The Teaching of Science.* Cambridge: Harvard University Press, 1962, pp. 3-103.

Suchman, Richard. "Learning Through Inquiry." *Childhood Education* 41 (February 1965): 289-91.

Collecting Information

Objective

To identify how children collect information (data) for resolving their inconsistent observations.

In order to resolve the inconsistency that he perceives, the child needs information (data). In too many classrooms, the teacher resolves the inconsistency by answering the child's question or by directing him to a book.

In an inquiring classroom, the student resolves the inconsistency with a minimum amount of help from the teacher. To do this, the child needs information, which he obtains by observing, measuring, comparing, and identifying

FIGURE 2-2
Children Collect Information Through Their Senses (Frank Ross, Photography).

components in the environment (some of the *inquiry skills* to be discussed later). The child usually collects this information through the use of his five senses. Children must be given the opportunity to use their senses to collect information.

As the child observes, measures, compares, and identifies, he may have to use certain tools, such as a ruler, microscope, or some other piece of equipment. The child must be taught how to use these tools, but first he must have specific abilities, or *psychomotor skills.* Even after collecting all of this information, the child will still perceive the inconsistency unless the information obtained makes sense to him. In other words, he will still perceive an inconsistency unless he reorganizes his conceptual framework in order to accommodate the information.

Activity

Have a child take one of his inconsistent observations from the activity on page 22 and collect information through the use of his senses, using any psychomotor skills that are necessary.

Resource Material

See resource material listed under "The Inconsistent Observation."

Processing Information

Objective

> To identify the skills that are needed by children in order
> to resolve an inconsistent observation.

With practice, each individual may acquire the *inquiry skills* necessary to *process* collected data and thus resolve an inconsistent observation. The child may begin this process by classifying the collected information. He may then find it necessary to make more observations. This does not mean that the information already collected is correct, but only that more is being gathered. Once the child feels he has collected sufficient observations and classified these data, he may then formulate inferences or hypotheses about the inconsistency.

After formulating hypotheses to explain an inconsistency, the child tests them. He may eliminate hypotheses and formulate new ones on the basis of the test. Eventually the child reduces the number of hypotheses to one. If extensive testing, through controlled experimentation, proves the hypothesis false, the learner may have to collect more data. Once having accepted a hypothesis, the child can make and verify predictions based on the hypothesis.

There is no particular order for developing or using these inquiry skills. However, some or all of them will be used in the solution of a problem, provided the child actually possesses the skills. Children do not spontaneously develop the necessary skills; they must be given opportunities to acquire them. We have identified the following inquiry skills[12] as necessary for the inquiry process.

1. *Observing:* the ability to
   (a) Collect data through the use of the five senses.
   (b) Construct statements of observations in qualitative and quantitative terms.
2. *Comparing:* the ability to recognize and state similarities and differences among objects, events, and places.
3. *Identifying:* the ability to
   (a) Name objects, events, and places.
   (b) Select from the several alternates the designated object, event, place, or sequence.
   (c) Devise a method to measure the properties of objects.
4. *Classifying:* the ability to
   (a) Form groups based on one or more observed common properties.
   (b) Construct a graph from a table of data.
5. *Measuring:* the ability to quantify an observation using a frame of reference.
6. *Inferring:* the ability to
   (a) Construct a nonobservable judgment from a set of observations and comparisons.
   (b) Interpret a table of data.

[12] Kenneth D. George et al., *Science Investigations for Elementary School Teachers* (Lexington, Mass.: D. C. Heath, 1974).

FIGURE 2-3
Children Mentally Process Information (Frank Ross, Photography).

7. *Predicting:* the ability to state a future occurrence on the basis of previous observations.
8. *Verifying:* the ability to check or test the accuracy of a prediction.
9. *Hypothesizing:* the ability to construct an answer to a problem from generalized observations and comparisons.
10. *Isolating* the variables: the ability to
    (a) Discriminate among factors that will, and will not, affect the outcome of an experiment.
    (b) Identify which factors are held constant and which factors are manipulated.
11. *Experimenting:* the ability to
    (a) Recognize and formulate a problem.
    (b) Plan and conduct a test of an hypothesis.
    (c) Use the collected results to pose possible answers to the problem.

Activity

Encourage the child who collected the information in the activity on page 23 to process this information. Identify any inquiry skills the child used in processing this information.

Resource Material

See resource material identified in "The Inconsistent Observation."

Discovery

Objectives

1. To define the term *discovery.*
2. To identify what happens when a child makes his own discovery.

The inquiry process permits incorporating apparent inconsistent observations into the child's conceptual framework. This happens—when the child suddenly makes sense out of what had been an inconsistent observation—the child has *discovered* for himself. *Discovery involves assimilation and accommodation of a perceived inconsistent observation into the conceptual framework.*

Not everyone agrees on a definition of discovery. We do not believe there is a teaching method called "discovery teaching"; discovering is something that everyone must do for himself. You can utilize teaching techniques that encourage children to inquire, and, therefore, make their own discoveries. But this is not discovery teaching; it is discovery learning.

As previously stated, a child in the preoperational stage of development believes that when a sugar cube disappears in a glass of water, it is gone. The child in this case assimilates the following observations and inferences:

1. The sugar cube has disappeared in the water.
2. The sugar cube is gone.
3. The water tastes sweet.

However, the child never sees the relationship between the first and third observations. He simply assimilates them into his conceptual framework and infers that the sugar cube is gone.

As the child enters the concrete operations stage of development, he learns the concept of "conservation." This new understanding makes his inference that the sugar cube is gone an inconsistency. During some period of inquiry, the child *discovers* the relationship between his two observations (1 and 3). He reorganizes his conceptual framework, relating these two observations. A new inference is then made: The sugar is not gone, it is still in the water.

This reorganization of the conceptual framework establishes a relationship between those previously known concepts and the inconsistency. Discovery helps the child to see relationships between observations. These relationships then become concepts and principles; ultimately, the relationship between observations, concepts, and principles becomes a conceptual scheme.

We hope you will encourage in your classroom the type of inquiry that culminates when the child discovers that an inconsistent observation is really not an inconsistency. This is the time that a child will exclaim, "Aha, I know an answer." This "aha" is what science teaching is all about. You will find nothing more exciting in your teaching experiences than this exclamation by a child who has made his own discovery.

Activity

Record any discoveries made by the child who processed the collected information in the activity on page 25.

Resource Material

See the resource material listed under "The Inconsistent Observation."

Atkin, J. Myron, and Karplus, Robert. "Discovery or Invention." *The Science Teacher* 29 (September 1962): 45-51.

Bruner, Jerome S. "The Act of Discovery." *Harvard Educational Review* 31 (1961): 21-32.

Taba, Hilda. "Learning by Discovery: Psychological and Educational Rationale." *The Elementary School Journal* (March 1963): 308-316.

Inquiry in the Classroom

Objectives

1. To describe the role of a teacher who encourages children to inquire.
2. To describe the kinds of activities that take place in an inquiring classroom.
3. To identify what a child acquires as a result of inquiring.

There are two techniques commonly used in teaching elementary school science: (1) didactic teaching, which is under the control and direction of the teacher, book, or curriculum; and (2) inquiry teaching, in which the learner makes his own discoveries. In most classrooms, science is taught didactically. Children do not ask questions, or, if they do, they are not permitted or encouraged to find the answers on their own. The answers or conclusions to problems are given to the children by the teacher or the textbook. The teacher assumes that the children will accept all that he teaches as fact and will look to him or the book as the provider of the answers to questions.

The advantages of teaching science as inquiry, rather than teaching it didactically are that science learned through inquiry (1) is retained over a longer period of time; (2) can be used in situations that are different from the situation in which the material was learned; (3) is more exciting for the child, just as this type of teaching is more exciting for the teacher; and (4) the child is rewarded intrinsically, by his discovery itself, which encourages him to pursue additional learning through further explorations.

According to one's definition of inquiry, one's approach to the teaching of science varies. For example, some teachers may provide activities so that the child will perceive inconsistencies, and the ensuing inquiry will lead him to discover certain science concepts. On the other hand, some teachers will tell the children the concept and have them use the inquiry process to discover an application of the concept. We do not favor one approach to the exclusion of the other, because both are important approaches when used properly.

If you encourage children to manipulate materials and to investigate problems that arise from such manipulation, the majority of the children in your classroom will be active inquirers. Most children are intrinsically motivated by their own interests and will pursue their own interest much longer than what is considered the "normal attention span" for a child of their age.

To encourage an inquiring classroom, you must give the children freedom to

FIGURE 2-4
An Inquiring Classroom (Frank Ross, Photography).

collect and to process data. You must provide the necessary materials for the children to manipulate in order to observe inconsistencies, collect data, and use the skills of inquiry. In this type of classroom there is an absence of teacher pressure and of extrinsic rewards normally given for the "correct answer."

Your role is to provide the children with both the opportunity to inquire and the experiences that will help them to develop inquiry skills. You will need to know what questions to ask, when to ask them, and where to find the answers to the questions. Your role in the classroom is that of a guide. The important thing for you to remember is that the children in your classroom will not begin to inquire just by being told to inquire. Nor will they develop the necessary inquiry skills without experiences that help to develop these skills. Children must be taught how to observe, put into questions inconsistent observations, classify, infer, and predict, as well as all of the other skills of inquiry. This will take time; it will not be accomplished with just a few experiences. (The teaching techniques that encourage inquiry are presented in Sections II and III.)

Perhaps the question that arises most often with beginning teachers who are encouraging children to inquire is, "How do I know when the child has discovered?" The answer to this question is somewhat difficult to put into words (and is covered in greater depth in Section IV of this book), for many of us who have taught children use an "intuitive" kind of evidence to know when a discovery has been made. Some of the evidence follows:

1. Children become excited over their own discoveries; this excitement is often demonstrated by verbal exclamations, jumping up and down, running to tell the teacher what they have discovered, and proudly showing others their discoveries.

2. Children can use their discovery in different situations. If they cannot transfer the new insight to other applicable cases, the "discovery" was probably not a discovery at all, but only an accidental solution to a problem. In that case the child must continue his activities until he truly discovers.

Activities

1. Observe the teaching of science in an elementary school. Distinguish between didactic and inquiry teaching. Summarize the differences you observe.
2. In your observations of these classes, identify the inquiry skills that the children are using.

Resource Material

Feifer, Nathan. "The Teacher's Role in the Discovery Approach: Lessons from the History of Science." *The Science Teacher* 38 (November 1971): 27-29.

Gage, N. L. "Can Science Contribute to the Art of Teaching?" *Phi Delta Kappan* 49 (March 1968): 399-403.

Pearce, Lucia. "Exploration-Innovation: The New Learning Environment." *The Science Teacher* 36 (February 1969): 20-23.

Raun, Chester E., and Butts, David P. "The Relationship Between the Strategies of Inquiry in Science and Student Cognitive and Affective Behavioral Change." *Journal of Research in Science Teaching* 5 (1967-68): 261-268.

Renner, John W., and Stafford, Donald G. "Inquiry, Children and Teachers." *The Science Teacher* 37 (April 1970): 55-57.

Wilson, Evelyn, and Pallrand, George J. "The Tyranny of Terminology." *The Science Teacher* 36 (October 1969): 41-44.

The Nature of Science
Objective

To define the term *science.*

The objectives of the science program are determined by the definition of science and the goal of education, previously identified as the ultimate attainment of formal thought. We must now define what is meant by the term *science.* Then we can identify the objectives for teaching elementary school science.

Thomas Hobbes, as far back as the 1600s, called the laws of science theorems, or the dictates of reason, behind which was the word of God.[13] Some people may still agree with that definition; however, most do not include religion in their definition. Science is frequently defined as an organized body of facts and the

---

[13] Thomas Hobbes, "Leviathan: Other Laws of Nature," in *Modern Classical Philosophers,* ed. Benjamin Rand (Boston: Houghton Mifflin Company, 1924).

generalizations based on these facts. Some definitions also take in those facts obtained through observation, experimentation, and reasoning.

We do not define science as an accumulation of facts. Therefore, we do not define the objectives of an elementary school science program in terms of scientific facts. We do not deny the importance of facts, but the facts are not the end products of the science program. Facts are the building blocks of the concepts and principles that make up the conceptual schemes of science.

What then is science? *Science is a body of content and the methods used to generate, organize, and evaluate that content.* These methods involve the interaction of physical manipulations and mental processes. The mental processes are those needed for assimilation and accommodation. Therefore, the child must possess certain psychomotor skills, inquiry skills, and certain attitudes, appreciations, interests, and content. The objectives of the science program must then be defined in terms of

1. Psychomotor skills.
2. Inquiry skills.
3. Attitudes, appreciations, and interests.
4. Content.

Activity

Examine various elementary school science textbooks. After this examination, try to identify how the authors would define science. Discuss these definitions with the members of your class.

Resource Material

Conant, James B. *On Understanding Science.* New York: Mentor Books, 1951.

Conant, James B. *Science and Common Sense.* New York: Yale University Press, 1951.

Goran, Morris. "The Goal of Science and Scientists." *School Science and Mathematics* 64 (October 1964): 592-593.

Robinson, James T. "Science Teaching and the Nature of Science." *Journal of Research in Science Teaching* 3 (March 1965): 37-50.

The Nature of the Elementary School 3
Science Program

Many children begin to attain formal thought at the end of the elementary school years; however, this goal can only be achieved through the combined efforts of each administrator, teacher, and curriculum coordinator of the school. This goal should guide the total school program as well as the day-to-day lessons of the classroom.

Does knowing this goal help you to be a better teacher? Does it help you to answer the following questions?

1. What should I teach today? Tomorrow? During this school year?
2. How should I teach what I am supposed to teach?
3. How should I evaluate my students to know if they learned what I intended to teach?
4. How should I evaluate myself to find out if I am teaching what I want the students to learn?

In order to answer these questions, you must have objectives. Objectives give you more specific direction in what to teach, how to teach, and what to evaluate. The goal of education helps you to determine your objectives, but the objectives are different from the goal, in that they indicate what a child should be like or what he should be able to do as a result of his learning. For the purposes of this book, objectives will be classified as either terminal or instructional. Both types of objectives, however, will guide you in planning your lessons and evaluating your students.

Terminal Objectives

Objectives

1. To explain the function of terminal objectives.
2. To classify and give examples of the various types of terminal objectives.

The *terminal objectives* of a science program are objectives that usually take the child a period of time for attainment. This period of time may vary from objective to objective: it may take a few days, a year, or even the entire span of the elementary school years. For example, the ability *to collect data through the use of the five senses* is a terminal objective that can be acquired by children during the first grade. However, another terminal objective, the ability *to discriminate among factors which will, and will not, affect the outcome of an experiment,* cannot be attained until about the fifth or sixth grade.

The terminal objectives of the science program are determined by (1) the goal of an elementary school education and (2) the definition of science. Terminal objectives answer the question, "Why teach science to children?"

The terminal objectives of the science program can be classified into the following categories:

1. Skills.
   (a) The physical manipulation of equipment, including measuring instruments (psychomotor skills).
   (b) Skills that are necessary for children to solve problems (inquiry skills).
2. The attitudes, appreciations, and interests of a person who inquires.
3. The conceptual schemes of science (content).

Terminal psychomotor objectives indicate certain manipulative skills that children will acquire as a result of the science program. These skills could include manipulating a microscope, using a spring balance, or measuring with a ruler.

Terminal inquiry skill objectives include skills that enable children to solve problems. Without these skills, children are limited to memorizing facts from outside sources. As we mentioned before, children are not always students in a classroom; they also live, and will be living, in a world that presents many problems to them. Each child will have to solve these problems in his own way. It is

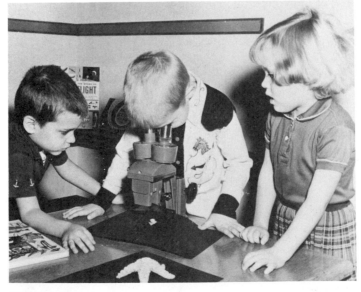

FIGURE 3-1
Using a Psychomotor Skill. (Courtesy of the University of Kansas.)

essential that inquiry skills be acquired by the children during the elementary school years, for they are also the prerequisites for formal thought. Terminal inquiry skills were identified earlier, but will be repeated here to emphasize their importance as terminal objectives of an elementary school science program.

1. *Observing:* the ability to
   (a) Collect data through the use of the five senses.
   (b) Construct statements of observations in qualitative and quantitative terms.
2. *Comparing:* the ability to recognize and state similarities and differences between objects, events, and places.
3. *Identifying:* the ability to
   (a) Name objects, events, and places.
   (b) Select from the several alternates the designated object, event, place, or sequence.
   (c) Devise a method to measure the properties of an object.
4. *Classifying:* the ability to
   (a) Form groups based on one or more observed common properties.
   (b) Construct a graph from a table of data.
5. *Measuring:* the ability to quantify an observation using a frame of reference.
6. *Inferring:* the ability to
   (a) Construct a nonobservable judgment from a set of observations and comparisons.
   (b) Interpret a table of data.
7. *Predicting:* the ability to state a future occurrence on the basis of previous observations.
8. *Verifying:* the ability to check or test the accuracy of a prediction.
9. *Hypothesizing:* the ability to construct an answer to a problem from generalized observations and comparisons.
10. *Isolating the variables:* the ability to
    (a) Discriminate among factors which will, and will not, affect the outcome of an experiment.
    (b) Identify those factors that are held constant and those factors that are manipulated.
11. *Experimenting:* the ability to
    (a) Recognize and formulate a problem.
    (b) Plan and conduct a test of an hypothesis.
    (c) Use the collected results and pose possible answers to the problem.

Terminal affective objectives include the attitudes, appreciations, and interests of a person who thinks scientifically. Children must be encouraged to develop a curiosity about the world, to be willing to avoid making decisions until as much evidence as possible has been collected, and to change their minds if new evidence is found. Children must be willing to allow others to challenge and question their ideas; they must respect others for their ideas. They must be unwilling to accept statements as facts unless they are backed by sufficient evidence. They must be careful not to allow decisions to be affected solely by personal likes, dislikes, anger, fear, or ignorance. Children should develop an appreciation for the ways science can be used to describe our environment, for the influence of science on man's way of thinking and our civilization, for the beauty of nature, and for the contributions scientists have made. Children should also be encouraged to develop interests in areas of science for hobbies or future vocations. These are some of the terminal affective objectives of an elementary school science program. Following are some examples of attitudes identified by the Education Policies Commissions:

1. Longing to know and to understand.
2. Questioning of all things.
3. Search for data and their meaning.
4. Demand for verification.
5. Respect for logic.
6. Consideration of premises.
7. Consideration of consequences.[14]

Probably less needs to be written about the importance of content objectives in science, as compared to skill objectives and affective objectives. Traditionally, the emphasis in the science classroom has been on content, which encompasses the facts, concepts, principles, and conceptual schemes. However, the terminal content objectives include only the conceptual schemes that will help unify the elementary school science program. These conceptual schemes should help children understand the relationships among the facts, concepts, and principles of science that they acquired during the lessons of the science program.

Children should be able to use the content they acquire in situations other than those in which they first encountered it. In order to be available for future use, the content of science needs to be resistant to forgetting. At the same time, it must be held with some level of tentativeness. This balance can be accomplished if the content of science is organized in the learner's conceptual framework around conceptual schemes. Even though conceptual schemes may differ with each learner, we have identified the following conceptual schemes:

1. Matter and energy interact between living organisms and their environment.
2. Matter can be measured in mathematical units, and these units exist in orderly systems.
3. Changes in matter require energy, and the totality of matter and energy are conserved.
4. Living organisms are a product of heredity and environment.
5. The physical universe, and all systems in it, are constantly changing.[15]

Activities

1. Identify some terminal psychomotor skills that are important for primary-grade children to develop.

[14] Educational Policies Commission, *Education and the Spirit of Science* (Washington, D. C.: National Education Association, 1966), p. 15.

[15] Kenneth D. George et al., *Science Investigations for Elementary School Teachers* (Lexington, Mass.: D. C. Heath, 1974).

2. Examine an elementary school science textbook series to determine what terminal inquiry skills it develops.
3. Talk to various teachers to determine what they believe are the terminal affective objectives of their science program.
4. Compare the conceptual schemes in various elementary school science methods books with those presented in this book.

Resource Materials

Bruner, Jerome S. *The Process of Education.* Cambridge: Harvard University Press, 1960.

Bruner, Jerome S. "The Process of Education." *Phi Delta Kappan* 53 (September 1971): 18-21.

Diederich, Paul B. "Components of the Scientific Attitude." *The Science Teacher* 34 (February 1967): 23-24.

Educational Policies Commission. *The Central Purpose of American Education.* Washington, D. C.: National Education Association, 1961.

Educational Policies Commission. *Education and the Spirit of Science* Washington, D. C.: National Education Association, 1966.

Fox, Fred W. "Education and the Spirit of Science—The New Challenge." *The Science Teacher* 33 (November 1966): 58-59.

Hawkins, David. "Education and the Spirit of Science." *The Science Teacher* 33 (September 1966): 18-20.

Kessen, William. "Statement of Purposes and Objectives of Science Education in School." *Journal of Research in Science Teaching* 2 (March 1964): 3-6.

National Science Teachers Association. "Conceptual Schemes and the Process of Science." *The Science Teacher* 31 (October 1964): 11.

National Science Teachers Association. *Theory into Action.* Washington, D. C.: National Science Teachers Association, 1964.

National Science Teachers Association Committee on Curriculum Studies: K-12. "School Science Education for the 70's." *The Science Teacher* 38 (November 1971): 46-51.

Russell, James E. "Theory into Action." *Science Teacher* 32 (May 1965): 27.

Instructional Objectives

Objectives

1. To explain the function of instructional objectives.
2. To compare the function of terminal objectives with instructional objectives.
3. To write instructional objectives.
4. To write a lesson based on these instructional objectives.

You must have clearly identified instructional objectives in order to plan the lessons of the science program. These objectives will help you to select the appropriate teaching methods and student activities; they will also serve as useful criteria for evaluation.

A lesson consists of activities through which the children will reach the specified instructional objective. Therefore, a lesson may be planned for one day or for many days. Some lessons cannot be completed in just twenty minutes— for example, some of the activities in a lesson on plant growth may take several weeks. These activities, however, are still a part of just one lesson.

When objectives are not clearly identified, it is difficult to plan a lesson. The objectives will help you to select what to teach, what materials you need, which teaching methods to use, and how to evaluate the learning of the children, the program, and the teaching methods.

Instructional objectives come from the terminal objectives, but unlike the terminal objectives, they include both content and skills, which must be taught in relation to each other. Instructional objectives must specify what the child should be able to do after he has attained the objectives. Following are some examples of instructional objectives for one lesson. Students should be able to

1. Grow plants in red, green, and blue light, sunlight, and darkness.
2. Compare the characteristics of plants grown in red, green, and blue light, sunlight, and darkness.
3. Formulate hypotheses regarding the differences in the characteristics of plants grown in red, green, and blue light, sunlight, and darkness.
4. Isolate the variables that affect the characteristics of plants grown in red, green, and blue light, sunlight, and darkness.
5. Plan and conduct an experiment to explain the differences in the characteristics of plants grown in red, green, and blue light, sunlight, and darkness.
6. Make predictions regarding the characteristics of plants grown in red-green, red-blue, and blue-green light.
7. Verify the predictions regarding the characteristics of plants grown in red-green, red-blue, and blue-green light.
8. Infer an explanation for the characteristics of trees growing in a dense forest.[16]

These objectives were derived from terminal objectives. A careful examination will indicate that the content part of each objective came from the terminal content objective, "Matter and energy interact between living organisms and their environment." Also, the objective, "grow plants," is related to psychomotor development. The remaining objectives came from the following terminal inquiry skills: comparing, formulating hypotheses, isolating the variables, planning and conducting an experiment, making predictions, verifying the predictions, and inferring an explanation.

After the instructional objectives are identified, the lesson is planned. The

[16] Kenneth D. George et al., *Science Investigations for Elementary School Teachers* (Lexington, Mass.: D. C. Heath, 1974).

following lesson was written from the preceding instructional objectives:

Materials Needed

1. Five shoe boxes.
2. Single-edged razor blade.
3. Cellophane tape.
4. Cellophane—red, green, blue, and transparent—enough to cover each shoe box lid.
5. Five paper cups (with holes in the bottom made with darning needles) on small containers to catch water.
6. Vermiculite or soil to fill at least five paper cups.
7. Fifty seeds (mung, pea, corn, or wheat).
8. Five rubber bands.
9. Water.

Procedure

A. How do the characteristics of plants grown in red, green, and blue light, sunlight, and darkness compare?
   1. Using a single-edged razor blade, cut out most of the centers of four of the five shoe box lids.

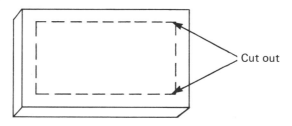

FIGURE 3-2
Shoe Box Lid.

   2. Tape red cellophane over the cut-out portion of one shoe box lid. Repeat this procedure with each of the three other lids, using the green, blue, and transparent cellophane.
   3. Put vermiculite or soil in five paper cups and plant seeds in each cup. Put the same amount of seeds in each cup (there should be at least ten seeds in each cup). Water the plants, using the same amount for each cup. Why is it important to keep the number of seeds and amount of water the same? Place the cups on small containers so that the excess water will drain through the holes in the cup and be caught.
   4. Put one cup in each of the five shoe boxes and replace the lids. Use rubber bands to hold the lids on the boxes. Place all the shoe boxes on a window sill, with the lids facing toward the window. Four cups will then be exposed to red, green, and blue light, and sunlight, and one cup will be in darkness.

FIGURE 3-3
Cup in a Shoe Box.

5. Add the same amount of water to each cup about three times a week, being careful not to overwater.
6. Two weeks after the seeds germinate, remove the cups from the boxes. Observe and list any differences in the characteristics of the plants.

B. How can you explain the differences in the characteristics of plants grown in red, green, and blue light, sunlight, and darkness? Your answers to this question are hypotheses. Hypotheses are tested by doing an experiment.
1. What are the variables that must be controlled in order to test your hypotheses?
2. Plan and conduct an experiment (the test for your hypotheses) to explain the differences in the characteristics of plants grown in red, green, and blue light, sunlight, and darkness.

C. What predictions can you make regarding the characteristics of plants grown in red-green, red-blue, and blue-green light?
1. Predict the characteristics of plants grown in red-green, red-blue, and blue-green light.
2. Verify your predictions by growing plants in boxes that have openings covered with the following combinations of colored cellophane: red-green, red-blue, and blue-green.

D. What are the characteristics of trees growing in a dense forest? Based on data collected in this investigation, infer an explanation for these characteristics.[17]

Activities

1. Identify some of the instructional affective objectives of this lesson.

[17]Kenneth D. George et al., *Science Investigations for Elementary School Teachers* (Lexington, Mass.: D. C. Heath, 1974).

2. From the terminal objectives presented earlier, write some instructional objectives for a lesson.
3. Using these instructional objectives, write a lesson.
4. Teach the above lesson to a class of children.

Resource Material

Bloom, Benjamin S., ed. *Taxonomy of Educational Objectives, Handbook I: Cognitive Domain.* New York: David McKay Co., Inc., 1956.

Krathwohl, David R., et al. *Taxonomy of Educational Objectives, Handbook II: Affective Domain.* New York: David McKay Co., Inc., 1964.

Behavioral Indicators of Learning

Objectives

1. To explain the function of behavioral indicators of learning.
2. To identify the guidelines for writing behavioral indicators of learning.
3. To identify some of the overt behavior exhibited by children who have attained the instructional objective.
4. To identify some examples of behavioral indicators of learning.

A behavioral indicator of learning is essentially a restatement of the instructional objective. However, the restatement *includes an overt behavior* to be exhibited by the child after attaining the instructional objective. Therefore, before behavioral indicators can be written, instructional objectives must be identified. The behavioral indicator includes both the content and skills of the instructional objective and the overt behavior to be demonstrated by the child.

The following steps are necessary in writing behavioral indicators of learning:

1. Identify the terminal objective.
2. Identify the instructional objective, skills, and content.
3. Describe the behavior of the child that has attained this instructional objective. This behavior must be overt and, therefore, seen by both the teacher and the child. Select a verb to describe this behavior, such as *write, orally describe, point, state, construct,* or *illustrate.* (Tables 3-1 and 3-2 indicate some behaviors that can be used for behavioral indicators of affective objectives.)

In writing behavioral indicators of learning, it is important to choose words that clearly describe the overt action of children. For example, words such as *names, selects, measures, groups, compares, estimates, writes, orally describes, rejects,* and *interprets* are not generally subject to misinterpretation. These words describe some observable action of the child, by which you can infer that learning has taken place. However, if your behavioral indicators include words such as *appreciates, understands,* or *believes in,* you will not be able to discern when or if learning has taken place.

TABLE 3-1
Behaviors of Affective Objectives

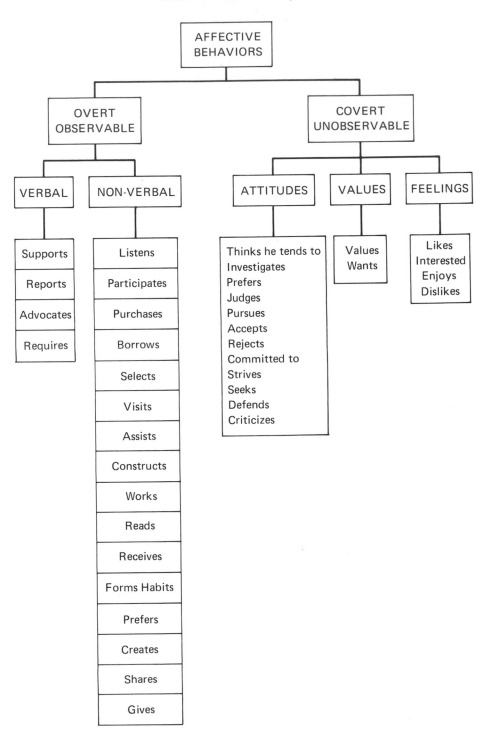

SOURCE: Robert B. Sund and Anthony J. Picard, *Behavioral Objectives and Evaluational Measures: Science and Mathematics* (Columbus, Ohio: Charles E. Merrill Publishing Co., 1972), p. 54.

TABLE 3-2
Observable Behaviors of Certain Attitudes

Attitude	Behavior
I Curiosity	A Expresses a desire to investigate new things or ideas. B Expresses a desire for additional information. C Asks for evidence to support conclusions made from scientific materials. D Expresses interest in scientific issues in the public domain. E Expresses a desire for explanations.
II Openness	A Demonstrates willingness to subject data and/or opinions to criticism and evaluation by others. B Seeks and considers new evidence. C Expresses the realization that knowledge is incomplete. D Expresses knowledge of the tentative nature of conclusions as products of science.
III Reality orientation	A Demonstrates knowledge and acceptance of his limitations. B Expresses awareness that change is the rule rather than the exception. C Expresses awareness of several sources of knowledge. D Expresses awareness of the fallibility of human effort. E Expresses belief in science as a means of influencing the environment. F Does not alter his data. G Demonstrates the realization that research in science requires hard work. H Demonstrates awareness of the limitations of present knowledge. I Expresses awareness of the historic development of patterns of inquiry and of the processes and characteristics of science. J Demonstrates belief that the search for desirable novelty should be tempered by awareness and understanding of traditional concepts.
IV Risk-taking	A Willingly subjects himself to possible criticism and/or failure. B Expresses his opinions, feelings, or criticisms regardless of the presence of authority. C Participates freely in class discussions. D Indicates a willingness to try new approaches.

(Continued)

41

TABLE 3-2 (Continued)

Attitude	Behavior
V Objectivity	A Indicates a preference for statements supported by evidence over unsupported opinion. B Indicates a preference for scientific generalizations that have withstood the test of critical review.
VI Precision	A Indicates a preference for coherent statements. B Seeks definitions of important words. C Demonstrates sensitivity to the appropriateness of general and/or specific statements in a given context. D Expresses the need to examine a problem from more than one point of view.
VII Confidence	A Expresses confidence that he can achieve success at inquiry. B Demonstrates willingness to take "intuitive leaps."
VIII Perseverance	A Pursues a problem to its solution or to a practical point of termination.
IX Satisfaction	A Expresses satisfaction with the process of inquiry. B Expresses confidence that his inquiry experience will enable him to attain future goals.
X Respect for theoretical structures	A Demonstrates awareness of the importance of models, theories, and concepts as means of relating and organizing new knowledge. B Demonstrates awareness of the importance of currently accepted theories and concepts as a framework or basis for the emergence of new knowledge. C Demonstrates awareness of the importance of scientific procedures to the generation of new knowledge, theories, and concepts.
XI Responsibility	A Is active in helping to identify and establish learning goals. B Demonstrates willingness to work beyond the assignment. C Insists upon adequate evidence on which to base conclusions. D Suggests changes to improve procedure. E Shows respect for the contributions of others. F Demonstrates willingness to share knowledge with others. G Offers a rationale for criticism.

TABLE 3-2 (Continued)

Attitude	Behavior
	H Initiates action for the benefit of the group.
XII Consensus and collaboration	A Demonstrates willingness to change from one idiom, style, or frame of reference when working with others.
	B Calls upon other talent from within the group when opinions and help are needed.
	C Seeks clarification of another person's point of view or frame of reference.

SOURCE: Richard M. Bingman, ed., *Inquiry Objectives in the Teaching of Biology* (Kansas City: Mid-Continent Regional Educational Laboratory and Biological Science Curriculum Study, 1969), pp. 34-37.

Behavioral indicators will be useful to you and worth the time spent in writing them only to the extent that they specify what the child should be able to do after he has attained the instructional objective. Most important, behavioral indicators identify the kind of *behavior* that will be an acceptable *indication* that the child has attained the objective of the lesson. Deciding on these indicators takes time and effort, but the outcome is well worth the effort. Following are the behavioral indicators of the instructional objectives identified on page 36. The student will:

1. *Demonstrate* the proper procedure for growing plants in red, green, and blue light, sunlight, and darkness.
2. *Describe* the differences in the characteristics of plants grown in red, green, and blue light, sunlight, and darkness.
3. *State in writing* hypotheses that explain the differences in characteristics of plants grown in red, green, and blue light, sunlight, and darkness.
4. *Design and carry out* an experiment in which the variables are controlled in order to test the hypotheses regarding the differences in characteristics of plants grown in red, green, and blue light, sunlight, and darkness.
5. *Select* the stated hypothesis that has the most supporting data; then identify the data that supports this hypothesis.
6. *State in writing* predictions regarding the characteristics of plants grown in red-green, red-blue, and blue-green light.
7. *Demonstrate* which predictions were correct regarding the characteristics of plants grown in red-green, red-blue, and blue-green light.
8. *Write a report* to explain the characteristics of trees growing in a dense forest.

These behavioral indicators should help you to evaluate what the children are able to do as a result of the lesson. Would these behavioral indicators help you to infer whether you had accomplished your instructional objectives? Could you infer how successful the student has been and how successful you were in

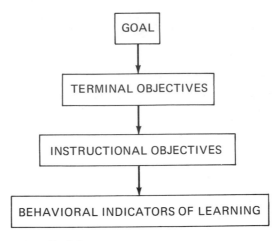

FIGURE 3-4

planning the lesson? How would your students evaluate their own progress, if they were given a copy of these behavioral indicators prior to the actual lesson?

Activity

Write behavioral indicators of learning for the instructional objectives you wrote in the previous activity.

Resource Material

Mager, Robert F. *Preparing Instructional Objectives.* Palo Alto, California: Fearon Publishers, 1962.

Montague, Earl J., and Butts, David P. "Behavioral Objectives." *The Science Teacher* 35 (March 1968): 33-35.

Having decided upon the objectives of instruction, you must then decide how to arrange the student learning activities to achieve the desired objective. To do this, you must know what types of learning activities are available and what advantages and disadvantages they have. This knowledge of learning activities is important, because not using them properly may result in little or no learning.

There has been much research on effective teaching, most of it confusing, but there appear to be at least two things a teacher does that effect student achievement. The first is variation. Students taught by teachers who use a variety of approaches and techniques seem to achieve better than students taught by teachers who do not use this variety. The second is clarity of presentation. If the teacher presents the material to be learned clearly, the students learn it.[1] This section of the book is designed to help you use a variety of learning activities and to present clearly what is to be learned.

The terms "discovery method," "inquiry method," "lecture method," "recitation method," and "demonstration method" are fraught with multiple meanings and have led to much confusion in the literature. Often these terms are not clearly defined. To avoid this confusion, we introduce and define here two terms that will be used throughout the remainder of this book. The first term is *strategy,* which means the *plan* a teacher has in mind to reach an instructional or terminal objective. The second term is tactic, which means the *maneuvers* a teacher makes in the classroom in order to implement the plan.

An analogy will help to clarify the difference. In tennis, the objective is to win. Each player has a plan for winning, called a strategy. Your winning strategy might be to manipulate your opponent so that he is out of position. The tactics to implement this strategy might be to keep hitting the ball to the same side of the court until your opponent plays only that side. Then, when he is on one side, you hit the ball to the other side of the court.

A teaching strategy is your plan to help students achieve your objectives. It is meaningless to discuss teaching strategies if no objective has been stated. Similarly, it is useless to discuss teaching tactics without having in mind the direction these tactics will take. However, before a strategy (plan) can be developed, you must be thoroughly familiar with the various tactics (maneuvers) you can use and where these tactics will lead.

Teaching tactics involve the presentation of concepts and principles through action, imagery, language, or any combination of these three.[2] *Action-oriented* presentations arc direct experiences in which children can manipulate, smell, taste, and in general observe objects involved in the learning experiences. In the *imagery-oriented* presentations, children deal with pictures or representations of the actual objects. In *language-oriented* presentations, depending primarily on verbal communication, children talk about and act on the objects of experience through language. According to Piaget's stages of development, before a young child can talk about an event or phenomenon, he must directly experience it.

[1] Barak Rosenshine and Norma Furst, "Research in Teacher Performance Criteria," in *Research in Teacher Education,* ed. B. O. Smith (Englewood Cliffs, N. J.: Prentice-Hall, 1971), pp. 44-46.

[2] Jerome Bruner, *Toward a Theory of Instruction* (Cambridge, Mass.: Harvard University Press, 1967), pp. 10-11.

This implies that for young children, action-oriented instruction is most appropriate, since it is quite likely they have not had any experience with the concept or principle to be studied. On the other hand, children in the upper elementary grades may have had direct experiences with the phenomenon to be studied, and imagery- or language-oriented instruction would be appropriate. As a general rule, the fewer experiences the children have had with the phenomenon to be studied, the more important it is to have extensive action-oriented instruction.

4 Verbal Communication

Since a large part of learning takes place through language, this topic will be discussed first. Much philosophical work has been done on language meaning and how words change in meaning in a given context,[3] but an adequate discussion of this topic would be inappropriate here. For our purpose, the effect that communication has on the learner is the aspect of language we will focus upon.

It has already been mentioned that student achievement is related to variety. This is especially true for verbal communication. Lecturing or asking questions all the time would probably be quite boring. Using variety in your verbal communication is necessary for successful lessons. But in order to achieve variety it is important to know what types of verbal communications are possible. Two broad categories of verbal communication are *monologues* and *dialogues.*[4]

Monologues

Objectives

1. To list three different types of monologues.
2. To give reasons why each type of monologue is used.

Verbal statements, made by either the teacher or the student, that require no direct verbal response will be called monologues. There are three types of monologues. The first type *summarizes or reviews* information previously presented. For example, at the beginning of the lesson: "Now yesterday we discussed various aspects of plant growth." In the middle of a lesson: "Up to now I have presented ways to measure length indirectly." At the end of a lesson: "Today we've been investigating the question, 'Can mealworms see?' "

Reviewing statements can be made at the beginning, middle, or end of a lesson. Such statements made at the beginning remind students of what has happened in previous lessons. A brief review in the middle or at the end of a

[3]See, for example, Irving M. Copi, *Introduction to Logic* (New York: Macmillan, 1967).
[4]Adapted from B. O. Smith and M. Meux, *A Study of the Logic of Teaching* (Urbana: Bureau of Educational Research, University of Illinois, 1962).

lesson can tie together points previously made and focus attention on the important aspects of the lesson, as well as add clarity to the lesson.

The second type of monologue *presents new material.* "In our solar system there are nine planets. The names of these planets are . . ." "The chemical symbol for hydrogen is H." There are many facts, concepts, and principles which would take the child too long to discover himself, but which he may need to resolve a problem on which he is working. The right time and place to provide students with such information comes with practice, although later on in this section suggestions will be made as to when to present new material using a monologue.

A third type of monologue *gives directions* on how to proceed: "Measure out three grams of salt." "Wear your safety glasses." "As you pour the two solutions together, observe what happens." Like the previous monologues which present new information, instruction monologues are important for giving direction to student work. To have a child "discover" how to use a scale or thermometer might result in breaking the equipment or in personal injury. Directions most likely would be given just prior to laboratory situations where students need guidance in how to proceed. These statements might also direct attention to an important aspect of a film or demonstration.

Unfortunately, most of the statements made in a classroom are of the monologue type and are usually made by teachers. As a matter of fact, researchers who have recorded classroom interaction have developed what is known as the Rule of Two Thirds. During a class period, two-thirds of the time someone is speaking; usually two-thirds of the speaking time, it is the teacher talking; two-thirds of the time that the teacher is speaking, he is lecturing.[5] In classes where achievement is low, the Rule of Two Thirds becomes the Rule of Three Fourths. Such a division of time ought not to occur in a science classroom. If the teacher is encouraging children to inquire, both the students and the teacher should be asking many types of questions. We are not saying that new material should never be presented by monologues. Rather there is a time for monologue and another time for *dialogue,* which involves an interaction with students.

Activities

1. List three different types of monologues.
2. After each monologue listed in Activity 1, give a reason for using it.

Dialogues

Objectives

1. To identify focusing questions and reactions.
2. To identify the different types of focusing questions and reactions.
3. To state why a focusing question and a reaction are used.

---

[5] Edmund Amidon and Michael Giammattee, "The Verbal Behavior of Superior Elementary Teachers," in *Interaction Analysis: Theory, Research and Application,* ed. Edmund Amidon and John B. Hough (Reading, Mass.: Addison-Wesley, 1967).

To involve students in the inquiry process, you must keep them mentally and physically active with the concepts being investigated.[6] Questions are an effective means of doing this. However, stimulation of inquiry with questions involves much skill and maneuvering. It also involves knowing what types of questions to ask and how to react to student responses.

To see clearly what is involved in a questioning technique, it is helpful to think of it as a process with an initial question, followed by a response, which in turn is followed by a reaction to the response. In the ensuing presentation in this book, the initial questions are called *focusing questions,* while the reactions to responses are called *reactions.*[7]

Types of Focusing Questions

While there are many ways to categorize questions, most are too complex to assimilate or use.[8] To be consistent with the model of inquiry teaching and learning presented in this book, we group focusing questions into four main areas: recall, data collecting, data processing, and evaluating or verifying. This category system corresponds to the types of mental processes required for inquiry in science and is also consistent with the definition of science proposed earlier. Note also that the system is based on the type of mental processes the teacher hopes to elicit from the students. Although this presentation is made from the teacher's point of view, that is, the teacher asks the questions and reacts to student responses, there is no reason why this process should be limited only to the teacher. Strategies will be illustrated later on that help students to ask questions and to react to the responses.

Recall

Recall questions require the responder to remember specific information either from past classroom experience or from past personal experience. They are relatively easy to answer and require little original thought on the student's part. Some examples are: "How many of you have been to the zoo?" "How many blocks do you live from school?" "How old are you?" "What did we do yesterday?" Recall questions are an important part of the foundation work on which a lesson is built. Using such questions, the teacher can quickly assess how much content a student remembers.

One important feature of a recall question is that there is usually a single right answer, and consequently only one way to evaluate an answer—right or wrong. This feature in itself is neither good nor bad, but when the majority of questions asked in a classroom have a single right answer, and only the teacher knows that answer, students begin to look to the teacher as the authority, whom they do not question.

[6] John H. Flavell, *The Developmental Psychology of Jean Piaget* (Princeton, N. J.: Van Nostrand Co., 1963), p. 367.

[7] Adapted from Arno A. Bellack et al., *The Language of the Classroom* (New York: Teachers College Press, 1966), Chapters 4 and 6.

[8] To see the variety of ways to categorize questions, examine Anita Simon and E. Gil Boyer, eds., *Mirrors for Behavior: An Anthology of Classroom Observational Instruments* (Philadelphia: Research for Better Schools, 1967).

FIGURE 4-1
Children and Teacher Discuss a Laboratory Activity. [From Herbert D.
Thier, Teaching Elementary School Science, A Laboratory Approach
(Lexington, Mass.: D. C. Heath, 1970), p.60.]

Data Collecting
Data collecting questions require the responder to provide specific information
based on direct observations. The object or phenomenon from which data is
being collected must be present in order for a response to be made. Some examples of data collecting questions are, "Looking at the graph on the board,
how many bushels of wheat were grown in 1945?" "How many fish do you see
in this aquarium?" "How would you describe this plant?"

One difference between a recall question and a data collecting question is
that, for the latter, the stimulus object is present. Another difference is that
data collecting questions may have several correct answers. Consider the following dialogue:

Teacher: "Jim, what observations did you make about your mealworm?"
Jim: "It's brownish white, has brown rings circling it, and it
looks as though it has six legs."
Teacher: "What observations did you make on your mealworm, Larry?"
Larry: "Mine seems to have two feelers at the top of its head.
In the box I have it in, it continually walks along the
edge between the walls and floor."

Notice that the multiple answers given by the students are all correct in each
particular case. It would be highly unusual to evaluate responses to this type of
question as "right" or "wrong."

Data Processing
The third type, data processing questions, require the respondent to put the
information collected into some new form. Such questions may require the

respondent to compare, classify, quantify, infer, predict, or hypothesize. As examples: "From the graph, what do you predict will happen when the rubber band stretches to 15 cm?" "Looking at the cricket and the grasshopper, how are they alike?" "What do you suppose is in the box that would make a sound like that?" These types of questions have multiple answers; it might be quite difficult to judge responses as "right" or "wrong." If a teacher did make such arbitrary judgements, he would be encouraging the students to guess rather than think. Perhaps a more appropriate reaction to a data processing response might be "How did you arrive at that answer?" Data processing questions play an important part in the inquiry process, for they help the student to piece together the information—to see relationships in the data that has been collected.

Evaluating
The last and most difficult type of question is the evaluating or verifying question. This type requires the responder to judge a hypothesis or inference on some specific criteria, such as devising a test of the hypothesis. Some examples: "How could you find out if the mealworms were hungry?" "What could you do to test the effect of pouring the chemicals into the water?" In addition to having multiple answers, these questions require students to think about the logic of an experiment—an important part of science. Researchers have found that teachers seldom, if ever, ask such questions.[9]

The mental processes required to answer a question become more difficult proceeding from recall questions to evaluating or verifying questions. The more difficult the question, the more time the student requires to think about the answers before responding. Ample time should be allowed for the student to think about difficult and thought-provoking questions. Variation is needed not only in types of questions, but also in the length of time necessary to think about a question before responding to it.

Types of Reactions
Having asked a focusing question and obtained a response, the teacher should react to the response. If the response could be right or wrong, the reaction would reward the responder if his answer were correct, or "punish" him if his answer were incorrect. Teachers become the authority in the classroom when they use *only* this type of reaction. Reactions to responses should keep learners mentally active—one of Piaget's tenets for implementing his ideas in the classroom.[10]

Inquiry discussions, which can involve all the types of focusing questions already discussed, also involve at least five different types of reactions to responses: accepting, rejecting, asking for clarification or elaboration, asking for evidence to support what has been said, and asking another person to evaluate the response.

[9] John R. Moyer, "An Exploratory Study of Questioning in the Instructional Process in Elementary Schools" (Ph.D. diss., Teachers College, Columbia University, 1965).
[10] Flavell, *Developmental Psychology,* p. 367.

Accepting

The first type of reaction, *accepting a response* or agreeing with it, can be done in multiple ways. One is just a cursory remark such as "Fine," "Good," "That's right," or "OK." Such remarks require little thought on your part and provide minimum reinforcement for correct answers. Another way to accept is to repeat the student's response. In so doing you are helping other students to hear the response and you are emphasizing the contribution. Still another way of accepting a student's contribution is to elaborate on it in the discussion. Consider the following dialogue:

(*Focusing Question*)	Teacher:	How many pairs of wings do your insects have, Sue?
	Sue:	Mine have one pair.
(*Reaction*)	Teacher:	Yes, insects typically have one pair of wings, and by looking at more examples, you would find that most animals called insects have one *or* two pairs of wings.

In this interchange the teacher has not only used the student's contribution but has also added some new information.

Another way to accept responses is to tell the student why his response is acceptable, giving either the reasons or the criteria for your judgment. Consider this exchange:

(*Focusing Question*)	Teacher:	How many of you found that hot water freezes faster than cold water?
	Students:	(Respond by raising their hands.)
(*Reaction*)	Teacher:	Others who have investigated this phenomena have found similar results. Most scientists think that the hot water, in cooling, sets up currents, which in turn speed the cooling.

Of course, combinations of these reactions are also possible, such as cursory acceptance followed by a repetition of the student's remarks.

At this point, we wish to emphasize the importance of variety. By reacting positively, and in a variety of ways, to student responses, you let the student know that you heard what he said and that you think it is important. For children who need to develop a good self-concept, such recognition is very important.[11]

Rejecting

An obvious reaction to an incorrect response would be to reject it—the second category of reactions. As there are several types of accepting reactions, so there

[11] For a more penetrating analysis of accepting and clarifying responses, see Louis E. Raths et al., *Values and Teaching* (Columbus, Ohio: Charles E. Merrill Publishing Co., 1966), Chapter 5.

are similar types of *rejecting reactions.* These types are a cursory reaction "No," "That's not right"; a cursory rejection followed by a repetition of the student's response; or rejection reactions which give reasons why an answer is incorrect. If the teacher has to react to student responses by rejecting many of them, he should carefully consider the type of focusing questions being asked. The questions may be too difficult, or the teacher may not have properly prepared students to answer the questions.

Asking for Clarification
Asking for clarification or elaboration is a reaction that asks that the response be more fully explained. Your purpose in doing this is to ask for more information and/or more meaning. By asking for clarification or elaboration, you can quickly determine if the student is just repeating what he has heard, or if he really knows what he is talking about. Some examples of this kind of reaction: "I don't understand what you mean." "Could you put that in other words to make clearer what you mean?" "Can you explain that further?" "What do you mean by the term . . .?" You may use this reaction even if you think you know what the student means. By playing "dumb" you give the student an opportunity to become an authority.

Asking for Evidence
Asking the responder for evidence to support his previous statements requires him to supply the rationale for the response. A statement not supported with appropriate evidence is, at best, a form of guessing. Examples of this type of reaction: "How do you know?" "Can you give me some experimental evidence to support your statement?" "What are your reasons for thinking this way?" "Why do you say that the mealworm is hungry?"

Asking Another Person
Asking that another individual evaluate or react to the previous response helps to stimulate student interaction. Too often students listen only to what a teacher says—because he is supposed to be an authority—rather than to a peer's ideas as well. Use of this type of reaction often enough, and in the appropriate place, helps students to listen to each other and to evaluate each other's comments. Eventually students will no longer need this type of "priming" and will readily react to each other's statements.

What type of reaction should follow a given focusing question? A partial answer was given under "Focusing Questions"; a more thorough explanation follows. For most recall questions there is a right or wrong answer, so that accepting and rejecting reactions are appropriate. For responses to data collecting questions, accepting reactions seem to be the most appropriate, unless a response is completely "off base."

Asking a student to clarify his response to a recall or data collecting question gives the teacher an opportunity to determine just how well he understands what was said. If a student is just repeating what he has heard others say, this type of reaction will help to point his actual lack of understanding. In addition, a student who has given the correct response may have done so for the wrong reason.

When the teacher asks another student to evaluate a previous response to a recall or data collecting question, the students, rather than the teacher, have an opportunity to be authorities. The reactions of other students also provide the teacher with information on how many others agree or disagree with the initial response. If the initial response was correct, but many students disagree with it, this information would tell you to reteach the material or elaborate on it.

The only reaction which might be inappropriate for responses to recall or data collecting questions would be that which asks the student to support his answer with evidence. A reaction of this sort to a recall or data collecting response could be extremely frustrating to a student. Consider the following exchanges:

(*Focusing Question*)	Teacher:	What do you observe about these rocks, Shelly?
	Shelley:	Mine are blue.
(*Reaction*)	Teacher:	Why do you say that?
	Shelley:	(Silence.)
(*Focusing Question*)	Teacher:	Shepley, how would you define a centimeter?
	Shepley:	A centimeter is 1/100th of a meter.
(*Reaction*)	Teacher:	Why do you say that?
	Shepley:	(Silence.)

In both cases the teacher's reaction is met with silence, although the teacher expected an answer. Probably the student did not know how to answer the question. Would you? In the first case a more appropriate reaction might have been to accept the answer, while in the second case a simple acceptance followed by ". . . that is the way in which scientists have defined a centimeter," would have been enough.

For data processing and evaluating and/or verifying questions, most reactions would be appropriate, except possibly for accepting and rejecting reactions. A teacher may want to limit the number of inferences or devised tests because of time considerations, and might reject responses that are not easily testable. Certainly the most appropriate reaction to a data processing question would be to ask the student to supply evidence in support of what he has said. With such a reaction, you are permitting the student to explain his inquiry process and consequently giving other students insight into the inquiry process. Providing children with examples of the inquiry process plays an important part in developing the skills and attitudes of inquiry. If they are given these examples often enough, students quickly learn how to reason in a scientific manner.

A variety of focusing questions has been presented and categorized according to a definition of science and a model of the inquiry process. Many reactions to responses were also presented, along with some indication of when to use them. You might naturally ask if there isn't any more to know about questioning techniques. There is, and it is perhaps the most important part of a teaching tactic— the sequence in which questions are asked. This topic is presented in the remaining pages of this chapter.

Activities

1. Since focusing questions and reactions play an important part in what is to follow, here is an exercise to see if you can recognize both. Immediately following is a typescript of numbered classroom interchanges. On a blank sheet of paper, number from one to twenty-seven. After each number write an F if the statement is a focusing question, an R if the statement is a reaction to a response.

1.	Teacher:	How many of you have ever been to the zoo?
2.	Students:	(Students raise their hands.)
3.	Teacher:	Good, I see that more than half of you have.
4.	Teacher:	What kinds of things do they have at the zoo, Lou?
5.	Lou:	Lots of animals.
6.	Teacher:	What kinds of animals?
7.	Lou:	Bears, lions, tigers.
8.	Teacher:	Fine.
9.	Teacher:	Are there any other kinds of animals? Shelley?
10.	Shelley:	At the zoo I went to, they had a bird house with at least fifty different types of birds.
11.	Teacher:	Do you remember what some of them were?
12.	Shelley:	Well, I think I saw some macaws, bird of paradise, a toucan.
13.	Teacher:	Ethan, you said that you went to the zoo; what do you remember about it?
14.	Ethan:	I remember the hippopotamus.
15.	Teacher:	Can you describe it?
16.	Ethan:	It was huge, and it stayed in the water.
17.	Teacher:	The rest of you. Did you see the hippo?
18.	Students:	Yes.
19.	Teacher:	Was he in water?
20.	Students:	Yes.
21.	Teacher:	Why do you suppose he was in the water? Sue?
22.	Sue:	He was staying cool.
23.	Teacher:	Why do you say that?
24.	Sue:	It was a hot day when I visited the zoo, and the water probably was cool.
25.	Teacher:	Gene, you saw the hippo in the water too. Why do you think he was in it?
26.	Gene:	He was getting a drink of water.
27.	Teacher:	What makes you think that?

2. Now go back over the statements. For each one labeled as a focusing question, decide which type it is and assign to it one of the letters below. Do the same for each reaction.

Focusing Questions		*Reactions*	
Rc	Recalling	A	Accepting
C	Data collecting	R	Rejecting

P	Data processing	Cl	Clarifying
V	Evaluating and/or verifying	E	Asking for evidence
		Ap	Asking another person

Resource Material

Carin, Arthur A., and Sund, Robert B., *Developing Questioning Techniques.* Columbus, Ohio: Charles Merrill Publishing Co., 1971.

Hunkins, Francis P. *Questioning Strategies and Techniques.* Boston: Allyn and Bacon, 1972.

Sanders, Norris M. *Classroom Questions: What Kinds?* New York: Harper and Row, 1966.

Verbal Aspects of Teaching Tactics

Objectives

1. To state the meaning of a given discussion paradigm.
2. To construct a discussion paradigm representing discourse in a science classroom.

Through a conscious arrangement of statements or questions, you can control the direction a lesson takes. This sequencing plays an important part in communicating during a teaching tactic.[12] Each aspect of a teaching tactic—the action, imagery, and language modes—complements the other. Consider the difficulty in just telling a young child how to tie his shoe. One must show as well as tell; a lecture or discussion without some type of physical or visual aids is not usually as meaningful. In this section only the language aspects of teaching tactics are presented, while in the following sections actual teaching tactics combining the language, action, and imagery modes will be presented.

Because the verbal aspects of a lesson are quite lengthy and sometimes boring to read, we will use a type of shorthand that will convey the *intent* of a classroom dialogue—what the teacher is attempting to do. The letters T and S will represent a teacher and a student, respectively. An arrow will indicate a verbal transaction, the head of the arrow pointing away from the person speaking. Thus T $\longrightarrow$ S indicates that the teacher is talking to a student, and T $\longleftarrow$ S represents a student talking to the teacher. To represent all of the students in a classroom at once would be extremely difficult, so the convention will be adopted that only three students will be shown at one time. *This does not mean that only three students are participating, but rather that three or more are participating.*

How can the type of dialogue taking place be represented? The three types of monologues presented earlier were reviewing (Rv), presenting new information (I), and giving directions (D). Thus, a teacher who sequenced a series of reviewing statements together would be conducting a review, and it would be presented as

---

[12] Hilda Taba et al, *Thinking in Elementary School Children,* U. S. O. E. Cooperative Research Project No. 1574 (San Francisco: San Francisco State College, 1964).

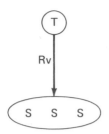

FIGURE 4-2
Representation of a
Teacher Review.

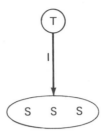

FIGURE 4-3
Representation of a
Teacher Presenting
New Material.

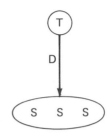

FIGURE 4-4
Representation of a
Teacher Giving
Directions.

in Figure 4-2. The arrow indicates that the teacher is talking to the students. The letters to the left of the arrow indicate that review statements are being made. Similarly a teacher who was sequencing a series of statements that presented new material to the students would be lecturing and could be represented as in Figure 4-3. Giving directions would be represented as in Figure 4-4. Dialogue is a little more complicated to represent, but the same shorthand will be used, with two additions. The first is a double-headed arrow representing a question and answer (◄────►). A reaction to a response is indicated by a dashed arrow (◄────►).

Using the focusing questions and reactions presented above and assigning a letter to each type, many kinds of verbal transactions can be represented.

Types of focusing questions
(◄────►) and their responses

Rc   Recall
C   Data Collecting
P   Data Processing
V   Verifying

Types of reactions (◄────►)

A   Accepting
R   Rejecting
Cl   Clarifying
E   Asking for evidence
Ap   Asking another person

Dialogue   *Representation*

Teacher: What did we do yesterday, Jim?
   Jim: We talked about air pressure.
Teacher: Right. What else did we do, Sandy?
  Sandy: We did an experiment to see the effects
           of air pressure.
Teacher: We didn't do an experiment in the true
           sense of the word. It was really a series
           of demonstrations. What were some of
           the effects we observed? Laura?

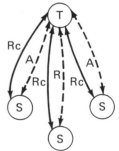

FIGURE 4-5

In this series of verbal exchanges the teacher is asking recall questions, represented by the Rc's to the left of the solid arrows (Figure 4-5) and reacting to student responses by accepting or rejecting them (represented by the A's and R.s

to the left of the dashed arrow.) To help understand what the topic of the interchange was, a few brief words could be written beneath the representation as a
description; for Figure 4-5 this would be

Focus: Reviewing previous day's lesson.

For a teacher who has just completed a demonstration on floating and sinking,
the verbal interchanges might be represented as follows:

Dialogue   *Representation*

Teacher: What observations did you make about
            the demonstration I've just done?

Student: When you dropped the egg into the glass
            on the right, it sank.

Teacher: OK. What else did you observe?
            Jerry?

Student: There was more liquid in the beaker on
            the right.

Teacher: Fine. Susan?

Student: The egg you dropped into that glass
            floated.

Teacher: Which glass?

Student: The one on the left.

Teacher: Mary?

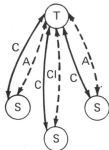

FIGURE 4-6

In this series of interchanges, the teacher is asking and the students are responding to data collecting questions (C's to the left of the solid arrows). The
teacher is reacting to the responses with acceptance and clarifications (A's and
Cl's to the left of the dashed arrows). Remember that even though only three
students are represented in the diagram, it means that three or more students
participated. Further, the representation means that only data collecting questions
were asked and answered, and that the only types of reactions used were accepting or clarifying.

Activities

1. Below you will find two typescripts of classroom interchanges. Read
    them carefully and then draw a representation of the transaction on a
    separate piece of paper. Underneath the representation, summarize what
    the interchange is about.

    (a) Teacher: For the past week or two we have been studying
                      the reactions plants have when grown in sun-
                      light, in darkness, in red, green, and blue light.
                      Some of the things we've found are that plants
                      grown in darkness look white compared to those
                      grown in the sunlight. In addition, the plants
                      grown in darkness are much taller and more
                      scraggly looking than those grown in light.

(b)   Teacher: What did we find out about plants grown in different colored lights? Ethan?

Ethan: The plants grown in green light looked completely different from those grown in red and blue light.

Teacher: How could you explain those differences?

Ethan: It had something to do with the way in which light was reflected from the leaves.

Teacher: Sue, do you agree with that?

Sue: Yes, the green light was reflected from the green leaves. In order for the plant to make food, the light had to be absorbed. Those plants grown in the green light weren't getting any light to make food.

Teacher: Shep, do you agree with what Ethan and Sue have said?

Shep: Yes.

2.   As further practice, write a brief description of what Figures 4-7 and 4-8 mean. Include the types of focusing questions asked and the reactions used.

3.   Observe a science teacher at work and represent his verbal communications with the symbols explained in this chapter.

As you read on, further practice interpreting these diagrams will be given. A thorough understanding of these representations is a key to comprehending the teaching strategies developed later. By using such representations, large volumes of typescript can be avoided, and yet the types of verbal transactions necessary for the teaching strategy can be summarized using diagrams. Every statement does not have to be represented in the diagram.

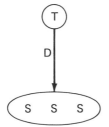

Focus: how to weigh an object
using a balance

FIGURE 4-7

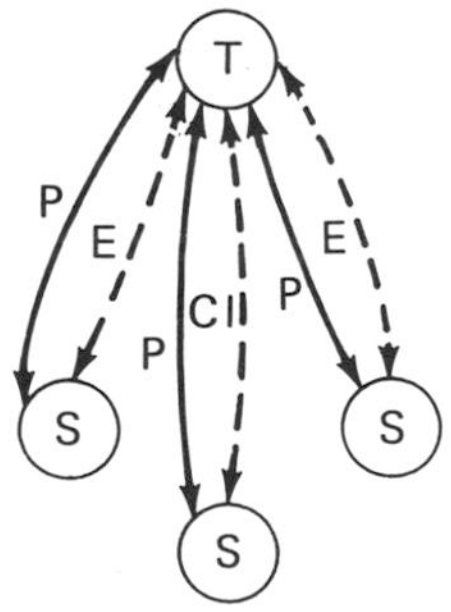

Focus: to develop a concept
from the experiment

FIGURE 4-8

Initiating
Tactics 5

In this chapter we put the language part of a teaching tactic together with the action and imagery parts in different types of teaching tactics or maneuvers. Teaching tactics may be divided into four types—initiating, focusing, extending, and terminating. Each has its own place in a teaching strategy. Each is used to direct the students a little further towards an instructional objective.

Your intent in an initiating tactic is to gain students' attention *and* to relate to their past experience what is about to be studied. An effective initiating tactic must include *both* the attention-getting aspect and the relating aspect. Attention getting is an obvious ingredient, because if you do not have the students' attention, you may as well stand in a closet and teach! On the other hand, if you have the students' attention, but in no way relate the material to student experiences, the lesson will have little meaning to the students. With these two purposes in mind, there are at least four different ways to initiate a lesson: (1) apparent inconsistencies, (2) creating competition, (3) problem creation, and (4) setting expectations.

Apparent Inconsistencies

Objectives

1. To state reasons for utilizing an apparent inconsistency as an initiating tactic.
2. To construct an apparent inconsistency which would serve to introduce a science concept or principle.

Recall that one of the first steps in the inquiry process is the creation of an inconsistency.[13] The inconsistency initiates a sense of surprise or frustration in the child and, ultimately, a desire to find out why he was surprised at his observations.

[13] Edward Palmer, "Accelerating the Child's Cognitive Attainments Through the Inducement of Cognitive Conflict: An Interpretation of the Piagetian Position," *Journal of Research in Science Teaching* 3 (1965): 320.

A child can be surprised, and sometimes frustrated, if he is confronted with an observation that is the opposite of what he would expect. Such an observation is called *inconsistent.* It is inconsistent to the *child's* conceptual framework; that is, to his idea of how the event should have happened. In order to create an inconsistent observation, you must know the child's past experiences. If the child has little or no experience with the phenomenon you are presenting, he has little knowledge of what to expect; hence, surprise is unlikely. In other words, the attention-getting aspect of an inconsistency must relate to the students' past experiences.

For an analogous situation, imagine a physicist telling you that he found one of the phonons of lead telluride to have an energy of 20 electron volts. You would not be surprised or frustrated if you did not know (1) that the phonons of lead telluride occur at 13.6 ev and/or (2) what phonons are! The point here is that *past* experience with a phenomenon determines to a large extent whether or not it seems inconsistent.

Such observations suggest that a teacher should use familiar materials, such as household items, and common experiences in constructing inconsistencies. The use of common experiences and familiar materials, coupled with the manner in which the teacher presents the event, should help to produce surprise and frustration for the child.

One method of presenting an inconsistency is to do so in silence. In order to get students' attention, your movements may be exaggerated, as illustrated in the following way. After the opening bell has rung or at some other convenient time, produce with a flourish a board three feet in length, three inches wide, and one-eighth inch thick, and a newspaper. Test the strength of the board by attempting to bend it or by tapping it on the edge of a table. Tapping on the table will naturally attract students' attention, if they are not already watching. You can then lay the board on a table so that the length of the board is towards the class and about six inches of the board extends over the table edge. Then take a single sheet from the newspaper and lay it across the board carefully, smoothing down the paper. Repeat this several times so that the board, except for the six inches extending over the table, is covered with the newspaper. (See Figure 5-1.) Then produce a board, similar to the one on the table, turn the board on edge and station yourself to hit the six-inch portion of the board. After taking several practice swings with the board, finally strike the six-inch portion with a quick motion.

The result will be an inconsistency that should get the students' attention, assuming they know from experience that when an object extending over the edge of a table is struck, the object will fly up. If students have not had this experience, of course, the demonstration with the board will not seem inconsistent to them.

As another inconsistency presented silently, consider this: You have on the table at the start of the lesson a clean, dry one-gallon metal can that can be sealed with a stopper or lid. (A carefully rinsed empty duplicating fluid can, commonly available in schools, is perfect for this.) Again with a flourish, draw a thimbleful of water from the tap and pour it into the empty can. Tilting the can to accumulate the water in one corner, bring the water to a boil by holding the corner

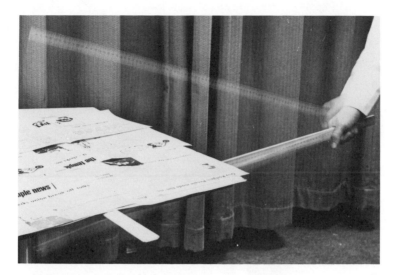

FIGURE 5-1
A Teacher About to Present an Inconsistency to Children. (Courtesy of Ronald Kalstein, Temple University.)

over a Bunsen burner or propane torch. When the water is boiling rapidly in the can, as indicated by the noise and steam emitted from the unsealed opening, remove the can quickly from the heat and seal it tightly, leaving the can in full view of all students. The events that follow will lead to an inconsistency for many students.

If you don't object to teaching science at any time during the school day, the following is another good example of how to present inconsistencies. At milk time on a cold day, produce these materials: a nonwaxed paper cup; a source of heat with an open flame, such as a candle, Bunsen burner, or propane torch; some type of stand on which to rest the cup while it is heating; and a carton of milk. Again with a flourish, set up the stand, place the paper cup on it, pour a small amount of milk into the cup, ignite the flame, and place it in a position to heat the milk. The result—milk warmed in a paper cup over an open flame—is an event completely inconsistent with almost everyone's past experience.

Another technique in developing situations leading to inconsistencies is to have the event in operation as the students enter the classroom. In this situation you do nothing verbally and may not even be present when the children enter. For example, as an introduction to moving air and its effects on pressure, connect one end of the flexible tube of a tank type vacuum cleaner to its exhaust, while the other end is held rigid and pointed vertically upward. Turn the vacuum cleaner on and place a beach ball in the air stream; it will soon remain suspended in the air stream. When the students enter the room, they will gather around and start asking questions.

As an introduction to the effects of cooling, "Albert" can be used. Albert is the name given to a glass or metal bird who apparently keeps dunking his head in a glass of water. If one of these is set up on a table before the class enters, students will gather around to watch "Albert" as they enter the room.

FIGURE 5-2
"Albert," the Dunking Bird. (Courtesy of
Ronald Kalstein, Temple University.)

In order for a silent presentation to develop inconsistencies, it must attract students' attention. You can attract their attention, as illustrated above, either by your exaggerated movements or by the puzzlement induced by the event itself. But it is difficult to generate events that, when performed silently, will attract students' attention. An alternative method of introducing the event is to cue students verbally. For instance, you might say, "Today we are going to start a new unit. Right now I'm going to do something related to this new unit, and I want you to watch carefully." Then proceed to perform the following, silently.

Clearly visible to all, cut four three-foot lengths of string. Show the class two objects of the same type but different sizes—two stones, one large and one small; or two hammers, a tack hammer and a large carpenter's hammer; or two weights a 100-gram weight and a 500-gram weight. Fasten two strings to each object so that when one string is picked up, it supports the object, and the second string hangs directly below the first (See Figure 5-3). Then tie each object by one string to an immovable support clearly visible to all, so that the support strings are of equal length and the strings below the objects are hanging freely. Then wrap the freely hanging string from the small object several times about your fingers. With a slow steady pull, increase the force exerted until a string breaks. (Watch your fingers so that they are not hit by the falling object.) You can repeat the procedure for the larger object, but this time quickly jerk the freely hanging string.

As an introduction to microscopic animals, you might present situations in which an inconsistency develops by giving each group of two or three students

FIGURE 5-3
To Produce an Inconsistency, Jerk the Loose String on
the Right and then Pull Steadily on the Left String.
(Courtesy of Minaruth Galey, Temple University.)

a small amount of pond water. Also, give each student a hand lens and tell him
to make observations of the pond water.

In all of the examples so far, the actual equipment was present when the
inconsistency developed. This method of presentation has the advantage that
students can, if they wish, manipulate the materials in order to verify the observed results. But sometimes it is possible to construct inconsistencies through
films or pictures. J. Richard Suchman has developed a series of short (2-3 minute)
film loops that present events for upper grade schoolchildren or middle schoolchildren. Many of the film loops show phenomena inconsistent with the children's
past experience.[14] Some of these film loops are perfect for use as initiating tactics.
Along with these film loops, Suchman has a problem book and idea book containing many more examples of presentations to develop inconsistencies. The
references to these works are given in the resource material following this discussion.

[14] J. Richard Suchman, *The Inquiry Development Programs in Physical Science* (Chicago:
Science Research Associates, 1966).

FIGURE 5-4
An Inconsistency Presented in Picture Form.

Inconsistent observations can also be developed via pictures, an example of the imagery-oriented presentations discussed earlier. For young children, such presentations are quite abstract. In order for them to absorb the presentation, the same equipment shown in the film or picture should be available for them to manipulate. For older children, abstract methods of completing the lesson could be used and will be described later.

Any type of event that is inconsistent with the students' conceptual framework is an excellent method of initiating a lesson. However, if it is done in excess, students expect this type of treatment every day. Then science becomes entertainment rather than a learning experience. Another disadvantage to using inconsistencies is that they may be difficult to devise. If you are interested in constructing some, here are a few suggestions.

First, state the instructional objectives of your lesson. Second, using a resource book with demonstrations, scan it for topics related to the topics you wish to teach. Usually the resource book will show complex laboratory equipment in the demonstration. You needn't use this complex equipment; for example, if the demonstration calls for a beaker, you can use a styrofoam or paper cup. If it calls for a thermometer, you could use a household thermometer. If it calls for a bunsen burner, a candle or a hot plate will usually do. It is important, when developing events that might be inconsistent with students' past experience, to use equipment familiar to all students. This is one way of relating the event to the students. Third, convert the demonstration into a situation that you believe will be unexpected by the students.

Here are more examples of events that your students may perceive as inconsistent.

1. Wet a sponge with water and erase the board. Ask the children to observe what happens to the water.
2. Place a radiometer in the sunlight and ask the children to observe what happens.
3. Drop an ice cube in a glass container that has alcohol in it, and drop another ice cube in a glass container that is filled with water. Be sure the students do not know what liquid is in each container.
4. Have two glass containers of water—one salt water and one regular water. Drop an unshelled egg into each one.
5. Briskly comb your hair and then hold the comb next to a stream of water coming from the faucet.
6. Fill a bucket with water and whirl it over your head.
7. Hang two balls from strings so that the balls are one inch apart. Blow between the two balls.
8. Place a piece of aluminum foil between two rectangular pieces of paraffin as if you were making a sandwich, holding the sandwich together with two rubber bands. Then hold the sandwich next to a light source. Rotate the sandwich 180° and again hold it next to the light source.

FIGURE 5-5
A Radiometer Can Be Placed in a Window to Produce
an Inconsistency.

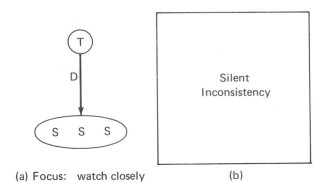

(a) Focus: watch closely   (b)

FIGURE 5-6

9. On a cool, dry day blow up some balloons. Rub them briskly on a wool sweater and let them adhere to the walls or ceiling before the children enter the classroom.

The resource material given below is an additional source of events that could cause an inconsistency in the child's conceptual framework.

In summary, if an event is to be inconsistent with the child's past experience, it must be presented in such a manner that the child expects one thing to happen, but another happens instead. In order to set up such a situation, you must know what types of experiences the children have had and use this information to the fullest when developing an inconsistent event. A general method of verbally presenting inconsistencies has been developed and is summarized in Figure 5-6. Another method of presenting inconsistencies will be included under the next type of initiating tactic.

Activities

1. Give some reasons for utilizing an apparent inconsistency as an initiating tactic.
2. Using the resource material below, construct an apparent inconsistency for the following science concepts and principles.
   (a) For a sixth-grade class.
       Principle: two objects of equal weight and the same material may float or sink, depending on the shape of the object.
   (b) For a first-grade class.
       Concept: evaporation.
   (c) For a fourth-grade class.
       Principle: an object will remain at rest unless acted upon by some force.
   (d) For an eighth-grade class.
       Concept: phototropism.
3. Present one of your inconsistencies developed in Activity 2 to a group of children. Note their reactions to determine if the event was inconsistent with their past experiences.

Resource Material

Kadesch, R. R. *The Crazy Cantilever and Other Science Experiments.* New York: Harper and Row, 1961.

Piltz, Albert, and Sund, Robert. *Creative Teaching of Science in the Elementary School.* Boston: Allyn and Bacon, 1968, pp. 131-153.

Suchman, J. R. *Teacher's Guide: The Inquiry Development Programs in Physical Science.* Chicago: Science Research Associates, Inc., 1966.

Suchman, J. R. *The Problem Book: The Inquiry Development Program in Physical Science.* Chicago: Science Research Associates, Inc., 1966.

Sweezy, K. *After-Dinner Science.* New York: McGraw-Hill, 1952.

Sweezy, K. *Chemical Magic.* New York: McGraw-Hill, 1956.

Sweezy, K. *Science Magic.* New York: McGraw-Hill, 1952.

Creating Competition

Objectives

1. To explain why creating competition is a good initiating tactic.
2. To construct a competitive situation to introduce a science concept or principle.

As with other initiating tactics, the purpose of creating competition is to get students' attention and to relate to their past experiences. The principle under- lying a tactic that creates competition is to divide the class into several opposing points of view, thus stimulating interest. One method of doing this is to describe what you are about to do, and then ask the students to predict what will happen. By accepting answers given by students, you will be able to establish several points of view.

Any one of the events described under the topic of apparent inconsistencies can be implemented in this manner. As an illustration of this way of creating competition, consider one teacher's tactic:

> Today we are going to begin a new unit on the properties of matter. As an illustration of one of these properties, I am going to take this egg and drop it into this glass container (the teacher points to a glass filled with a clear liquid on the table). What do you suppose will happen when I drop it in? (The teacher then asks several students to make a prediction. Two of the possible answers are that it will float or that it will sink. After getting several predictions, hopefully several that conflict with each other or with the actual outcome, the teacher drops in the egg and it floats—the liquid is salt water.)

If students have had experience with eggs and know that they sink when placed in water, this event will be inconsistent with their conceptual framework. If students have had no experience with eggs sinking in water, the event will most likely not seem inconsistent to them. An alternative method to demonstrate this concept uses ice cubes colored with food coloring, in order to make them visible to the class, and ethyl or methyl alcohol as the liquid. The ice cubes would probably relate more to the students' experience, since almost everyone has seen ice floating on water.

During a unit on gases and gas pressure, you might produce a device similar to that shown in Figure 5-7. After permitting several students to examine the apparatus, state that you will release the pinch clamp and would like the students to predict what will happen. If you ask several students and do not give any indication of who is right, several different opinions will be offered. The verbal aspects of this tactic can be conceptualized as presented in Figure 5-8. Note in

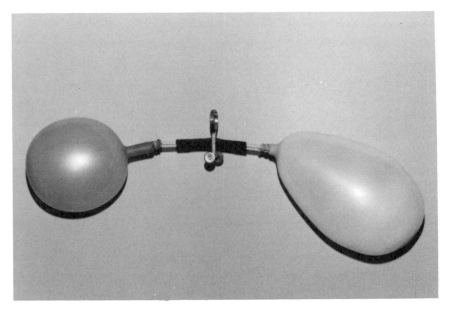

FIGURE 5-7
Asking Students to Predict What Will Happen When the Pinch Clamp Is Released Is a Sure Way to Develop Interest.

(a) Focus: description of
what will be done

(b) What will happen
if I do this?

FIGURE 5-8
Representation of an Initiating Tactic Designed to Create Competition.

Figure 5-8 that the teacher does *not* react to student responses. In this way, interest is developed.

In the examples above, competition was developed through a lack of knowledge of what would happen, or through some misconception held by the students. Artificially induced competition can be developed by appointing students to take sides in a manner similar to debates, where one side argues for a given resolution while the other team argues against it. This type of initiating tactic would work well with role-playing activities and quests, which are presented later. As with most initiating tactics, the past experiences of students play an important part in determining the success of the tactic. In assigning roles for the students to play, you must be sure that students have had experience that would enable them to successfully carry out their designated role.

For most children, the type of competition described here is a good way to develop interest and enthusiasm. However, if it is done to excess, an unhealthy relationship between members of the class can develop. In addition, not all lessons can be started with either apparent inconsistencies or competition, so other types of initiating tactics must be employed.

Activities

1. Explain why creating competition is a good initiating tactic for children.
2. Develop an initiating tactic that creates competition while presenting the following science concepts or principles.
   (a) Air pressure.
   (b) Acids.
   (c) Plants do not need soil in order to grow.
   (d) Weathering.
3. Present the initiating tactic developed in Activity 2 to a group of children and note their reaction.

Problem Creation

Objectives

1. To explain why presenting a problem is an initiating tactic.
2. To construct an initiating tactic that presents a problem to the students.

Another initiating tactic that can be used to some advantage is to present the children with a problem and have them work toward its solution. As an illustration, suppose your students have some mealworms to observe for a day or so. For this lesson you might begin by saying:

> For the past two days we've been observing mealworms. We found that these animals have 6 legs, 13 body segments, and 2 antennae, and that they move rather slowly. We've also found that mealworms seem to eat cereal such as bran or corn flakes. Many of you have asked the question, "Can mealworms see?" Some of you say yes, but

others say no. You've noted further that, using a hand lens, you can see something that looks like eyes. Today we're going to try to answer the question, "Can mealworms see?"

In this particular example, the problem investigated relates to student past experiences because it has grown out of their observations, and it should attract their attention because several of the students, as noted by the teacher, were curious about this problem. So, in this particular example, the problem has both the ingredients necessary for an initiating tactic—it gets students' attention and relates to their past experiences.

As another illustration of a problem used as an initiating tactic, consider the following situation. After your students have studied density and learned how to determine the density of regularly shaped objects, you might present the problem in the following manner. Using a cassette tape recorder, you might play a prerecorded tape. If five minutes of silence were put on the tape, the teacher could be out of the room when the tape starts. The commentary might be something like this:

> Good morning class. Your task this morning is an unusual one. If you remember, the past few days you have been studying density, and you have actually determined the densities of several objects. However, most of them have been cubes, spheres, or cylinders made of different materials. At this moment you are being given an irregularly shaped object. Your task, class, is to determine its density, using any of the methods presented previously. Do not ask your teacher for help. Your teacher will only give you the equipment you need. When you think you have determined the density of your object, write your name on a sheet of paper, record the density and the method you used to determine it, and give the paper to your teacher. Good luck.

A common method of presenting a problem is to give the children something to observe and have the problem evolve from their observations. For instance, you might present each student with a hand lens and a glass of pond water and give these directions: "I want you to look at this glass of water. As you look, be thinking about the different questions you could ask that might be interesting to solve." In this method the problem evolves from the student's own observations, but the teacher has initiated those observations by giving the students a task to perform. Typically, students may observe the same phenomena but make conflicting observations. This conflict is the start of a problem.

In presenting a problem as an initiating tactic, you should carefully choose a problem that has evolved from the students' past experiences. This means that you listen carefully to what the children are saying as you move about the classroom.

Activities

1. Using your understanding of science, explain why presenting a problem is a good initiating tactic.

2. For each of the science concepts or principles given below, develop a problem that could be used as an initiating tactic.
    (a) Density.
    (b) Erosion.
    (c) Heat.
    (d) Bacteria can be controlled by disinfectant chemicals.
    (e) Muscles fatigue after constant exercise.
    (f) Plants grow differently in different types of soil.
3. Present a problem you have developed from Activity 2 to your class and note their reaction.

Resource Materials

See the resource materials for laboratory activities and demonstrations, pages 89-90 and 100.

Setting Expectations

Objectives

1. To state reasons why expectation setting is an initiating tactic.
2. To construct an initiating tactic that uses expectation setting as a means of introducing a given science concept or principle.

It is almost impossible to constantly provide students with such exciting initiating tactics as previously presented. A more common method of starting a lesson is to refresh student memory regarding past experiences, and then to show how these experiences are related to what will be studied. Too often teachers plunge into a lesson without giving students any background on how the day's work fits in with past experiences. Students not given this tie-in with past experiences view each lesson as a distinct entity without any connection to previous work. This lack of continuity could easily happen in the elementary school, where science is sometimes taught only twice a week, or less. Therefore, students need to be reminded of how prior lessons fit in with the present lesson.

There are two ways by which you might relate the students' past experiences to the day's lesson. The first way is to directly remind students of what has happened. For example, you might start off by saying:

> For the past three days we have been studying mealworms. We have found that these animals have six legs, thirteen body segments, and two antennae. We have also found that mealworms seem to eat cereal, such as bran or corn flakes. Many of you have wondered if mealworms can see. You've noted that, using a hand lens, you can see something that looks like eyes. Today we're going to try to find out if the mealworm can "see." And what we will try to do is design an experiment to find out if mealworms can "see."

As another example of expectation setting, you might say the following:

> As part of our unit on plant and animal relationships, we are going to see a film today that describes what types of animals depend on plants for food. After we discuss this film, you will have the opportunity to observe your crickets and mealworms to see what type of food they have eaten.

The second method is to review by a question and answer mode. Using the same topic—"Can mealworms 'see'?"—you might ask these questions: "What have we been studying the past few days?" "What have we found out about mealworms?" After asking each question, it is important for you to accept answers from as many students as possible and perhaps to write various responses on the chalkboard. The questions you ask will gradually lead to the problem, "Can mealworms see?" This procedure serves two purposes. First, it refreshes students' memories and reminds them of their past experiences. Second, it provides you with some information as to where the lesson should begin. If students failed to remember or learn some important point on which the day's lesson is built, the lesson would be a failure. Teaching is somewhat like building a pyramid with blocks; if the foundation is not properly constructed, the upper portions will not stand. Each lesson should be a foundation for the next lesson. The verbal aspects of this type of initiating tactic are represented in Figures 5-9 and 5-10.

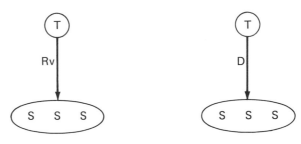

(a) Focus: review past lesson   (b) Give directions

FIGURE 5-9
Representation of an Initiating Tactic That Sets Expectations.

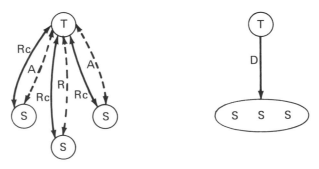

(a) Focus: review past lesson   (b) Give directions

FIGURE 5-10
Representation of an Initiating Tactic That Sets Expectations.

Activities

1. Using your understanding of science teaching, explain why expectation setting is a good initiating tactic.
2. For each of the science concepts or principles presented below, describe how you would introduce them, using expectation setting.
   (a) Plants give off oxygen in the presence of light.
   (b) Termites react negatively to light.
   (c) Periodic motion.
   (d) Magnetism.
   (e) Diatropism.

6 Focusing Tactics

The teacher's intent, when using an initiating tactic, is to gain students' attention and to relate the concepts, principles, or other material to be learned to past student experience. Four different types of initiating tactics have been presented, with examples of each type. Each initiating tactic—apparent inconsistencies, problem presentation, competition setting, and expectation setting—has two common ingredients. Each relates in some way to student past experience, either in the equipment used or with the type of experiences provided; each gains the students' attention in some manner. In using a variety of initiating tactics, you increase the probability of getting all the students involved in the lessons.

After obtaining students' attention with an initiating tactic, you must then provide a common base of experiences that are related to your instructional objectives. These experiences are extremely important, since they are the only events that all your children will have had in common. These shared experiences enable you to communicate more effectively with all the children and get the class moving toward the instructional objectives. All the focusing tactics must take into account the children's past experiences and their stage of development. For this reason, the focusing tactics will be categorized as action, imagery, or language modes of instruction.

Laboratory Activities

Objectives

1. To state a rationale for using each one of the five types of laboratory activities.
2. To construct a laboratory activity as a focusing tactic for a given instructional objective.

When a child thinks of science, he most often thinks of experimentation—pouring things together to create explosions, foaming liquids, and so on. However, a child is experimenting when he turns a rock over to see what is under it, or when he touches a leaf to see how it feels. If one accepts the view that science is a body of content, as well as the methods of collecting, organizing, and evaluating that content, then children are constantly "doing" science. By pushing, touching, smelling, tasting, or hearing the things in their immediate environment, children are continually collecting information and organizing it to build a conceptual framework. Piaget postulates that this is how children learn.[15]

The laboratory experience in a science classroom can play an important role in helping children learn by giving them the opportunity to acquire a body of content, and by giving them practice with the methods of collecting, organizing, and evaluating that content. Moreover, laboratory activities provide common experiences that focus students' attention on a specific event or phenomena. For this reason, laboratory activities are excellent focusing tactics.

Laboratory experiences are considered to be the most action-oriented instructional mode a teacher can use. There are at least five different types of laboratory activities, which differ in purpose and in the amount of teacher control exerted during the activity.

Type I

A teacher who uses this type of laboratory activity wants students to develop and practice such psychomotor skills as measuring length, mass, volume, or density. Or he may want students to practice using a particular type of equipment, such as a double pan balance, graduated cylinder, or dissecting equipment. In order to provide such practice, you must control the laboratory activity by giving directions on how to proceed, what to do, and how to hold the equipment. If you do not have this control, or if the students are permitted to discover on their own how to use the equipment, there will be much equipment broken and possibly some students injured. In this type of laboratory activity, it is important and proper for you to be in control and to tell the students how to proceed.

In designing a Type I laboratory activity, it is important to provide as much practice with the skill as possible, and to let the student know how well he is doing, in much the same way as when you drill students on certain mathematical or spelling skills. However, to keep the child from getting bored, a variety of situations in which the skill is used should be provided. If the child is asked to measure the length of the same table eight times, he can easily become bored. On the other hand, if the child is asked to measure the length of eight different objects, he not only gets more practice measuring, but also is kept from getting bored. The less prior experience a child has with the equipment or the skill, the more you need to provide practice. All too often a teacher will show a student how to perform a particular task, give him the opportunity to practice it once, and finally evaluate the students on his performance of that task. This kind of teaching is analogous to showing a person how to type and then expecting him to type a perfect letter after only one practice session.

In the following example, a Type I laboratory activity is used to focus students' attention on the skill of weighing with an equal arm balance.

> Suppose that you are investigating the properties of matter, and you
> would like your children to be more quantitative in their observations.
> One of the principles you wish to present is that equal volumes of

---

[15] John H. Flavell, *The Developmental Psychology of Jean Piaget* (Princeton, N. J.: Van Nostrand Co., 1963), p. 367.

FIGURE 6-1
Proper Use of a Spring Scale Is an Important Skill to Develop. (From Thier,
Teaching Elementary School Science, p. 61.)

different substances weigh different amounts. Furthermore, you find
that none of your third graders have had any experience weighing
with an equal arm balance. After carefully showing the students how
to use such a balance, and after several students have repeated back
to you a general procedure for determining the weight of an object,
you then focus their attention on the skill of weighing. With the students working in pairs or groups of four, you give each group a small
paper cup with a capacity of one fluid ounce. These cups can be made
by cutting down a four-ounce paper cup, obtainable at a grocery
store. Then you ask each group to weigh a paper cup full of salt,
leveled at the top. As students do this, you circulate among them to
help those who are having trouble. When each group has weighed the
salt, you ask them to report what they found. You permit enough
students to give an answer to assure you that most have determined
the weight in the proper manner.

Completing this task, you ask them to empty their cups and determine
the weight of the same volume of baking soda. As you circulate among

the children this time, make sure that those children who did not use the balance the first time did so the second time. You will still need to help individuals who are having trouble. You could keep repeating this procedure with different powders, such as flour, brown sugar, white sand, or epsom salts.

Note how this tactic provides much varied practice with the skill of weighing. Moreover, students quickly learn how well they are using the skill.

As indicated above, there are two types of verbal communications used during a Type I laboratory activity. The first is a monologue that gives directions on how to proceed. The directions must be clearly understood by the children. How to do this is discussed under Demonstrations, page 96. After the students have collected data and reported it to the class, correct answers should be praised, while students giving grossly incorrect answers might be asked to repeat their measurements. Notice that in the verbal aspect of this tactic the teacher's main focusing questions are of the data collecting type, and the reactions to the responses are accepting or rejecting. This aspect of a Type I laboratory activity is quite important, because it focuses students' attention on the obtained data and provides them with immediate feedback on their performance of the task. The direction-giving aspect focuses students' attention on the task to be performed. Using the diagrams presented in Chapter 4, an appropriate arrangement of the verbal and physical aspects of a Type I laboratory activity used as a focusing tactic is shown in Figure 6-2.

A Type I laboratory activity is a good way to introduce and practice a needed psychomotor skill in an interesting manner. But if a Type I activity is the only encounter a child has with the laboratory, he is not practicing science. That is, he is not involved in the organization and evaluation of data.

Type II
A Type II laboratory activity is quite similar to Type I in the amount of teacher control. It is different, however, in purpose. The main aim of this type of laboratory activity is to verify a concept or principle already studied in a textbook or presented in a class discussion, or to replicate an experiment already performed

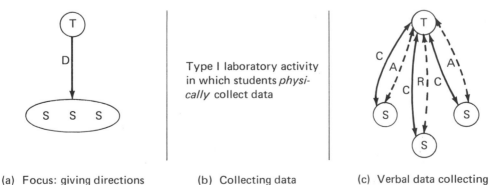

(a) Focus: giving directions   (b) Collecting data   (c) Verbal data collecting

FIGURE 6-2
Focusing Tactics for a Type I Laboratory Activity.

FIGURE 6-3
Giving Directions on How to Proceed Is an Important Part of a Type II
Laboratory Activity. (Courtesy of Ronald Kalstein, Temple University.)

by someone else. In this type of activity the problem, the materials needed, the
procedures to follow, and the type of data to collect are all given to the student.
Usually he also knows what the results will be—what to conclude. It is indeed
unfortunate that most of the laboratory activities done in many classes are of
this type. While a Type II laboratory activity has an important place in the science
program, it should not be used to the exclusion of other types.

In a Type II laboratory activity, it is important for you to guide students by
stating the problem, the procedure to follow, and the data to collect, and by
providing the materials. If such information were not provided, the students
would probably not be able to replicate the experiment and consequently verify
the principle. Before commencing the laboratory activity, you should give directions in the form of a monologue, followed by a brief question-and-answer period
regarding the procedure. The questions might be (assuming the students have
been given material to read beforehand): "What are we trying to do today?"
"How are we going to proceed?" "What data will we collect?" "What precautions
must be followed?" The purpose of reviewing the directions is to be certain that
they are clear and that everyone understands them. Using the paradigms presented earlier, this procedure can be represented as in Figure 6-4.

Many teachers have the students write a formal laboratory report stating
whether or not the principle was "proved," rather than discussing what was
done. For some types of laboratory activities, this formal report is necessary.
However, for a Type II laboratory activity, this is not necessary, since all parts
of the activity are actually given to the student. Having the student copy what
was given him should be considered "busy work." The value of a class discussion
is this: if an individual is asked to collect three to five sets of data and to conclude
something from it, he is being forced to make conclusions from limited data. The

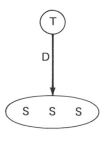

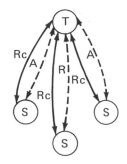

(a) Focus: giving directions   (b) Reviewing directions

Key: D   Giving directions
      Rc   Recalling questions
      A   Accepting reactions
      R   Rejecting reactions

FIGURE 6-4
Representation of Two Sequential Tactics Used to Give Directions.

more replications of a given experiment, the easier it is to see trends and relationships in these data. Since a class performing this activity is some thirty children
working on the same problem and following the same procedure, it would seem
reasonable to pool the class's data. Then the entire class can discuss the observable trends and draw conclusions, rather than each student generalizing from his
own limited data. In a post-laboratory discussion of the pooled data, the tentative
and searching nature of science can be shown. In addition, to see relationships or
trends by looking at one individual's data is difficult, but by pooling data collected in the same manner it is easier to see relationships.

The first part of the postlaboratory discussion can be considered as part of
the focusing tactic. Your main purpose is to find out what data the students have
collected and to arrange the data in such a manner that the students can determine whether the principle has been verified. The verbal aspect of this tactic
should utilize data collecting questions and reactions that accept and/or clarify
student responses. Using the diagrams presented earlier, a focusing tactic that
uses a Type II laboratory activity preceded by verbal interactions can be represented as in Figure 6-5.

It is not difficult to find examples of this kind of laboratory activity; any
high school or college laboratory guide contains many examples. An advantage
in using a Type II activity lies in the amount of teacher control. Direction following is quite important in these activities, especially if you believe that repli-
cating an experiment can contribute to the instructional objectives. But if a Type
II activity is used to the exclusion of others, or if the majority of laboratory
exercises are of this type, students get a distorted view of science and never have
a chance to practice its processing or evaluating aspects.

Type III
Otherwise known as a guided discovery activity, a Type III laboratory experience
has much teacher control. The student is not told and does not know what the

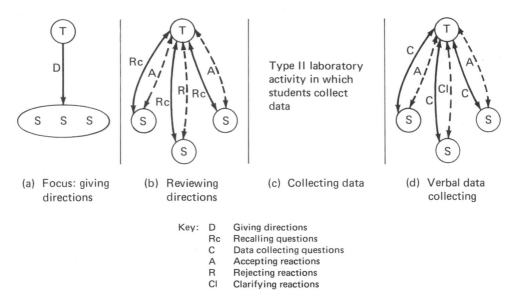

(a) Focus: giving   (b) Reviewing   (c) Collecting data   (d) Verbal data
     directions   directions   collecting

Key: D   Giving directions
      Rc   Recalling questions
      C   Data collecting questions
      A   Accepting reactions
      R   Rejecting reactions
      Cl   Clarifying reactions

FIGURE 6-5
Focusing Tactics Used with a Type II Laboratory Activity.

conclusions may be. The purpose of using a Type III laboratory activity is to give students practice in seeing relationships in the data collected. From this data a generalization, previously unknown to the students, can then be made. The main difference between Type II and Type III laboratory experiences is the student's prior educational experience. For a Type II activity, the students have had previous experience with the concept or principle from reading, discussions, or lectures, and therefore know what the outcomes may be.

It is not easy to construct activities of this type; however, there are some guidelines to follow. First, decide on your instructional objectives. For each lesson that uses a Type III laboratory activity, *one* concept or principle should be chosen. Second, using resource materials, choose five or more activities that illustrate the relationship to be "discovered." The younger the child, the more numerous should be the examples. One reason for using many examples is that it is quite difficult to generalize from one example—it can only be done if one has had much past experience to draw upon. Very often a series of demonstrations found in a resource book can be converted to a series of laboratory activities suitable for a Type III laboratory, as discussed on page 134.

The following are examples of Type III laboratory activities. In order for children to discover the concept "insect," obtain speciments of insects—enough for each group of three or four children to observe. You might start out by having students find out how many legs each insect has. Then have the students find out how many body parts each insect has. This examination is continued until the characteristics of insects are developed—three pairs of legs, all attached to the central body part; three separate body parts; one pair of antennae attached to the head; none, one, or two pairs of wings. After having the children discover these characteristics, you tell the students that these are the characteristics of an animal that is called an *insect.* In the remainder of the laboratory activity, present other examples and have the students tell you whether or not they are insects—making sure that they give reasons for their responses.

To discover a more complex relationship, such as a principle, the students could try the activities below:

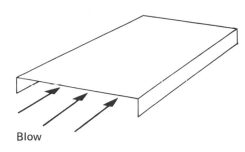

Bend down one-half inch on two sides of a three-by-five card and place it on the table, as in the picture. Try to blow the card over. What do you observe?

Blow

FIGURE 6-6

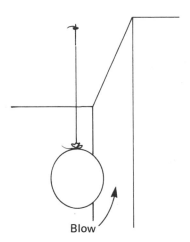

Blow up a balloon and tie it closed with a long piece of string. Hang the balloon about six inches from a vertical wall and blow between the balloon and the wall. What do you observe?

Blow

FIGURE 6-7

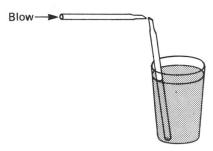

Blow→

Flatten one end of each of two straws. Stand one straw in a glass of water and hold the other horizontally, flattened ends together. Blow hard through the horizontal straw, aiming the air from it directly across the top of the other. What happens?

FIGURE 6-8

Place a thumbtack in the center of a three-by-five card. Place the card against a spool of thread so that the thumbtack point is inside the hole of the spool. Try to blow the card away from the spool by blowing into the other end of the hole. What happens?

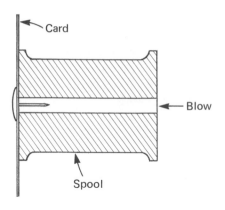

FIGURE 6-9

Connect the hose of a tank-type vacuum cleaner to the exhaust of the vacuum cleaner. With the cleaner turned on, place a ping-pong ball in the air stream and record your observations.

All these examples have something in common. What makes them similar? Note that if you were to try to discover the relationship between the activities given above just by doing them, you probably could not. This indicates the importance of teacher guidance.

As with a Type II laboratory activity, the class's data should be pooled and discussed by the group. Again, since everyone will be collecting the data in approximately the same way, it would be easier to observe trends and relationships in group data than in individual data. The data must be made visible by putting them on the chalk board or on display so that all may see. Also, these data should be displayed in such a manner as to make relationships more evident to the student. Figure 6-10 illustrates this idea. Since Type II and Type III laboratory activities are similar, the focusing aspects of these tactics, including the verbal interactions, can be generalized as in Figure 6-5.

The experience of the process of seeing new relationships in data is an advantage in a Type III laboratory activity. For students inexperienced in data processing, a certain amount of teacher direction in this type of activity is needed and important in helping them discover the relationships. The major disadvantage of such an activity, like Types I and II, comes with overusing it. If you consistently use this activity, the amount of material you can cover in a year is more limited; in addition, it would be frustrating for the students to have to "discover" everything.

Type IV
In a Type III laboratory activity, the teacher is primarily in control. In a Type IV laboratory activity, the child is primarily directing his own experience. In the latter case, only the problem to investigate is presented; and the child's task is to develop the methods for collecting data. As in a Type III activity, the laboratory work precedes the discovery of the concept or principle. The purpose of this

FIGURE 6-10
Recording Data in Histogram Form Helps Students to See Relationships.
(From Thier, Teaching Elementary School Science, p. 145.)

activity is to provide practice with such data-collecting skills as measuring, identifying, and controlling variables, and to discover a science concept or principle.

From the teacher's point of view, it takes courage to utilize a Type IV laboratory experience. Most teachers like to think they are in control all the time. Moreover, it is much easier to have thirty students doing the same thing than to have thirty students doing thirty different things. With a Type IV experience, you will assume the role of a patient and careful listener and a resource person. You must have the insight to know when to tell a student what to do and when not to tell him what to do. You must be extremely adaptable to shift from one student to the next, helping and encouraging each one. At first glance, one might think that little preparation is needed for a Type IV activity; actually, you must be well prepared in order to handle the problems that may, and usually do, arise.

Since each child develops his own method of collecting data, and consequently his own solution to the problem, an individual report, either in oral or written form, should be required. This report might include a statement of the problem, the methods used to collect data, the data, and some conclusions supported by the data. Which form of report the students will do depends on their grade level and the precise purpose of the Type IV laboratory activity.

Here are some guidelines for constructing a Type IV laboratory experience. Decide on the content and the inquiry skills you want the children to acquire. As a rule of thumb, only a limited number of concepts or principles and skill objectives should be attempted for each laboratory activity. For ideas on what topics to investigate in this manner, refer to the resource material at the end of this topic. Next, decide on an initiating tactic that will gain the students' interest. Then present the laboratory activity to your class. The activity may be presented verbally or given to the students on paper, as in the example following.

FIGURE 6-11
A Teacher Must Be a Patient and Careful Listener. (From Thier, Teaching
Elementary School Science, p. 150.)

Investigation of a Pendulum

A pendulum can easily be made using a piece of string attached to a
weight, such as a stone. The free end of the string can then be attached
to a support. A sample pendulum is on my desk. I'll provide you with
the materials to make your own.

Once you have made your own pendulum, pull the weight to the right
or left about two inches and then release it. Notice how it swings back
and forth. Using the classroom clock, you can easily determine how
long it takes to make ten swings.

Your task is to answer this question: How many different ways can
you find to change the amount of time it takes for ten swings? Devise
a laboratory procedure for determining an answer to this question. Be
sure to identify first the factors you think will make the pendulum
swing longer.

When you have made your plans, see me. I will then arrange for you
to work with another student. With your partner, modify plans as necessary in order to reach agreement on a laboratory procedure.

While you are working and collecting your data, pay particular attention to any circumstances which cause trouble and interfere with your
getting exactly the data you hoped to acquire. Try to develop ways to
eliminate these troubles or ways to make allowances for their effects
on the data. Use these revised techniques if you have time. Be prepared
to discuss the ones you were unable to use.

Make careful notes of all procedures used and of the data collected;
you will use them in presenting an oral report to the class.

Because of the individualized nature of this activity, the verbal aspects of this focusing tactic are primarily of the direction-giving type, in order to introduce the topic. Then the students would be permitted to work individually. However, if your purpose in using a Type IV laboratory activity is to provide practice in the inquiry skill of controlling variables, an appropriate verbal interaction, after the students have collected data in the laboratory, is to have a group of students present what they did. The ensuing discussion would focus on whether or not the students controlled relevant variables. A focusing tactic emphasizing this is illustrated in Figure 6-12.

This type of laboratory activity is quite similar to the activities undertaken by most scientists, in that a problem is developed, and the researchers attempt to find a solution for it. If this type of activity is the only experience students have with science, it can be frustrating and time-consuming, because a satisfactory solution to the problem may be a long time in coming. Poorly motivated students, or those who need more immediate rewards for learning, find Type IV activities quite boring and frustrating. From the teacher's point of view, Type IV laboratory activities require much planning and patience.

Type V

This laboratory activity has the least teacher direction of any type so far presented. It places the entire burden of investigation on the student, because he formulates the problem and the methods of collecting data. He also interprets the data, arriving at conclusions based on what he has done. A Type V laboratory investigation most closely approximates that which is done in a research laboratory.

In order for this experience to be productive for the student, he must have already gained some competency with the inquiry skills of science as well as with the science content he wants to investigate. Otherwise, he is likely to flounder and become discouraged easily. Today some educators argue that this floundering is what learning is all about, and some strongly advocate this method of teaching

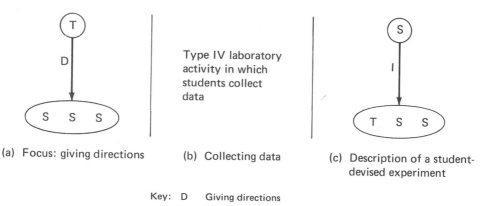

(a) Focus: giving directions   (b) Collecting data   (c) Description of a student-
                                                                           devised experiment

Key: D   Giving directions
       I   Presenting new material

FIGURE 6-12
Representation of the Focusing Tactics Used with a Type IV Laboratory Activity.

FIGURE 6-13
Basic Skills Are Needed Before Type V Laboratory Activities Can Be Used Successfully in the Classroom. (From Thier, Teaching Elementary School Science, p. 125.)

and learning. The sink-or-swim method of learning, as this is commonly called, can waste time in the classroom. Furthermore, for a student with an average or below amount of motivation, such an experience can be frustrating. It is one thing to be frustrated and have some idea of how to proceed, but it is another to be frustrated and not know what to do. It is strongly recommended that this type of activity be used only after students have acquired sufficient familiarity with the skills of inquiry. A Type V laboratory activity gives a student the opportunity to focus on a problem that he has identified, and to use the skills and content already acquired to solve the problem. This is not to imply that first or second graders cannot successfully participate in this type of laboratory activity. Sometimes they can do independent work successfully, although not with the adeptness that older children might.

As in a Type IV laboratory experience, you must be well prepared to act as a resource person and to feel comfortable in permitting students to work in an area unknown to you. In a sense, you permit the *child* to become an expert in the area he chooses to investigate. The topics a student investigates can be logical extensions of the material presented in class or ideas obtained from the students' own reading or experiences. The most difficult task for a student is limiting a problem to a size commensurate with his stage of development. A good resource book to have in the classroom for you and your students to read before attempting this type of activity is Phillip Goldstein's book, *How to Do an Experiment.*[16]

A key ingredient in motivation and learning is variety. Variation in the types

[16] Phillip Goldstein, *How to Do an Experiment* (New York: Harcourt, Brace, World & Co., 1957).

of laboratory activities can play an important part in developing enthusiasm for a science program. Five types of laboratory activities have been presented and were characterized by the teacher's purpose in employing them and by the amount of teacher control. Type I is concerned with developing psychomotor skills. Verification of science concepts or principles previously known to the student is the emphasis of a Type II laboratory activity. The discovering of a science concept or principle previously unknown to the student is the purpose of a Type III laboratory activity. These three types of laboratory activities must of necessity include much teacher control. The two remaining types place the burden of direction and learning on the student. In a Type IV laboratory activity, the student is given a problem, and his task is to devise a method of solving it— collecting his own data and analyzing it himself. The most student-directed laboratory activity is a Type V, in which he selects his own problem and the methods of solving it. For young and/or inexperienced children, the Types I, II, and III are the most appropriate, while for individuals who have some experience with the content as well as inquiry skills, Types IV and V are the most appropriate.

Using the different laboratory types as focusing tactics, you can verbally focus students' attention on the task to be performed, permit the students to perform the task, and then refocus their attention on the data collected, helping them to assimilate the material or accommodate their conceptual framework.

Activities

1. Describe the rationale for using the five types of laboratory activities discussed.
2. Using the resource material given at the end of this topic, construct the laboratory activity suggested by each of the following instructional objectives.
    (a)   To measure the weight of an object (Type I).
    (b)   To state evidence that matter has holes in it (Type III).
    (c)   To design an experiment in which controls are used (Type IV).
    (d)   To determine if starch is present in a leaf (Type II).
3. Find an experiment in any elementary science textbook, change it into a Type III laboratory activity, and present it to a class.
4. Find an experiment in any elementary science textbook, change it into a Type IV laboratory activity, and present it to a class.

Resource Material

Any elementary school science textbook has a plethora of examples of Type I and Type II laboratory activities. Although there are many sources of laboratory activities, we have been selective in choosing the following list. The sources presented here are very suitable for developing Type III laboratory activities.

Cornell Rural School Leaflets. Ithaca, New York: New York State College of Agriculture, Cornell University.

George, Kenneth D. et al. *Science Investigations for Elementary School Teachers.* Lexington, Mass.: D. C. Heath, 1974.

Joseph, Alexander et al. *A Sourcebook for the Physical Sciences.* New York: Harcourt, Brace & World, 1961.

Lynde, C. J. *Science Experiences with Home Equipment* Scranton, Pa.: International Textbook Co., 1941.

Lynde, C. J. *Science Experiences with Inexpensive Equipment.* Scranton, Pa.: International Textbook Co., 1941.

Morholt, E., Brandwein, P., Joseph, A. *A Sourcebook for the Biological Sciences.* New York: Harcourt, Brace, & World, 1958.

National Science Teachers Association. *Investigating Science with Children:* vol. 1, *Living Things;* vol. 2, *The Earth;* vol. 3, *Atoms and Molecules*; vol. 4, *Energy in Waves*; vol. 5, *Motions*; vol. 6, *Space.* Darien, Conn.: Teachers Publishing Corp., 1964.

Science Curriculum Improvement Study (SCIS). Numerous volumes of science material suitable for elementary school, taking into account the child's intellectual development. Chicago: Rand McNally.

UNESCO, *700 Science Experiments for Everyone.* Garden City, New York: Doubleday and Co., 1958.

UNESCO, *UNESCO Sourcebook for Science Teaching.* France: UNESCO, 1970.

Any of the above are good sources of problems suitable for Type IV laboratory activities. The Elementary Science Study (ESS) materials published by Webster Division, McGraw-Hill Book Co., St. Louis, are especially suited for Type IV investigations. The teachers' guides give countless suggestions for problems a child may investigate.

Field Trips

Objectives

1. To state the rationale for using field trips as focusing tactics.
2. To construct a focusing tactic that uses a field trip to provide experiences for an instructional objective.

Most of you have been on what is called a "field trip." Unless this trip was atypical, it was conducted in tour fashion: a guide pointed out and explained the facility being toured—arboretum, zoo, museum, or factory. The participants had little opportunity to become physically or mentally involved, other than by listening and walking from place to place. Such an activity should be called an off-campus *lecture.* But if used properly, an off-campus lecture can be an effective teaching tactic.

As used in this text, field trips are outdoor *laboratory activities.* In the preceding topic, the laboratory activities were assumed to take place in a classroom. But a field trip can also be a useful focusing tactic. If properly designed, these

FIGURE 6-14
The Outdoors Can Provide Many Science Experiences, if the Teacher Plans
for Them. (From Thier, Teaching Elementary School Science, p. 119.)

experiences can keep students mentally and physically involved with the material
presented. The main difference between a field trip and a laboratory activity is
that in the former, more planning is required, since students will be spread over
a larger area than in a classroom.

As with the previously described laboratory activities, field trips can be classified into five types—the same five as classroom laboratory activities. The ideas
presented in the preceding pages regarding laboratory activities also apply to
field trips. Similarly, the advantages and disadvantages for each type are the same.
However, on field trips you must be in better control of the class and know what
the students are doing at all times. Only *examples* of different types of field
trips will be presented here.

A Type I field trip is appropriate to develop selected psychomotor skills.
Skills that could better be developed out-of-doors are insect or plant collecting,
various types of sampling techniques to determine animal and plant populations
in land and aquatic environments, or observations of plants or animals in natural
habitats. To find areas where such skills may be practiced is a difficult task for
a busy teacher. A local high school biology teacher, a science consultant, a nature
group, or one of the resource books given at the end of this topic are excellent
starting points for finding such areas.

Verification of concepts or principles presented in class can be completed
out-of-doors with a Type II field trip. In a study of astronomy, you may describe
certain constellations in class, then assign the students to locate the described
constellations that night. In class you may use slides to present certain species
of trees and their distinguishing characteristics. You can then take your class
outside to verify these characteristics.

FIGURE 6-15
Zoos Can Be Good Places to Observe Animal Behavior. (Photo by Miles Nelson.)

Selected concepts and principles can also be discovered out-of-doors, using a Type III field trip. For example, several points around the school may illustrate the concept of weathering. Your class may be able to observe a tree whose roots are penetrating the sidewalk, feel the well-worn stone steps of the school, or observe a small gully formed when water ran off the dirt playground. Animal behavior studies, too, can best be completed outside. The children may be able to observe squirrels, pigeons, ants, or spiders, carefully noting what the animal is doing—feeding, hunting, carrying food, nesting—and when the animal is actually performing these activities. Such activities can help the children to discover new principles regarding animal behavior.

A well-planned trip to the zoo or horticulture garden could also be used as a Type III discovery-oriented field trip. You might specifically ask students to visit, or take them personally to, specific places in the zoo, having them carefully take notes on a specific type of plant or animal characteristic. When the students return to the school, a post-field trip discussion would pull together everyone's observations. Subsequently, a concept or principle new to the students might be developed.

Presenting your students with a problem and permitting them to collect data outside of the classroom provides an opportunity for a Type IV field trip. Even though you present a problem to your students, inconsistencies can arise from careful observations. The solution to these inconsistencies may come only if the students are permitted to collect data outside of the classroom. For example, you could ask students to determine how many different kinds of plants or animals live in a designated area near the school. Such a problem could be solved by a Type IV field trip. You may be surprised at the variety of plants and animals living in the city.

Identification of microscopic and macroscopic animals, using a key, would also be a suitable Type IV field trip. Or conversely, having students classify the material gathered on a field trip would be an excellent way to organize data.

Problems evolving out of students' observations of natural phenomena can lead to Type V field trips. A group of students walking to and from school may have noticed a line of flowers growing in a rain gutter, and wondered where they came from or why they are growing there. A teacher who hears this phenomenon discussed by students entering the classroom could use it as a topic for a field study.

It is not important that you remember the names of the different field trip types, but it is important to remember the different ways in which you can use a field trip to focus students' attention on science concepts, principles, and skills.

Activities

1. Describe the rationale for using each of the five types of field trips.
2. Using the resource material following this activity, construct a field trip as a focusing tactic for the following instructional objectives:
   (a) The students should be able to collect and identify the insects found in a field (Type I).
   (b) The students should be able to identify examples of erosion outside of the classroom (Type II).
   (c) Given a series of examples of rotting logs, the students should be able to order them chronologically (Type III).

Resource Material

Hurd, Paul D. *How to Teach Science Through Field Studies.* Washington, D. C.: National Science Teachers Association, 1965.

National Science Teachers Association. *Living Things.* Investigating Science with Children, vol. 1. Darien, Connecticut: Teachers Publishing Corp., 1964, pp. 74-94.

Demonstrations

Objectives

1. To state the rationale for using a demonstration as a focusing tactic.
2. To construct a demonstration as a focusing tactic for an instructional objective.

Simply stated, a demonstration is an illustration. In science classes, focusing tactics that use demonstrations are intended to draw attention to one or two things. First, you may use a demonstration to illustrate a science concept, such as solid, bird, fish; or to illustrate a principle, such as "Objects in a vacuum fall at the same rate of speed." Second, the teaching of skills needed in the laboratory, such as how to collect data, duplicate observations, weigh an object, heat a beaker, or dissect a worm, can be done with a demonstration. Demonstrations

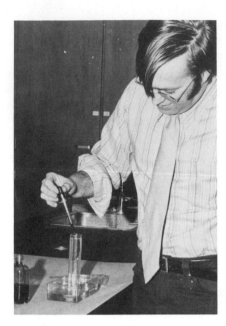

FIGURE 6-16
Demonstrations Can Be Good Focusing
Tactics if Equipment Is Limited. (Courtesy
of Minaruth Galey, Temple University.)

differ from laboratory activities in the amount of student involvement. Typically, demonstrations actively involve only a small portion of the class. For those involved in presenting the demonstration, it is an action mode of learning, while for the remainder of the class, demonstrations are an imagery and/or language mode.

Demonstrations performed primarily by the teacher make it difficult to keep students physically *and* mentally involved. They also become passive observers when the demonstration is not clearly visible from their seats, or if it is not a clear example of the concept, principle, or skill. Thus demonstrations can lose their focusing efficiency. If demonstrations are to be used to focus attention on a concept, principle, or skill, the observers should be directed to watch for the particular event. The easiest way to do this might be to say, "I'd like you to watch closely what is going to happen when I mix these two liquids in this beaker." To aid your students in seeing the demonstration, it could be performed several times in different places in the room. Or, if your room has moveable seats, have the children gather around you or whomever performs the demonstration. Using equipment familiar to your students also lends clarity to the presentation and helps to dispel the illusion that science is mysterious or gadgety.

The following are sample demonstrations illustrating a concept or principle—first, examples of ways to obtain maximum student involvement and then examples that are more teacher centered. Of course, demonstrations that could possibly harm a child while performing them should not be done by him.

Perhaps the simplest type of demonstration is one a child can do by himself:

An aquarium in your room has some snails in it. You have noticed a deposit of eggs on one wall of the aquarium, so you draw a circle around the egg mass with a magic marker and post this sign above the aquarium: "What is going on here?" A magnifying glass could also be handy for closer observation.

Another self-demonstration could be a table on which several different types of lenses are displayed. A sign on the table might read: "Can you make this sign look bigger, smaller, or upside down?"

These are examples of self-demonstrations for which you have set up the situation and the students are asked to perform some operation. Only the simplest of equipment should be used to demonstrate concepts or principles in this way.

Another procedure to follow in obtaining student involvement with a demonstration is to have the child perform it under your direction.

On the playground you can demonstrate many types of forces through a child's experience. You might have a child describe what he feels while riding on a merry-go-round, or how "hard" he is sitting on a swing when it is at the top and then at the bottom of its climb. These are ways to have one or several children inform the others of the experience, rather than have you explain it. For another example, if a child sits in the bottom of a wagon and throws bricks out the back of it, he can feel the forces that cause the wagon to go forward.

Having several children perform the task, and then having them describe what they feel, will help the nonparticipants to verify and assimilate the information. Another example may help to explain this:

Have a child put one hand in a bowl of warm water and the other hand in a bowl of ice water. Leave both hands there for about one to two minutes. Then have the child place both hands in a bowl of water at room temperature. Ask him to describe what he feels.

Having the children tell you what to do during a demonstration is another way to obtain student involvement, even though they are not directly manipulating the equipment.

Suppose you are demonstrating a pendulum. A child asks, "What would happen if you used a heavier weight for the bob?" You try it, and the students note the effects. If another student says, "Make the string shorter," you follow his suggestion.

You are demonstrating the effects of an object's shape on its ability to float. A child asks to see what would happen if the object were made into a ball; you respond by trying the child's suggestion.

All of the above are excellent methods for obtaining student involvement while focusing student attention on a concept or principle. Most of the preceding examples of demonstrations are from the physical sciences. In some areas of the biological or earth sciences, demonstrations are difficult to do, because it takes some time before a change can take place or be observed. It is easy to adjust the length of a pendulum and immediately notice the effect it has on the time to make one swing, or to see the results of mixing two chemicals. But within a short period of time it is difficult to change the amount of light a plant gets and see the resulting effects, or to give an animal a particular type of food and see the effects the same day. However, with careful planning, you can bring to class examples of plants grown under different amounts of light, or animals fed different diets, and use these examples to focus attention on a concept or principle. For example:

Bring to class two of the same types of plants and allow one to become wilted before you display it. Place the plants side by side on a table and use them to draw attention to the principle that plants need water in order to survive.

Slit the stem of a carnation half way. Place one half in a jar filled with water colored red and the other half in a jar filled with water colored blue, or any other color. Wait a day or two, until the flower is colored, and then present it to the class to show how water gets to the blossom.

The examples presented above are methods you might employ to focus attention on a concept or principle. To get students involved in demonstrations, you might have them record data on the chalkboard, watch the clock to note how long something takes to happen, or observe color changes.

On the other hand, student involvement in presenting a psychomotor skill could be detrimental to a clear presentation of the skill. Another problem with "live" demonstrations of some skills, such as how to weigh an object, measure length using a ruler, or inoculate Petri dishes, even if performed by the teacher, is that they are difficult to perform so that all may see. Repeating the demonstration to several small groups would overcome this problem, but might create another—what to do with students who aren't involved.

One solution to this dilemma is to illustrate the skill through a film. There are many skills recorded on 8 mm single-loop films, which run from three to five minutes in length, and can be shown over and over again without rethreading a machine. The ease with which such film loops are shown makes them suitable for self-instruction purposes. Therefore, using a single-loop film, rather than a "live" illustration, as a demonstration of a skill has more than one advantage. First, the skill is presented in a manner clearly visible to all. Furthermore, the skill can be illustrated several times without wasting time setting up the equipment again, or wasting live materials.

Imagery modes of presenting demonstrations are usually called audio-visual aids. However, in science classes, most of such aids are used to illustrate a science concept or principle, so we will call them demonstrations. Films, charts, models, and chalkboard sketches are all typical means of illustrating concepts, principles, and skills. Yet, even though we have classified all of the above as imagery modes of demonstrations, there are subtle differences. Films and some types of models can be very lifelike and require little, if any, imagination to understand what is being represented. On the other hand, some charts or chalkboard sketches can be quite abstract and require much thought for the student to determine that they represent a concrete object. The examples below should help to clarify this point.

Films showing real people, as opposed to animated films, give more realism to the demonstration. In addition to presenting the concept or principle in a manner visible to all, films enable you to present some important ideas which you otherwise could not. A film demonstrating bird habitats or the predator-prey relationship can be far more effective than any display you could put together in a classroom.

A dimension of realism is added to any lesson when representations, or models, of a concept can be utilized. Plastic models of a flower, eye, human skeleton, and so on, help students to understand things not ordinarily available to them for examination.

Mechanical models and animated films, on the other hand, help students to visualize information that scientists have not directly seen but have much data to support. The sun-centered theory of the solar system, for instance, can be demonstrated with a mechanical model or an animated film. Theories involving the atom or a group of atoms can similarly be represented. Such modes of representation do not depict the actual objects, like a skeleton or the eye, but rather summarize evidence in such a manner that predictions and hypotheses can be made.

More abstract demonstrations may use maps representing the distribution of vegetation in an area or geological features; or charts representing an idealized digestive tract, or a leaf cross-section, or atomic size. All these examples require more experience on the child's part before he is able to understand them. Likewise, your chalkboard sketch must represent an object the children are familiar with before they will be able to understand it. Using Piaget's ideas, the younger or more inexperienced child needs demonstrations using real objects, while the experienced child will be able to cope with the more abstract representations.

What types of monologues or dialogues should be employed when using a demonstration as a focusing tactic? In contrast to some of the initiating tactics that could be thought of as demonstrations, a demonstration is used to draw attention to a concept, principle, or skill. Whereas with the inconsistencies presented earlier, your objective is to initiate the inquiry process. With this change in purpose comes a change in verbal interaction patterns. There have been many studies on the effects of cuing or not cuing an observer when he is attempting to inquire. Most of these studies clearly indicate the necessity to cue the observer. So, applying these findings to demonstrations and their focusing aspect, you should provide the child with some cues before presenting the demonstration.

In all the examples of "live" demonstrations given previously, the child was cued. Likewise, when showing a chart or map, you should direct your pupils to look for the specific parts that you wish to illustrate. Most teachers do this by pointing or through some other gesture directing attention to the pertinent object or event. When you show a film, the children should be directed to look for examples of the *one* or *two* concepts or principles on which the film will focus. Afterwards, the student's attention should be redirected to those one or two

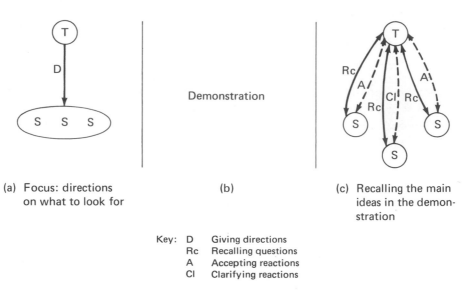

(a) Focus: directions   (b)   (c) Recalling the main
    on what to look for   ideas in the demon-
                                                 stration

Key: D   Giving directions
      Rc   Recalling questions
      A   Accepting reactions
      Cl   Clarifying reactions

FIGURE 6-17
Representation of the Focusing Tactics Used with a Demonstration.

concepts through a brief question-and-answer review. These focusing aspects of a demonstration can be conceptualized as in Figure 6-17.

To construct a demonstration is difficult, especially for someone who is not well acquainted with the content. Fortunately, there are many books available with ideas for demonstrations. Some of these are included in the resource materials. Assuming that some of these books are available to you, the following guidelines should help you use a demonstration as a focusing tactic.

To focus students' attention on a science concept or principle with a demonstration, first decide on your instructional objectives. Using the resource material, familiarize yourself with the demonstrations available and select several that are clear examples of the concept or principle you wish to present. Then, to decide between a laboratory activity or demonstration, ask yourself these questions:

1.   Is enough equipment available so all the students may perform the activity?
2.   Is the activity safe enough for a child to perform?
3.   Is the equipment simple enough to use?
4.   Is the activity easily observed?

If the answer to all four questions is *yes,* then you should use a laboratory activity. If the answer to item 4 is no, you should look for another concept or principle to demonstrate. Next, present the demonstrations, using equipment familiar to your students so that they are not awed or confused by it. Be sure to use methods of getting your students involved, especially if they are young or lack experience with the concept or principle to be presented.

To show how to perform a skill needed in the laboratory, such as weighing or measuring, you should choose a very simple one. After clearly showing how

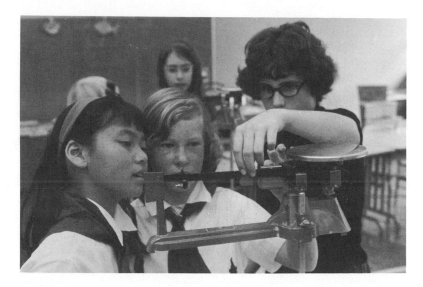

FIGURE 6-18
One Student Can Show Others How to Use a Balance. (From Thier,
Teaching Elementary School Science, p. 189.)

to perform the task, permit three or four children to practice the skill with everyone else watching. As each child demonstrates how to perform the skill, the rest
of the class should be encouraged to comment on the performance. In this
manner, both the child who is performing and the children watching obtain
constructive feedback on the performance.

To demonstrate how to weigh an object using an equal-arm balance, show
step by step, and in a part of the room where all could see, how to use the balance.
Then have a volunteer from the class demonstrate his ability to weigh an object
(Figure 6-18). While he is doing this, you can ask the rest of the class to watch
carefully and comment on whether or not he is following the correct procedure.
After this child completes a weighing, ask another. Repeat this until you are sure
most of the students can at least state the correct procedures to follow.

To demonstrate the performance of a skill used in science, first decide which
one is needed by students. The type of skill you choose should be commensurate
with the child's level of development. Then provide the opportunity for three or
four children to practice the skill, in view of all the children, with you providing
some constructive feedback on their performance.

Demonstrations used as focusing tactics are less active modes of instruction
than laboratory activities. Demonstrations provide some control over what a
child experiences, thus making them good focusing tactics to draw attention to
a single concept, principle, or skill. A wide range of realism exists in demonstrations; care must be taken to employ the right type of demonstration for the
child's stage of development and past experience with the phenomenon. With
due care, demonstrations are a valuable tool with which you can develop content
and skills in a variety of ways.

Activities

1. Give the rationale for using a demonstration as a focusing tactic.
2. Using resource material, construct a demonstration as a focusing tactic for the following instructional objectives:
   (a) The students should be able to identify the color of an object.
   (b) Given an angle, the student should be able to measure it, using a protractor.
   (c) The students should be able to infer the materials needed to support combustion.
   (d) The students should be able to identify the sepals, petals, stamens, and pistils of a flower.
3. Present a demonstration to a class of children and note their reactions.

Resource Material

American Geological Institute. *Geology and Earth Sciences Sourcebook for Elementary and Secondary Schools.* New York: Holt, Rinehardt and Winston, Inc., 1962.

Blough, Glenn O., and Schwartz, Julius. *Elementary School Science and How to Teach It.* 4th ed. New York: Holt, Rinehart and Winston, Inc., 1969.

George, Kenneth D. et al. *Science Investigations for Elementary School Teachers.* Lexington, Mass.: D. C. Heath, 1974.

Hone, Elizabeth et al. *A Source book for Elementary Science.* 2nd ed. New York: Harcourt, Brace, Jovanovich, Inc., 1971.

Joseph, A. et al. *A Source Book for the Physical Sciences.* New York: Harcourt, Brace, Jovanovich, Inc., 1961.

Morholt, E., Brandwein, P., Joseph, A. *A Source Book for the Biological Sciences.* New York: Harcourt, Brace, Jovanovich, Inc., 1958.

Victor, Edward. *Science for the Elementary School.* 2nd ed. New York: The Macmillan Co., 1970.

Role Playing

Objectives

1. To state reasons for using role playing as a focusing tactic.
2. To construct a role-playing situation as a focusing tactic for an instructional objective.

There are two types of concepts—observational and abstract. Young children's dependence on direct or concrete experiences often makes it difficult to teach them abstract concepts. Observational concepts can be learned through observing specific examples of the concept or by viewing phenomena directly related to the concept. Roundness, insects, birds, mammals, and plants are examples of concepts that can be formulated through observation. The focusing tactics of laboratory

FIGURE 6-19
Acting out the Meanings Helps to Make Abstract Words More
Meaningful to Young Children.

activities and demonstrations are useful for providing the experiences children
need in order to formulate such concepts.

On the other hand, abstract concepts that exhibit relationships formed by
definition might be quite difficult for young children to grasp, since they are
primarily presented through verbal means. Some examples of abstract concepts
are atom, pressure, and energy. In order to provide meaning to these abstract
concepts, role playing is a useful tactic. Having your children act out the meaning
of the words will help them to visualize them. In a unit on astronomy, for instance, the words "rotation" and "revolution" may not be understood by many
young children. However, by acting out these words and "feeling" them by their
actions, children can attach a meaning to these words. Similarly, to get students
to see the relationships among planets in our solar system, role-playing tactics
help. Students can be assigned different parts to play—the sun, Mercury, Venus,
Mars, and so on. If you utilize the playground and have children carry signs des-
ignating their roles, observers—the rest of the class—can see the solar system in
action. The planetary model of the atom could also be demonstrated in this
manner.

In order for such activities to be successful, there must be much teacher direction, and the children playing the various roles must understand their parts.
This suggests that the appropriate verbal maneuver to employ before using this
type of role-playing activity is a direction-giving monologue.

There is another use for role-playing tactics, involving helping children to be
less egocentric.[17] Egocentricity is a characteristic of young children in the stage
that Piaget refers to as preoperational, but many children, and even many adults,

[17] The child's egocentricity is well documented; see Jean Piaget, *The Child's Conception of the*
World, trans. Joan and Andrew Tomlinson (New York: Littlefield, Adams and Co., 1965).

find it difficult to see an event from a point of view other than their own. For instance, children may argue over a toy, each wanting sole possession. Or two adults may argue over an environmental issue, one wanting to dam up a river that annually floods him out of his home, the other claiming that damming the river will spoil several wild bird rookeries. Role playing is a focusing tactic that can help children see a problem or issue from another perspective.

Using the issue presented above—whether a particular river should be dammed to avoid flooding—you can develop a situation in which role playing would be an excellent focusing tactic. Four or five students could be assigned to play the role of farmers whose hard work—their land and homes—is annually destroyed by this flooding river. A similar number of students could be assigned to play the role of environmentalists whose research has shown the river to be a nesting grounds for several species of wild birds. It should be noted that, in order for the students to successfully fulfill their roles, they must have studied or read some material on the farmers' and environmentalists' points of view. If no preparation or background information data are given, the students would be guessing, at best, and the role-playing activity would not be as successful as possible.

To involve the remaining students, one small group of students could be given the task of deciding whether or not the dam should be built. They would base this decision on the arguments presented by the groups representing the farmers and environmentalists. The rest of the class could be assigned the task of identifying the feelings expressed by each group.

An alert teacher can identify many controversial issues in which science is involved. Many environmental issues can be presented and discussed, using role playing. "Should automobiles be banned from the streets because of the effect of the exhaust on the environment?" "Should a small industry in a rural community be prevented from discharging wastes into the local river?" "Should organ transplants be performed?" "Should our water supply be fluoridated?" All of these are suitable topics for presentation by role playing.

Once the issue has been presented and roles assigned, the students can then play out their designated parts. This sequence of presenting the issue, assigning tasks, and then playing out the role constitutes a focusing tactic using role playing. Role-playing tactics are excellent ways of showing the effects science has on society. Such tactics are equally effective in showing different attitudes about an issue. It may not change any attitudes, but it certainly will focus students' attention on the underlying reasons behind the attitudes.

When you employ this type of teaching tactic, care must be exercised. Usually the issues presented are controversial, and your children may be taken up in the emotion of the role. Before discussing the result of the activity, your children should be brought back to reality—calmed down. The students in the play may have criticized each other, and feelings may be hurt. It is important that the students be reminded that they were reacting to roles, not to an individual.

Role playing as a focusing tactic is an example of an action-oriented type of presentation. You may use role playing to make abstract concepts concrete or to identify attitudes behind social issues involving scientific findings.

Activities

1. Give the rationale for using role playing as a focusing tactic.
2. Construct a role-playing situation that will give the students a better understanding of the following science concepts and principles:
   (a) Air is made of small particles in constant motion.
   (b) An unbalanced force on an object results in motion or change in motion.
   (c) Force.
   (d) Water table.
   (e) Expansion.
   (f) Contraction.
3. Construct a role-playing situation to help children identify the attitudes behind issues such as the following:
   (a) Birth control.
   (b) Building atomic power plants in cities.
   (c) Limiting each family to owning only one car.
   Then try out this situation with a class.

Resource Material

Chesler, Mark and Fox, Robert. *Role Playing Methods in the Classroom.* Chicago: Science Research Associates, 1966.

Quests

Objectives

1. To give the rationale for using a quest as a focusing tactic.
2. To construct a quest as a focusing tactic for an instructional objective.

Too often science is taught as an unchanging body of content—as definite conclusions. The tentativeness and probabilistic nature of science, and the process by which concepts and principles arise from data, are rarely shown; yet this is the very foundation of science. As discussed in Section I of this book, the authors feel that a more realistic view of science stresses the ways of generating and organizing the content of science as well as the content itself. Focusing tactics emphasizing the development of concepts or principles from data that students have not collected themselves, we call *quests.*

This type of tactic is quite useful in immediately focusing students' attention on the skills of inquiry, such as inferring, predicting, verifying, hypothesizing, and isolating variables. In a typical laboratory situation, students' processing of the data is postponed until after the data has been collected. In this teaching tactic, the student is presented with a problem and a set of data, from which he can immediately begin solving the problem.

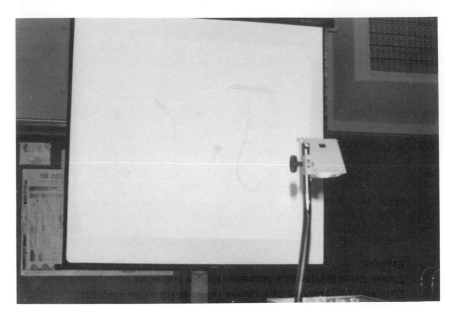

FIGURE 6-20
Shadow Projection Is One Method of Presenting Data to Students.

Experimentally collecting data in a laboratory situation sometimes is quite time consuming for children who have a short attention span; in addition, equipment may be too complex for youngsters whose coordination of motor skills has not yet developed. A quest is an effective means for skipping the actual data collecting process and focusing on data analysis. Since your students do not physically manipulate apparatus or directly experience the phenomenon, quests are typically imagery and/or language modes of instruction. One way of presenting data to students is shown in Figure 6-20.

> Suppose you are investigating plant growth, and you want to provide practice with the skills of observing and classifying. Using a styrofoam cup half filled with wet paper toweling, place pea seeds on top of the toweling. After one week of keeping the toweling wet, you will have several seeds sprouted. Carefully picking out seeds in various stages of development, place them on the stage of an overhead projector. While you project their shadows on a screen, ask students to make observations of them and also rank them from youngest to oldest.

> The data you are presenting to the students are plants in various stages of development. However, these data are primarily in image form, because the students see only the shadows. To focus attention on the data, you might use the following monologue: "I'd like you to observe carefully the shadows on the screen. After you have spent a few moments observing them, I will ask you to describe what you see."

> After several minutes, you could draw attention to the observations made by asking students to describe what they saw. Reacting to stu-

dent responses by accepting them or asking them to be clarified, you could then ask students to arrange the shadows according to which came first.

Some geological processes can be studied with quests. By projecting simultaneously two pictures taken in the same location but several years apart, you could have your children practice the inquiry skills of observing and inferring, and develop the concept of erosion. Figure 6-21 depicts erosion by wave attack.

A brief introduction, describing when the slides were taken, should be made before presenting them. The teacher should ask data collecting questions in order to be sure students have observed carefully. Reacting to student responses with acceptance or asking for clarification of responses is also important in the development of the quest. A dialogue illustrating this type of verbal communication is presented here:

Teacher: Who will describe what they see in the slide on the right? OK, Robin.

Robin: The ground looks flat and dusty.

Teacher: What do you mean dusty?

Robin: Well, I see a sort of dust cloud in the background.

Teacher: Judy, how would you describe the slide on the right?

Judy: About the same way in which Robin did, but I would add that no plants are present.

Teacher: How would you describe the slide on the left? Joe.

Data can also be presented in the form of tables or graphs. Figures 6-22 and 6-23 represent some examples. Again, a brief monologue describing the problem to be investigated should be given before presenting the table or graph. The dialogue following the data presentation should immediately focus students' attention on the data—*not* on the interpretation of the data. Interpretation should come after you determine that most of the students understand what data have been presented.

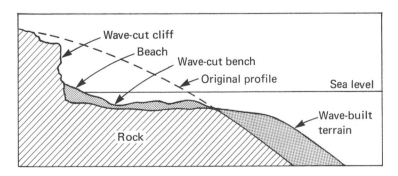

FIGURE 6-21
**Data May Be Presented by Pictures Taken at Intervals. Diagram
Shows Cross Section of a Shoreline Before and After
Erosion.**

D_o	D_i
1.20	4.58
2.02	2.71
3.89	1.41
7.98	0.69
10.03	0.53
14.38	0.38
16.36	0.34
18.11	0.30
27.0	0.25
42.25	0.13

FIGURE 6-22
Data Presented in
Tabular Form.

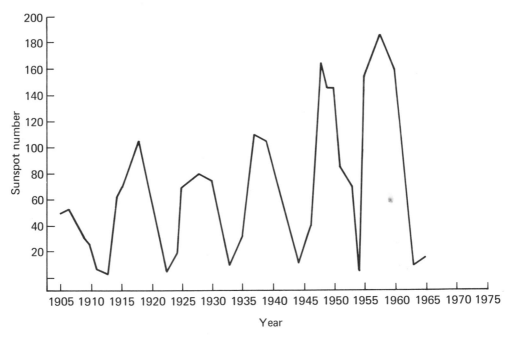

FIGURE 6-23
Data Presented Graphically.

Sometimes problems and data are presented in written form. You might introduce the example in Figure 6-24 like this:

We've been investigating different types of mystery boxes. Today I'm going to give you a mystery box that you cannot shake or pull. This paper that I am handing out has a mystery box on it, along with some observations. After studying the box carefully, try to determine how the pipes are connected inside the box.

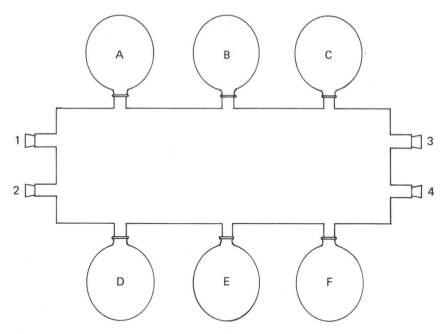

FIGURE 6-24
The following observations were made on the balloon box.

Balloons can only be inflated by blowing into pipes 1, 2, 3, or 4.
With all balloons inflated, when plug 3 is removed, balloon C deflates.
When plug 2 is removed, nothing happens.
With all balloons inflated, when balloon A is punctured, balloons B and E deflate.
When balloon D is punctured, balloon F deflates.
On the picture above, draw an inferred pattern of the connection of the balloons and pipes
   consistent with the observations.
What further tests could you make to determine whether your inferences are correct?

    The emphasis of this quest is to provide practice with the inquiry skills of
inferring or verifying. The skill of experimenting could easily be discussed using
the following example:

> Your class has been studying the factors that affect the growth of a
> plant. Your students have developed experiments to determine the
> factors influencing plant growth. To provide more practice with ex-
> perimenting, your students could be asked to read carefully the fol-
> lowing description of an experiment, keeping in mind the question,
> "Are the investigator's conclusions supported by his data?"

Is Wood Made of Water?

All earth, clay, and every body that may be touched is truly and materially the offspring of water only, and is reduced again into water,
by nature and art. . . . But I have learned by this handicraft-operation,
that all vegetables do immediately and materially proceed out of water
only. For I took a pot in which I put 200 pounds of dirt that had been
dried and I planted a willow tree weighing five pounds. After five years

of watering the tree and watching it grow, I reweighed it and found it to be 169 pounds. I watered the pot with rainwater, or distilled water (always when there was need) . . . and lest the dust should settle on the dirt of the pot, I covered the pot with an iron plate. I did not weigh the leaves that fell off in the four autumns. At length I again dried the dirt in the pot and found the same 200 pounds. Therefore 164 pounds of wood, bark, and roots arose out of water only. Therefore, wood is made of water.[18]

After the students have read this example, you bring to the students' attention, by asking data collecting questions, the important facts that would help students to answer the question, "Are the investigator's conclusions supported by his data? These focusing questions might be

1. What problem was this investigator trying to solve?
2. How did he go about collecting data relevant to his problem?
3. What data did he collect?
4. What were his conclusions?

All of the quests presented so far have emphasized interpreting data in order to arrive at a conclusion. Sometimes it is helpful to have students predict what will happen if the conclusions of an experiment are accepted as generally true. Such quests involve discussing the implications a scientific discovery might have on society as a whole. Too often science is taught as an individual endeavor, completely isolated from the rest of society. We teach science at 9 a.m., math at 10 a.m., social studies at 11 a.m., and never show students how these subjects interact with one another. Quests with the purpose of developing the social implications of a science discovery are an important factor in dispelling the illusion that science and society do not interact.

The following article, which appeared in *The Christian Science Monitor,* is an excellent source of data for this type of quest. Before presenting this article to the students, you might focus their attention by saying, "As you read this, think of the ways that this discovery could change our eating habits and the cost of food."

Plastic Ends Greenhouse Bee Strike[19]
By Ernest Douglass

A new discovery about bees has researchers at the University of Arizona buzzing with excitement. What they have found could change the eating habits of millions of Americans.

Horticulturists here have discovered—almost by accident—that bees will work busily and do a thorough job of pollination on plants in a greenhouse made of polyethylene.

What's so unusual about this is that bees normally drag their feet and work only reluctantly in a greenhouse of any kind. If it's made of clear glass, they will batter themselves against it trying to escape. If it is fiber glass, they will cluster in a corner and pay slight attention to the blossoms.

So pollination of most vegetables grown in greenhouses is done tediously and expensively by hand—greatly increasing the cost of greenhouse produce.

Dr. Mearle Jensen, research horticulturist at the Environmental Laboratory and Dr. L. N. Standifer, director of the United States Bee Culture Laboratory here in Tucson, are agreed that if bees can be induced to do pollinating, it will be a tremendous stimulus to the greenhouse industry. Far more, far cheaper, off-season melons and vegetables can be on millions of tables.

In fact, that stimulus is already being felt at Nassau, in the Bahamas. Resorts International is constructing a two-acre greenhouse complex producing cantaloupes for guests of a luxury hotel. Bees will do the pollinating. Dr. Jensen is a consultant as to design and operation.

And cantaloupes were the objective of the Tucson experiment that led to the discovery that bees will accept as normal an environment enclosed with polyethylene.

Greenhouse cultural experimentation is the main activity of the Environmental Research Laboratory, whose director is Carl N. Hodges. Its staff designed and put into operation a greenhouse at Puerto Penasco, on the Gulf of Mexico, that was turned over to the University of Mexico after it had gained worldwide attention. Later they designed and built a similar but much larger installation for the sheikdom of Abu Dhabi on the Persian Gulf.

Feasibility Test
Here it was decided to test the feasibility of growing off-season muskmelon, which bring fancy prices at expensive hotels and restaurants. The winter had passed but temperature and humidity are strictly controlled in greenhouses and the season doesn't matter. The test got under way in late spring.

The laboratory's greenhouses have no frames. They are big "balloons" of milky-white polyethylene 10 mils thick kept inflated by blowers that never stop.

The sticking point was pollination. The flower on the end of each tiny new melon must be fertilized with pollen from a male flower, or the melon doesn't develop. If that had to be done by hand the labor outlay would eat up any possible profits.

Could bees be persuaded to make that pollen transfer? All available information was discouraging. In the United States bees have generally been so disappointing in greenhouses that they are used scarcely at all. They are used on melons in France but only to a limited extent.

Advice Sought
Advice was sought from S. E. McGregor, former director of the apiary division of the Agricultural Research Service at Beltsville, Md. on

special assignment to write a book on the subject. Pollination is his special field of interest, and he is now at the Bee Culture Laboratory.

Yes, melon flowers were attractive to bees, Dr. McGregor said. But he had never seen them pay much attention to any kind of flower inside a greenhouse. They were too much disturbed by the restricted, artificial environment.

No one was more astonished than Dr. McGregor when the bee colony moved into the "cantaloupe greenhouse" went to work eagerly as soon as the first cantaloupe blooms appeared. Soon there was a "set" of seven melons to the vine, although under field conditions the average is only one per vine. A single watermelon vine had a similarly abundant set.

Although Dr. Jensen, Dr. McGregor and everyone else involved in the experiment cautions that there is a great deal of research yet to be done before the utility of bees in greenhouse culture can be determined, their jubilation could not be concealed.

The Tomato Question
Tomatoes are the principal greenhouse product in this country, and nobody knows whether bees will work on tomato blooms as industriously as on melon blossoms. The only printed information is from Ohio, where one trial several years ago was pronounced a failure. That testimony is doubted by Dr. Jensen and his associates, who are drawing plans for further experiments to be undertaken as soon as the laboratory's budget permits.

The biggest mystery is why bees accept the polyethylene-greenhouse environment so readily. It has been suggested that the dome shape of the roof may have something to do with it. William A. Iselin, young horticulturist in day-to-day charge of the cantaloupe greenhouse, thinks the quality of sunlight as strained through polyethylene is a more likely explanation. "Bees don't see light the way we do, but see and are influenced by colors invisible to us," he says.

One of the Bee Research Laboratory's entomologists, Joseph O. Moffett, has made a study of the 70-odd species of wild bees indigenous to Arizona, most of them much smaller than the honey bee. He conjectures that if a search were made, a kind of bee could be found that is especially adapted to the pollination of each vegetable, perhaps in a greenhouse of any type.

After the class has read the article, you could focus their attention on the important points of the article, using these data collecting questions:

1. Why are bees important to plant reproduction?
2. What was the important discovery presented in the article?

Quests are excellent ways to show students how concepts and principles can be generated from data. They are also important for exemplifying the effects scientific discoveries might have on different aspects of our society—the economy, our life style, or leisure time. A danger in using them is that you could, through the improper use of questions or reactions to responses, present only your ideas,

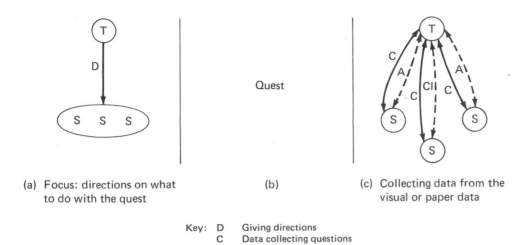

(a) Focus: directions on what   (b)   (c) Collecting data from the
    to do with the quest   visual or paper data

Key: D   Giving directions
      C   Data collecting questions
      A   Accepting reactions
      CI   Clarifying reactions

FIGURE 6-25
Representation of the Focusing Tactics Used for Quests.

and not encourage the students to process the data themselves. Another danger in using a quest is that students may not have had sufficient experience with the topic to be able to process the data or to discuss its implications.

To construct a quest for use as a focusing tactic, you should first state your instructional objectives. Choose only one or two inquiry skills to practice during the lesson. In choosing the form the data should be in when it is analyzed by the student, consider that interpreting a data *table* is different than seeing the data displayed in a *graph.* Likewise, seeing relationships in pictures is different than seeing a relationship in data on a graph. In general, pictures are less abstract than graphs, which in turn are less abstract than tabular data. Therefore, for younger children, pictures or graphs would be the best means for presenting the data.

After having stated your instructional objectives, find some data related to your objectives. Pictures from magazines or books, slides, and tables or graphs from science journals are excellent sources of data. Then develop a short problem statement to present to the class. Make sure that the problem relates to the material students have been studying and that they are familiar with it. In general, the focusing aspects of a quest can be presented as in Figure 6-25.

In summary, quests are one of several types of focusing tactics. By nature a quest is an imagery or language mode of instruction that provides specific practice with the skills of inquiry—the methods by which scientists generate concepts and principles from data. Quests are quick and easy methods of getting at the heart of science without the painstaking and time-consuming task of collecting data in a laboratory.

Activities

1. State the rationale for using a quest as a focusing tactic.
2. Find a table or graph in a newspaper, magazine, or book, and construct

a quest that provides practice in making predictions. Present this quest to a group of students.

3. Find a newspaper or magazine article that gives an account of a recent scientific discovery. Develop and present to a class a quest requiring them to infer the implications this discovery may have on society.

4. Find a data table in a magazine or develop your own table from an experiment you did. Using this data, construct a quest to focus students' attention on analyzing the data for relationships.

Resource Material

Klinckmann, Evelyn, Supervisor. *Biology Teachers' Handbook.* 2nd ed. New York: John Wiley and Sons, Inc., 1970, pp. 130-136.

Piltz, Albert, and Robert Sund. *Creating Teaching of Science in the Elementary School.* Boston: Allyn and Bacon, 1968, pp. 122-130.

Extending
Tactics 7

Objectives

1. To state reasons for using an extending tactic.
2. To construct an extending tactic appropriate for an instructional objective.

So far we have presented a variety of ways to initiate a lesson and to focus student attention on the topic under consideration. It is important that you now help the class organize the material so that it can be assimilated or so that their conceptual framework can be restructured to accommodate it. It is this assimilation and accommodation of material that leads to concept formation and learning other than recall of information. Piaget stresses that in order to do this, the learner must be physically and mentally involved with the material to be learned. The child should directly manipulate material and interact with his peers as he attempts to solve problems. *The focusing tactics presented earlier illustrated the variety of ways to obtain student involvement in a physical way. The extending tactics developed here will exemplify ways to keep students mentally involved with the material to be learned, thereby promoting assimilation and accommodation.*

Using Piaget's theory, extending tactics should keep the students mentally active through promoting group interaction. Since accommodation is the primary factor contributing to the extension of the learner's conceptual framework, discussions are excellent methods to speed reorganization. There are several ways to keep students mentally active by using inconsistencies.

1. One child compares his explanation to a peer's explanation.
2. The teacher feigns surprise at a faulty explanation.
3. The teacher does not accept a rote answer, but asks for proof or verification of an answer.
4. The teacher methodically goes around the classroom, drawing out observations and explanations, until two contradictory observations or explana-

tions have been given. Then the teacher builds a discussion on those conflicting ideas.[20]

These suggestions show the importance of a teacher's reactions to student responses. These suggestions also imply that a teacher should react by *asking for
evidence.* In asking a child to supply evidence or reasons for his response, you
are helping him to understand how a statement in science needs to be supported
with data.

A second type of reaction to keep students mentally active is to ask *another
student to evaluate* or judge the response. Such a reaction, used consistently, will
help to promote peer interaction. The authors' experience indicates that much
work and effort on the teacher's part is required in order that students interact
with one another. Usually students have not developed the ability of listening
to what a peer has to say. For example, when the teacher says, "Jim, do you
agree with what Joan had to say?" Jim will usually say, "I didn't hear her." Then
the teacher must back up and have Joan repeat what she said. This process takes
patience on your part and at first tends to slow down the discussion. A conserva-
tive estimate of how long it takes before students will respond spontaneously to
each other is about eight weeks, provided that you work on student interaction
each day.

Even before you begin to react to responses, you must initiate a question to
start students organizing the data they collect. These questions are the *data collecting* questions presented earlier. If you have properly focused students' attention on the data collected by writing it on the chalkboard, you can now ask a
data processing question and get a good response.

To illustrate the verbal aspects of an extending tactic, several examples follow.
Suppose you have just finished discussing the data obtained from a series of experiments, and your instructional objective includes developing a principle. This
objective may be to have students predict the rate of a chemical reaction when
the concentration of the reactants is changed. The principle to be developed is,
"As the concentration of the reactants is increased equally, the rate of reaction
will also increase." Students have completed several experiments illustrating the
principle and the data are displayed in written form on the chalkboard. At this
point the teacher begins an extending tactic by asking a question:

Teacher:	Can anyone see a relationship between the concentration and the reaction rate? Sue?
Sue:	As you increase the concentration the reaction rate de-creases.
Teacher:	Why do you say that?
Sue:	From the chart on the board you can see that as the con-centration numbers get larger, the time decreases.
Teacher:	Shelley, do you agree with what Sue has said?
Shelley:	No and yes. She's right when she says as the concentration rate increases the time for a reaction decreases. But she

[20] Edward Palmer, "Accelerating the Child's Cognitive Attainments Through the Inducement
of Cognitive Conflicts: An Interpretation of the Piagetian Position," *Journal of Research in
Science Teaching* 3 (1965): 324.

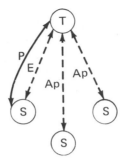

Focus: generating hypotheses

Key: P   Data processing questions
      E   Asking for evidence reactions
      Ap   Asking another person reactions

FIGURE 7-1

Teacher: said that means the reaction rate decreases. A smaller time
means a quicker reaction rate.

Teacher: Phil—

Phil: I agree with what Sue said. . . .

This is an example of an extending tactic conceptualized in Figure 7-1. The same
purpose could be achieved using a slightly different extending tactic.

After the teacher asks the same initial question, the dialogue might be something like this:

Teacher: Can anyone see a relationship between the concentration
            and the reaction rate? Roy?

Roy: As the concentration increases so does the reaction rate.

Teacher: What evidence do you have to support this hypothesis?
            (writing it on the board.)

Roy: As the concentration number in column one gets larger, the
            numbers in column two, the rate of reaction, get smaller.

Teacher: What is your hypothesis, Tim?

Tim: As the concentration decreases the reaction time increases.

Teacher: Why do you say that? (writing the second hypothesis on
            the board.)

Tim: The reaction time in our experiments increase as we de-
            crease the concentration of the reactants.

This type of extending tactic is represented in Figure 7-2. These two extending
tactics can also be used with quests when your objective is to develop a principle.
The use of these tactics will help students to organize the data into concepts or
principles and yet keep the students mentally active by having them supply
evidence to support what they say.

If your major objective is to provide practice in evaluating or verifying hypotheses, your plan could be to elicit as many hypotheses as possible and then
to evaluate them. The following dialogue illustrates this plan. After your class

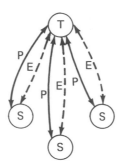

Focus: generating hypotheses

Key: P   Data processing questions
     E   Asking for evidence reactions

FIGURE 7-2

has observed mealworms and written on the board many observations, you may ask your students for a hypothesis to explain how mealworms find their food.

Shep: I think mealworms can see it.
         (Teacher writes on board.)
Ethan: Mealworms can't see but they feel it with their antennae.
         (Teacher writes hypothesis on board.)
Jane: Mealworms smell the food, because when I put ammonia close to them they jiggle around like I do when I smell ammonia.
         (Teacher writes hypothesis on board.) Now we have several hypotheses to account for the mealworms' behavior. Let's look at the first one and see if we can devise an experiment to determine if mealworms find food by using their eyes.
         (Long pause.)
Teacher: Jeff.
Jeff: We could put the food in the middle of a dark box and see if they find the food.
Teacher: Does that sound like a good idea? Mary.
Mary: Yes, 'cause when I'm in a dark room the only way I can find my way around is to feel my way, and this would help us test the second hypothesis, too.
Teacher: Nancy?
Nancy: I disagree, because after my eyes become accustomed to the dark, I can see a little bit. . . .

This type of extending tactic can be represented as in Figure 7-3. Notice that in this figure the teacher does not react to any of the responses. The purpose in not reacting is to help generate as many hypotheses as possible. If you were to accept or reject some, this extending tactic would become a guessing game—the students would try to guess which hypothesis the teacher is looking for. In addition, your lack of reaction helps to keep students mentally active, since you have not signaled which hypothesis is "right."

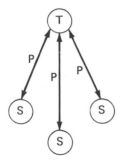 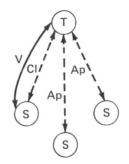

(a) Focus: generating hypotheses   (b) Evaluating hypotheses

Key: P   Data processing questions
      V   Verifying and/or evaluating
           questions
      Cl   Clarifying reactions
      Ap   Asking another person
           reactions

FIGURE 7-3

Extending tactics include not only the formation of concepts and principles, as just illustrated, but also the means for reinforcing the concepts or applying them to new situations. Once the concept, principle, or skill has been initially developed, it is a good idea to help students use it in different situations. When you use extending tactics in this manner, students must find out whether they are wrong or right. It would be quite easy for you to tell them whether they were right or wrong, but a threefold purpose could be achieved if the other students did the evaluating. First, the student giving the response would know what others thought about it. Second, you would be given the opportunity to assess how well the entire class has learned the concept, principle, or skill. Third, class members would practice evaluating evidence and inferences.

Suppose you have just completed a presentation on the characteristics of poison ivy. Your objective is to have students identify the poison ivy, in order that they may avoid touching it. A good extending tactic, to help them to as- similate the characteristics to a greater extent, is to present many other plants and ask students if they are poison ivy. After each student gives his response, you could react with, "How can you tell this isn't poison ivy?" or "How can you tell this is poison ivy?" Such reactions would require the student to respond with the identifying characteristics and thus reinforce them. By asking another student to evaluate the response of the first student, you obtain student interaction and provide additional opportunity to identify poison ivy. This extending tactic could also be used after the concept insect has been developed. You might present several different types of animals that look like insects and have the students in- dicate whether or not each one is an insect, and why. After one student has re- sponded, you could ask another to evaluate the first response. This type of extending tactic can be represented as in Figure 7-4.

Newly formed principles can be treated in a similar fashion. Referring back to the examples given on pages 83-84, the principle to be developed from the examples

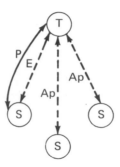

Focus: application of concept
to a new situation

FIGURE 7-4

is that air moving about an object reduces the pressure about the object in a direction perpendicular to the moving air. Of course students will not state the
principle as we have just done, but they will have the general idea. To help them
extend their learning, you might give several illustrations of that principle and
ask for an explanation of the results in terms of the principle. For example, "If
I blow between two balloons suspended an inch apart, they will move together
rather than apart. What could account for this?" "A convertible moving down the
street with the top up and all the windows rolled up will bulge outwards at the
top." These examples will provide the student with an opportunity to apply the
principle to new situations.

Field trips can also be good extending tactics. Having presented the concepts
shiny and *dull* to a first-grade class, you could take them outside the classroom
and have them identify objects that are shiny or dull. A fourth-grade class could
be given practice, using a classification key, to identify trees or insects in the
neighborhood. Again, it is quite important that students be given feedback on
their answers, so that they can determine whether they were right or wrong.

In summary, extending tactics can serve two functions. First, extending
tactics can help to formulate a concept, principle, or skill new to the student.
This process, which Piaget calls accommodation, may be accomplished during
data processing. Second, the application of a concept, principle, or skill to situations new to the students helps them to identify and interpret familiar situations
in the light of this newly developed idea. Such application helps students assimilate this familiar material into their reorganized conceptual framework. Extending
tactics are extremely important in learning, for they help to develop content beyond simple recall, as well as inquiry skills.

Activities

1. Give the rationale for using an extending tactic.
2. Develop an extending tactic for the following instructional objectives.
    In your development include the focusing questions you would use and
    the manner in which you would react to student responses. You may do

this either by writing a dialogue for the extending tactic or by drawing
a paradigm including a statement of the dialogue's focus.

(a)   Given a woody stem, the students should be able to infer how long
        it grew over the past year.
(b)   When presented with a flower, the students should be able to iden-
        tify the sepals, petals, stamens, and pistils, if present.
(c)   Using a mineral key, the student should be able to identify a mineral.
(d)   Given two soil types and two stream speeds, the student should be
        able to predict which conditions would modify the land at a greater
        rate.
(e)   Given an object, the student should be able to determine its density.

8 Terminating Tactics

Objectives

1. To state the rationale for using a terminating tactic.
2. To construct a terminating tactic appropriate for an instructional objective.

Terminating tactics are an essential part of any lesson. One reason for using such a tactic is to summarize the entire instructional sequence, to focus on the important points of the lesson or unit. Another purpose is to determine how well students have learned the material. The content of terminating tactics can be determined by completing the following statement: "If I could have my students remember one or two things from today's lesson tomorrow, or a week from today, it would be . . ." Usually in completing this sentence you will mention the content of the instructional objectives and the skills practiced. It is important to keep in mind that many things transpire during the lesson. The things you hope will be remembered should be those that stand out in the lesson. In this text we stress clarity and variety in presentation. Terminating tactics, used at the end of each daily lesson and at the end of each unit of instruction, will certainly clarify the important points.

The simplest and easiest type of terminating tactic to use is a teacher-centered review, in which you recapitulate the lesson with a series of summarizing statements. As an illustration, a teacher whose instructional objective was "Students should be able to remember at least four properties of acids," might make this summary: "Today we have investigated several properties of acids. Some of you found that very dilute acids taste sour, much like lemon juice. Those of you who tested several acids found that they turn blue litmus paper red. And using this same test on orange, lemon, and grapefruit juice, you found that these juices acted something like acids." This type of summary should take place immediately *after* a thorough postlaboratory discussion on what students discovered. The verbal aspects of this tactic are represented in Figure 8-1.

While using this type of tactic, you must be sure to include only the lesson highlights and not deviate from them. The nonverbal aspects of this tactic would be short, concise summary statements on the chalkboard, helping to reinforce

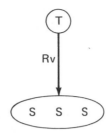

Focus: reviewing the day's
main points

FIGURE 8-1

the important concepts, principles, or skills developed. This type of summary should be used as a terminating tactic for a single lesson, but *not* for the review of an entire unit of work. While lending clarity to the entire lesson, the teacher's summary of important ideas in the lesson does not permit him to find out whether these ideas were grasped by the students.

A terminating tactic to help you determine whether students have recalled the lesson highlights is a question-and-answer review. You initiate questions focusing students' attention on the lesson highlights, and react to student responses by accepting or rejecting them. A teacher whose instructional objective was to have students hypothesize and devise a test for variables that affect the period of a pendulum, might conduct a terminating tactic in the question-and-answer mode as follows:

Teacher:	For several days we have been investigating the factors that affect the period of a pendulum. Name one variable we've tested that didn't have an effect on the period. Jim?
Jim:	The weight of the bob didn't have an effect, except when it was so heavy it broke the string, or so light the pendulum swung only once.
Teacher:	Right.
Teacher:	What was another variable that didn't have an effect? Nancy?
Nancy:	The size of the arc.
Teacher:	In general this is true for small arcs. However, when you swing a large arc, the period does change.
Teacher:	Who can name the one variable that did affect the period of a pendulum? Sam?
Sam:	The length of the string?
Teacher:	Good, and who remembers what we do to make the period longer? Mary?
Mary:	Lengthen the string.
Teacher:	Right, and what do we do . . .

Such a review should take place immediately after a discussion of the experiment, to tie together the many facets of the experiment. Notice also that it would tend

FIGURE 8-2
Summarizing an Investigation Is an Important Part of Learning. (From Thier, Teaching Elementary School Science, p. 148.)

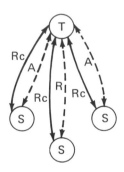

Focus: reviewing highlights of
the day's lesson

FIGURE 8-3

to clarify the entire proceeding. The verbal aspects of this type of review are represented in Figure 8-3.

This tactic, being more student-centered than the previous one, tells you how well the students are learning, since they are directly responding to questions dealing with the ideas in the lesson. This method, while directing students' attention to the significant aspects of the lesson, is still teacher controlled. It is the teacher who initiates the questions. Therefore, this tactic does not permit you to determine whether the main points of your lesson were obvious to the students.

In a third type of terminating tactic, you initiate the tactic, but then let the students discuss the lesson among themselves, while you direct participation in the discussion. Your primary role is to react in such ways as asking for clarification of responses, asking for evidence to support a response, or directing another student to evaluate a previous response. Your objective in using this type of terminating tactic is not only to summarize the highlights of the lesson, but also to evaluate the lesson's effectiveness in communicating to the class. An instructional sequence with an objective, such as having students hypothesize the variations in growth for plants grown under different-colored light, might be terminated in the following way. Students have just completed a somewhat rambling discussion on a series of investigations that you designed to achieve the objective: "The student should be able to formulate hypotheses regarding the differences in the characteristics of plants grown in red, green, and blue light, sunlight, and darkness." Not being sure what students have gleaned from the discussion, you might terminate the discussion in the following manner:

Teacher: Let's tie things together now. What have we found out about plants grown under different-colored lights? Rufus?

Rufus: I would say that what we've shown is that green light is the only colored light that makes a difference.

Teacher: Gay, do you agree with that?

Gay: Sort of. Our plants that were grown without any light at all looked just like the plants grown in green light.

Rufus: Yes, that's right. I forgot about that.

Teacher: Judy, do you agree with what Rufus and Gay have said?

Judy: Yes, but I don't think we've found out why green light makes the difference.

Rufus: Oh, yes, we did. Remember when we talked about reflected light? How an object's color is determined by the color of light that's reflected? Well, plants look green

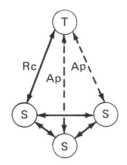

Focus: reviewing the main
points of the lesson

FIGURE 8-4

                    because they absorb all colors of light except green and
                    that's reflected.
    Teacher: So what difference does that make? . . .

This type of tactic can be represented as in Figure 8-4.

    As with other types of teaching tactics, a variety of terminating tactics can
be used. The use of this type of tactic at the end of instructional sequences provides you with an additional opportunity to clarify and reinforce your instructional objectives. Although there is not much research in this area, the few studies
available seem to indicate that summarizing at the end of a lesson is more effective
than summarizing the lesson at the beginning of the next class meeting.

Activities

1. Give the rationale for using a terminating tactic.
2. Using the paradigms presented earlier, show how you might terminate a
   lesson with each of the following objectives:
   (a) The students should be able to infer the conditions needed for a
        viable seed to germinate.
   (b) Given a picture of a bird's beak, the student should be able to predict
        what type of food it eats.
   (c) Given a graph, the students should be able to make predictions
        from it.
   (d) Students should be able to plan an experiment to show that
        mealworms do not see as humans do.

Teaching SECTION
Strategies III

FIGURE III-1
The Action Mode — These Children Are Working Directly with Objects.
This Is Most Effective for Children Entering, or Within, the Concrete Stage
of Development. (From Thier, Teaching Elementary School Science, p.93.)

We have just presented various types of teaching tactics, along with reasons for using them. You might ask, "What is the overall significance of this?" A little reflection will reveal that each type of teaching tactic plays an important role in the development of a lesson, and that several different tactics may be employed during an individual lesson. As we mentioned in the introduction to Section II, a planned arrangement of teaching tactics designed to reach an instructional objective is what we call a teaching strategy. Teaching tactics are not randomly combined; rather, each type of tactic plays an important role in the development of a lesson.

Are there guidelines for constructing a strategy? The research as to which combination of tactics would most effectively achieve a given type of objective is not conclusive. However, it is clear that different types of objectives require different types of strategies.[1] We will now develop teaching strategies for the various types of instructional objectives and for the model of science explained in Section I.

Piaget suggests two guidelines for incorporating his ideas into educational practice: (1) the learner should be kept actively involved, and (2) there must be peer interaction.[2] Attempting to extend Piaget's theories into classroom work, Bruner suggests that there are three modes of presentation that help to keep chil-

[1] Gregor Ramsey and Robert Howe, "An Analysis of Research on Instructional Procedures in Secondary School Science—Parts I and II," *The Science Teacher* 36 (March 1969): 62-70, and (April 1969): 72-81.

[2] Jean Piaget, "Development and Learning," *Journal of Research in Science Teaching* 2 (1964): 176-186.

dren actively participating during the instructional process. We have discussed these modes in detail in Section II. You will recall that the *action mode* allows the students to manipulate the actual objects under investigation. This mode is most appropriate for children entering, or within, the *concrete operational* stage of mental development, or for those with little experience with the concept being developed.

The *imagery mode* of instruction, in which the children work with pictorial representations of the actual objects, is most appropriate for children making the *transition from the concrete to the formal operations stage* of development.

FIGURE III-2
The Imagery Mode— This Student Is Working with Pictorial Representations of Objects. This Is Most Effective for Children Making the Transition from the Concrete Stage of Development to the Stage of Formal Operations. Note That She Was Previously Working with the Actual Objects Themselves. (From Thier, Teaching Elementary School Science, p. 155.)

FIGURE III-3
The Language Mode — These Students Are Working with Symbols
and Abstractions Rather than with Actual Objects. This Is Most
Effective for Children Using or Developing Formal Operations.

The *language mode* of instruction, in which the children work with symbols and abstractions, is most appropriate for students using or developing *formal operations.*[3]

The amount of time spent in each mode of instruction depends on the child's stage of development and his past experience. In any event, the prerequisites for symbolic manipulation are experiences in the action and imagery modes of instruction.[4] Using all of these ideas, effective teaching strategies start with initiating tactics that get the attention of the students and relate past experiences and previous information to the lesson. Next come focusing tactics designed to provide common experiences that help students collect data. After the students have collected sufficient data, the teacher employs extending tactics—having the students process the data and evaluate the concepts generated from the data. This process often leads to accommodation. The teacher then ties the main ideas together with terminating tactics, completing the strategy.

To illustrate the designing of teaching strategies, we will present examples for the four main categories of objectives. The strategies illustrated are relatively short term—for instructional periods of only a few days. Longer-term teaching strategies will be presented in detail later.

[3] Jerome Bruner, *Toward a Theory of Instruction* (Cambridge, Mass.: Harvard University Press, 1966).

[4] Jean Piaget, "Development and Learning," *Journal of Research in Science Teaching* 2 (1964): 176-186.

Short-Term
Teaching Strategies 9

Content Objectives

Objective

To construct a short lesson that has at least two content
instructional objectives, as well as the following:
(a) Behavioral indicators of learning.
(b) The instructional procedure, including all supplementary
materials.

One of the easiest things to do with content is to have students recall it. There
is nothing wrong with this, since the students must possess a background of
factual content in order to be effective problem solvers. However, it is extremely
limiting to have as your *sole* objective the recall of specific content. One effective
strategy for accomplishing this objective is the lecture-recitation strategy.

Suppose you were going to begin discussing the solar system with your third-
grade class. Two of your instructional objectives were that the students should
recall the names of the planets and state the order of the planets outward from
the sun. Realistically, there is no way that the children could "discover" this information. They could obtain this factual content from a chart or book, or it
could be given to them in the form of a short lecture with visual aids.

The strategy you might use to accomplish these objectives could include an
initiating tactic, followed by a focusing tactic, and concluded by a terminating
tactic. Your initiating tactic might begin with recall questions such as: "How
many of you have been outside at night and seen the stars?" "Have you ever seen
any of the stars moving?" These questions would help you to determine the student's past experiences at stargazing. Having students elaborate and explain their
answers in detail will give you further valuable information on their past experiences, from which you can develop future lessons.

Another initiating tactic that could be used in this situation is to inform the
students that they will be studying astronomy—the stars and planets and the ways
we determine what they are like—for the next several weeks. You might say:
"Today we will spend some time familiarizing ourselves with the names of the
planets, their sizes, and their order from the sun." This initiating tactic "sets the

129

FIGURE 9-1
Specific Factual Content That Would Be Either Impossible or Very Difficult
for Students to "Discover" for Themselves Can Be Effectively Transmitted
by the Teacher Using a Lecture-Recitation Strategy. (Courtesy of Minaruth
Galey, Temple University.)

stage" and gives the children a common experience upon which to build. But
this beginning of a unit on the solar system does not imply that the entire unit
will be conducted through lectures. You should present in lectures only the factual content that would be very difficult, or impossible, for the children to obtain
directly for themselves.

After gaining the children's interest and relating the topic to their past experiences, you could then focus their attention on the activities for the day. When
presenting content verbally, keep in mind that this is a highly symbolic mode of
instruction, and you should attempt to make it less abstract with accompanying
demonstrations, by writing the important points on the chalkboard, or by using
visual models of what you are presenting. The use of such visual aids helps to
focus students' attention on the important points. Researchers estimate that 70
to 80 percent of the information we assimilate is acquired visually. Relatively
speaking, verbal communication is quite ineffective. For the lesson we are discussing, a picture or model of the solar system, indicating the sizes and positions
of the planets, could be used.

To provide practice with naming the planets, and recalling their order from the sun, you could ask a series of recall questions such as: "What is the name of this planet?" (Point to the planet on the model or chart.) After a student answered, you would react by telling him whether he was correct or, better still, by asking another child whether his answer was correct. This latter reaction helps to keep all the children involved in the lesson.

You might conduct another short question-and-answer review of the content to terminate this strategy. Such a tactic provides feedback on how well the students recalled the content of the lecture.

The lesson just described is a specific example of a teaching strategy that emphasizes the recall of content. It can be generalized as shown in Figure 9-2.

Many teachers abuse the lecture-recitation strategy by using it to achieve a wide range of objectives. As stated earlier, a lecture-recitation strategy is a most effective way to transmit factual content, but research has shown that other strategies may be more effective for developing the inquiry skills described in Section I.[5] There are many occasions when students can collect data and make discoveries on their own—activities that are so essential for maximum inquiry skill development. Thus, even though you can inform students by lecturing, you will lose much of the benefit from direct student interaction with materials and with other students if you overemphasize this strategy. *You* must decide on *your* priorities. Are you *primarily* interested in your students' recall of content, or in

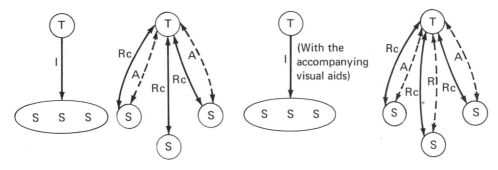

(a) Initiating tactics. The teacher (1) informs the class what is going to be done, and (2) relates the topic to previous classwork or personal experiences

(b) Focusing tactic. A presentation by the teacher of the characteristics of the planets in the solar system

(c) Terminating tactic. A review of the major points discussed

Instructional objective: After listening to a presentation of the characteristics of the planets, the student will recall at least three of the major points discussed.

FIGURE 9-2
A Paradigm Showing a Typical Lecture-Recitation Strategy.

[5]Gregor Ramsey and Robert Howe, "An Analysis of Research on Instructional Procedures in Secondary School Science—Parts I and II," *The Science Teacher* 36 (March 1969): 62-70, and (April 1969): 72-81.

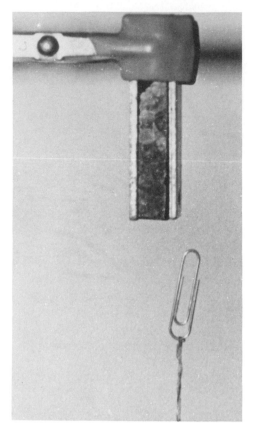 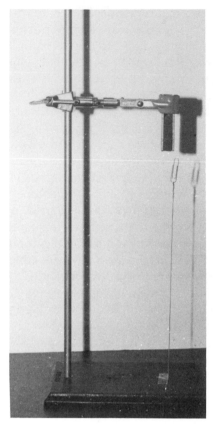

FIGURE 9-3
An Example of a Demonstration Designed to Create an "Inconsistency." (Courtesy of Minaruth Galey, Temple University.)

their development of the skills of inquiry while they are collecting and processing data on their own? The former takes much less time, but we believe that the latter, though more time consuming, will result in a much more permanent and applicable type of learning. Look again at the example presented in Figure 9-2. Could some of this content be discovered by the children as a result of their own work? Would you begin the topic on the planets in the same way as illustrated in Figure 9-2?

Some concepts can be "invented" for the students in the form of a lecture.[6] As a specific example, suppose you are teaching a unit to your fourth-grade class on magnets and magnetism. You might begin with an initiating tactic employing an inconsistency, such as the one shown in Figure 9-3.

To most children, the sight of a paper clip "floating" in midair would be very confusing and unexpected. You might allow the children to discuss possible

[6] J. Myron Atkin and Robert Karplus, "Discovery and Invention," *The Science Teacher* 29 (September 1962): 45-51.

reasons to explain the demonstration, and their suggestions might naturally lead to a discussion of magnets. Your focusing tactic might involve a Type IV laboratory activity, in which the children work with various magnets and other materials to discover as much about the behavior of magnets as they can. They will find out that the magnet attracts certain materials and has no effect on others. The principle that magnets seem to attract only certain metallic objects will probably be developed easily. The behavior of one magnet with another can also be studied. *After the children have gained considerable experience working with magnets,* there is nothing wrong with mentioning the concept of magnetic force to them. They can then return to their direct work with the magnets and discover many of the implications of this concept. It is important to remember, however, that the children must be given the opportunity to *explore fully the consequences and discover the implications* of the concept that you have "invented" for them. Too many teachers use the informing tactic (lecture) to explain the implications of the "invented" concept and thus, never give the students the chance to directly explore the phenomena themselves.

Even when the lecture-recitation strategy is the most appropriate, it should be used with care. Many of us can think of uncomfortable instances when we were students in a class where the teacher used recitation or drill very vigorously. Children have to be shown that there is no reason for being embarrassed if they answer a recall question incorrectly. Many teachers make the mistake of rejecting *both the child and the answer* when reacting to an incorrect response. This makes the child more hesitant about answering a question unless he is *absolutely certain* that he is correct. How often does this happen? Many children learn very quickly that it is far wiser not to raise their hands if they merely think they might be right. They have become unwilling to *take the chance of being wrong.* For many children, this is a very powerful motive.

We also have to be careful to give the student enough time to formulate his response. In many classrooms, correctness is not rewarded as much as correctness *and* speed. Is the child who gets the correct answer in three seconds really that much better than the child who takes ten? Maybe we don't think so, but we certainly teach as if we thought it were true. Research has shown that teachers tend to give the students less than three seconds in which to formulate a response and begin to answer a question.[7] For many students this is an impossible task, even though they do know the correct response. Teachers must consciously try to take the threatening aspects out of recitation by putting less emphasis on the speed of a response and paying more attention to its quality. Also, in rejecting an incorrect response, one must take care that it is the response that is rejected and *not* the child.

Summarizing, the lecture-recitation strategy is a very effective one for the transmission of factual content to the students. It is best employed when the students need information that they could not obtain directly themselves, or that

---

[7] Mary Budd Rowe, *Wait-Time and Rewards as Instructional Variables* (Paper presented at the national convention of the National Association for Research in Science Teaching, Chicago, Illinois, 1972). Also, "Silence and Sanctions," *Science and Children* 6 (1969): 11-13.

they could only obtain with difficulty. It is a limited strategy and should not be used to achieve more complex objectives that require the direct interaction of the students with the materials and with their peers.

Some research evidence suggests that for long-term retention of content, a discovery-oriented strategy is better than a rote memorization strategy such as lecture-recitation.[8] Suppose you were developing the topic of the structure of matter and specifically wanted your students to discover the principle, "Matter has holes in it." However, since your equipment is very limited, you must use a teacher-centered approach. A series of well-planned demonstrations can help in this situation. Here is a specific example of such a series designed to help students "discover" the principle, "Matter has holes in it."

> **Demonstration One:** Place a small amount of different "smelly" sub-stances in separate but equal-sized bottles, such as Coke bottles. You might use household ammonia, perfume, lemon juice, moth flakes, or cleaning fluid. Then blow up a balloon and hold the neck tightly with your fingers so that none of the air escapes. As you continue to hold the *neck* of the balloon, carefully place the end of the balloon over the end of one of the bottles. Now seal the connection with tape or cord so that none of the air escapes from the balloon. Place a balloon on each of the bottles, then set these aside for several days before your lesson.
>
> **Demonstration Two:** Blow up a balloon and seal it, then let it stand in your classroom for several days.
>
> **Demonstration Three:** Fill a bottle with a sealable lid half full of colored water. Then fill the remainder of the bottle with ethyl alcohol, *being careful not to mix the alcohol and the water.* Now carefully seal the bottle with the lid.
>
> **Demonstration Four:** Place some household ammonia in a drinking glass, then place a plastic bag in the glass so that it touches the am-monia. Next, place a small amount of phenolphthalein indicator solu-tion inside the plastic bag, making sure that the indicator solution does not drip into the ammonia. In other words, the indicator solution is *inside* the bag and the ammonia is touching the bag on the *outside.* This should be done at least two days before you do the demonstration.

The day you wish to present the lesson "Matter has holes in it," your strategy might be as follows. Begin with an initiating tactic that reminds the students of the content being studied, and review the material that they have previously covered. Briefly describe the day's lesson: "Today we are going to find out about a very important property of matter that is illustrated by the activities we will complete today." Follow with a direction statement to remind the students to observe closely. You may introduce Demonstration One by de-

---

[8] George Hermann, "Learning by Discovery—A Critical Review of Studies," *Journal of Experimental Education* 38 (1969): 58-72.

scribing to the students what you did a few days before. With the help of five volunteers, carefully open each balloon and have the students smell the contents, comparing the results with the odor in each jar itself. The students' observations should be written on the chalkboard.

Introduce Demonstration Two in a similar fashion, again recording the childrens' observations on the board. Demonstration Three can be done in front of the class with the aid of two helpers—one to fill the bottle half-way with the colored water, and a second to fill it to the top with ethyl alcohol. A rubber band is placed around the neck of the bottle to indicate the initial volume. After sealing the bottle, have a student shake it vigorously. Then ask the class to compare the resultant volume to the original volume. Demonstration Four is performed in a fashion similar to Demonstration One. The number of demonstrations to use is determined by the age, past experiences, and stage of development of your students. You should use no less than four, and the younger or less experienced your students, the greater should be the number of demonstrations. It is important to remember that this type of strategy should be used only if your equipment is too complex or limited to be used by all of the students. Also, even though the series of demonstrations is very teacher directed, the extending tactics should be much more student centered. Only the initial development of the principle, "Matter has holes in it" would be taught with demonstrations. This strategy is not unique to any particular topic. Many of the resource materials of Section II contain numerous examples of concepts and principles that can be effectively introduced with a series of teacher demonstrations. This strategy is illustrated in Figure 9-4.

This strategy is teacher centered, since the teacher directs the use of the materials. However, if you provide groups of three or four students with the same equipment, such a strategy easily becomes student-centered. As a matter of fact, a Type III laboratory activity or field trip (described in Section II) is student centered if performed by your children, but could easily become teacher centered if *you* demonstrate everything. Thus, a student-centered "discovery" approach, using a Type III laboratory activity or field trip in place of teacher demonstrations, still employs similar initiating, extending, and terminating tactics. Both teaching strategies can help students to recall important content.

Teaching strategies involving demonstrations and Type III laboratory activities or field trips are examples of strategies designed, in part, to achieve content objectives *without* relying heavily on the lecture-recitation strategy. Thus, content objectives do not necessarily indicate the exclusive use of the lecture. Furthermore, "lecture," as it is used here, does not necessarily indicate a long and time-consuming presentation. For very young children, it might only last a few minutes. Still, it is time in which the students are predominantly passive, listening as the teacher presents them with new content. In the example of a lesson on the solar system, the lecture part of the lesson would only last about five minutes. For young children, concept formation and abilities other than recall require the use of other strategies. The strategies thus far presented are not the most effective way to develop inquiry skills with children of relatively limited experiential background.

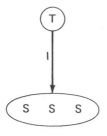

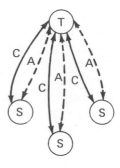

(b) The teacher performs a demonstration without any explanation

(a) Initiating tactic. The teacher explains the general topic and relates it to previous work

(c) Focusing tactics. The teacher performs the demonstrations (b) and the students collect data. [Steps (b) and (c) are repeated several times as the series of demonstrations are performed]

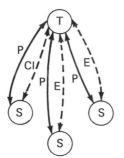

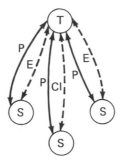

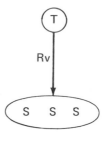

(d) Extending tactics. (1) "Did you see something similar in all of these demonstrations?" (2) "Based on what has been said, what conclusions can you make?"

(e) Terminating tactic. The teacher reviews the conclusions that were made

FIGURE 9-4
Paradigm Showing How a Series of Demonstrations Can Be Used to Develop a Concept if the Laboratory Is Too Limited or Complex for the Students to Use.

Activities

1. Develop a lesson plan meeting the criteria described in the objective on page 129.
2. Find a lesson from any science textbook series for children and write at least two content objectives for it.

Resource Material

Rockcastle, Verne. *Elementary School Science.* Menlo Park, California: Addison-Wesley, 1972.

Schneider, Herman and Nina. *Science.* Lexington, Mass.: D. C. Heath, 1973.

Inquiry Skill Objectives

Objective

To construct a lesson that includes the following:
(a) Instructional objectives that include inquiry skills.
(b) Behavioral indicators of learning.
(c) The instructional procedure, including the initiating, focusing, extending, and terminating tactics.

Since you are concerned with developing skills necessary for successful inquiry, you must consider the use of many teaching strategies. These strategies are not specific to any particular grade level or area of study. They apply to topics in earth science as well as topics in the biological sciences. With some modifications, they apply to third-grade children as well as to sixth-grade children. Specific examples in this section illustrate some strategies, but it is important to keep in mind that they only illustrate a general strategy. There are as many different types of effective teaching strategies as there are different teachers.

FIGURE 9-5
A Teacher Giving Directions During a Prelaboratory Discussion. (Courtesy of Minaruth Galey, Temple University.)

Many science lessons designed for students to practice and develop inquiry skills are structured in a *prelaboratory-laboratory-postlaboratory* format. As used here, the term "laboratory" does not mean a formalized experiment conducted in a science room with extensive laboratory equipment and facilities. "Lab" is used to describe any student activity in which the students are working directly with materials. This may be at their own desks, at a table or area of the classroom set aside for science work, or in a traditional science laboratory.

In general, the prelab is the most teacher-directed segment, and the postlab is much more student directed. In addition, the laboratory portion is the concrete portion of the lesson, while the postlab segment is the most abstract portion of the lesson. According to Piaget, this latter phase, leading to assimilation and accommodation, is crucial to the learning process.

A brief example of a prelab-lab-postlab sequence might be useful here. Investigation III-6 from *Science Investigations for Elementary School Teachers,*[9] involves the properties and reactions of basic solutions. During the prelaboratory segment, you might begin with a review of the results of the previous investigation on acids (George et al., Investigation III-5), and relate it to the work that the students are going to do on bases. The initiating tactic might be conducted in the following way:

Teacher:	For the past few days we have been studying the properties of acids. What are some of the things that we have found? Leslie?
Leslie:	Acids turn litmus paper red.
Teacher:	Right. What else have we found? Shelley?
Shelley:	Acids taste sour and dissolve some metals.
Teacher:	Good. For the next few days we will be investigating the properties and characteristics of liquids called "bases." To do this . . .

Here the teacher shifts to a direction-giving tactic that includes safety precautions.

The focusing aspect of this lesson could include directions given by the teacher and the ensuing laboratory activities of the students. After having collected the data in the laboratory, students could share their observations. This sharing is also a part of the focusing tactic, since its main purpose is to draw students' attention to the data collected during the laboratory activity.

If the teacher's instructional objective was for the students to discover the properties of bases, then the extending tactic—the postlaboratory discussion—could emphasize this objective. The questions asked by the teacher could direct the students to process the data collected for the purpose of developing the properties of bases. If, however, the objective of the laboratory activity was to determine whether or not a substance was a base, the questions during the postlaboratory discussion would direct the students towards this goal.

After developing the methods used to identify a base, the teacher would summarize the lesson with a terminating tactic. You might end the investigation

---

[9] Kenneth D. George et al., *Science Investigations for Elementary School Teachers* (Lexington, Mass.: D. C. Heath, 1974).

FIGURE 9-6
Children Collecting Data During a Laboratory Activity. (From Thier,
Teaching Elementary School Science, p. 134.)

by reviewing the results with the students. Part of the review might be something like this:

Teacher: What did you find were the main things to consider in
          determining whether or not a substance was a base?
          Dorothy?
Dorothy: We wanted to see whether it reacted with the indicators
          like the other bases or if it seemed to be more like the
          acids.
Teacher: Anything else? Shelley?
Shelley: Yes. We also checked to see if the solution had any effect
          on the grease stain.
Teacher: How did the bases react with the grease stain? Ethan?
Ethan: The weaker bases didn't do much to the grease stain, but
          the stronger ones did more.

It should be remembered that all of the information in this review was discovered by the students as a direct result of their lab work. It was *not* given to them by the teacher.

Using the paradigms developed earlier, a typical prelab-lab-postlab strategy, with the objectives of the development of concepts or principles and inquiry skills, is shown in Figure 9-7.

It is important to remember that each part of the prelaboratory-laboratory-postlaboratory sequence has its specific purpose and should be structured differently. The prelab segment is the initiating tactic, the time to relate the laboratory

Prelaboratory

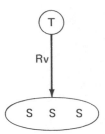

Laboratory

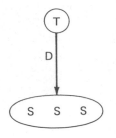

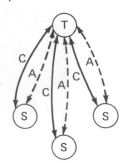

(a) Initiating tactic. The
teacher leads a pre-
laboratory review

(b) Focusing tactics. The
teacher gives direc-
tions, the students
work in the lab, and
their data is collected
and discussed

Postlaboratory

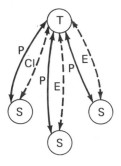

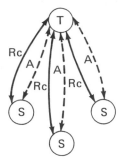

(c) Extending tactic. The
students are asked to
process and discuss
the data they collected

(d) Terminating tactic. A
review of the results
is made

FIGURE 9-7
Paradigm Showing a Typical Prelaboratory-Laboratory-Postlaboratory Sequence.

activity to past classwork or personal experiences. Then you should give the students directions or guidance before they begin working, to prevent any difficulties. This focusing tactic would be followed by the laboratory activities themselves, in which the students collect data as they interact directly with materials.

Following the collection of data, an extending tactic would help the students
discuss and process the data that they had collected. The extending tactics are
most important, since they lead to concept formation. Many teachers make the
mistake of summarizing the main points of the laboratory activity for the students
instead of permitting them to discuss and process the data for themselves.

Again, *you* must decide on *your* priorities. Are you *primarily* concerned with
the students' ability to recall certain specific content? Or are you primarily interested in having the students develop the skills necessary for the collection and

processing of data and for the attainment of formal thought? Your objectives will determine the type of teaching strategies you use. We have been emphasizing the development of the students' ability to solve problems *on their own.* After all, they won't always have you, or a book, to supply all of the answers. This ability to process data and solve problems is not limited to science, or to school, for that matter, but the science classroom is an excellent place for the children to develop these skills—*if we give them the experiences to practice and develop these skills.* There is a great difference between your solving a problem *for* the students and your serving as a guide while the children attempt to solve the problem for themselves. What we advocate is not a choice between content and inquiry skills, but rather that you give at least as much attention to the development of inquiry skills as you do to the acquisition of content.

A variety of strategies emphasizing different inquiry skills could be presented. Instead, however, we illustrate in detail three specific strategies involving the pre-lab-lab-postlab sequence, using the following sequence of inquiry skills:

1. Observing—comparing—classifying.
2. Observing—comparing—classifying—inferring.
3. Observing—inferring—hypothesizing—isolating variables—experimenting.

The first sequence is most appropriate for relatively young and untrained children entering the concrete stage of development, while the other two sequences would probably be more effective with older children who have had more experiences and are in the concrete stage of development or are making the transition into the stage of formal thought.

A teaching strategy emphasizing the inquiry skills of observing, comparing, and classifying is employed by several of the most widely used elementary school science curricula for the primary grades. The *Science Curriculum Improvement Study* unit on *Material Objects* and some of the early *Science—A Process Approach* lessons have the children observing the properties of materials in an attempt to make comparisons that would lead to various classifications. This strategy, based on the findings of Piaget, has young children spending much time working directly with objects. Children in the early primary grades are just entering the stage of concrete operations; they can work most effectively with objects they can directly manipulate.

In this observing, comparing, and classifying strategy the children practice observing, using all five senses as they describe the properties of objects. They compare these identified properties of the objects, and they begin to place the objects into groups based on one or more of the observed properties. For young children these classification systems may be very simple, usually based on only one observed property. As the children grow older, the classifications eventually become more complex, based on multiple properties or on more abstract properties.

Let's look at a specific example. Investigation I-5 from *Science Investigations for Elementary School Teachers*[10] has the students observing different fruits and

[10] Kenneth D. George et al., *Science Investigations for Elementary School Teachers* (Lexington, Mass.: D. C. Heath, 1974).

FIGURE 9-8
Children Observing and Comparing the Properties of Objects as They Attempt
to Classify Them According to Similarities and Differences. (From Thier,
Teaching Elementary School Science, p. 79.)

vegetables. The investigation involves presenting to the children both dry and
water-soaked lima beans, raisins, and prunes in order to observe and compare their
properties. A good initiating tactic for most age groups would be to present them
with the problem, "In how many different ways do you suppose these objects
are alike?" This question should arouse their interest, and using such familiar
objects helps to relate the lesson to their past experiences. Both the interest and
relevance, you will remember, are key ingredients of an initiating tactic.

Even though the initiating tactics are the same for most age groups, the focusing tactics would differ for children of different ability. For first or second
graders, you might ask the children to describe one object you have given to them.
After repeating this procedure several times with different objects, you might
then direct the students to form groups of objects with similar properties. For
more mature students, you could immediately ask them to develop groups based
on common properties.

After the students have had practice grouping the objects according to their
similarities, you could have several children describe how they classified their
objects. For the younger children, their grouping would be based on *one* observable property, such as color, size, or shape. The more mature children would form
groups according to multiple properties, such as color *and* size, shape or texture.
Even more abstract properties might be used, such as "fruit" or "vegetable," and
"edible" or "inedible." Of course, as the students suggest classifications, you

should be sure that they give reasons for their groupings. You should also make sure that many students had the opportunity to explain their classifications. This activity has a multiple purpose: first, the students can practice communicating with others; second, as descriptions are made by one student, the rest of the class can compare their groupings to the one being described. The students are also gaining experience in grouping objects in many different ways. To conclude this lesson, you might have several students tell what they learned as a result of the lesson. You will remember that the lesson was designed to help the children answer the question, "In how many ways do you suppose these objects are alike?"

The preceding examples were of a teaching strategy based on the inquiry skills of observing, comparing, and classifying. Using different content would not greatly change the structure of the strategy, which can be generalized as in Figure 9-9.

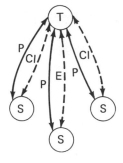

(a) Initiating tactic. The teacher introduces the topic by asking the class to suggest ways in which the objects are alike

Laboratory activity

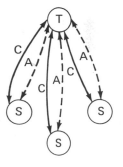

(b) Focusing tactics. The children work with the lima beans, raisins, and prunes, and the teacher helps them share their observations

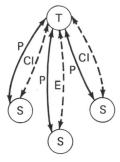

(c) Extending tactic. The children are asked to compare their observations and groupings

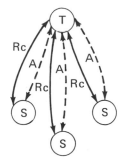

(d) Terminating tactic. A short review of the results

FIGURE 9-9
Paradigm Showing a Teaching Strategy Emphasizing the Inquiry Skills of Observing, Comparing, and Classifying.

A teaching strategy emphasizing the inquiry skills of observing, comparing, classifying, and inferring is similar to the one described previously, except that it tends to be more effective with older children who have had more experience with the inquiry process. The *Elementary Science Study* units on *Attribute Games* and *Tangrams* are examples of curricula with a strategy that involves observing, comparing, classifying, and inferring. As these units develop, the children make more subtle and complex comparisons, leading to the formation of some fairly sophisticated classifications. In this strategy, the discussion of the groupings is slightly changed. Each classifier, rather than describing the properties on which his groupings are based, tells what objects he has placed into groups. Then the rest of the class must infer the properties on which the groupings were based. Often the basis for the classification will be inferred rather than observed properties. This slight change in the discussion now places the emphasis on inferring rather than on observing and comparing. It is important to have those who are inferring the basis for the classification supply the reasons for their inferences. If these reasons are not discussed and explained, the lesson turns into a guessing game.

Once the children begin to infer the basis for a classification system, they can begin to attempt ways of testing their inferences. Now you need a more complex and advanced teaching strategy, concentrating on the generation and the *evaluation* of inferences.

A teaching strategy emphasizing the inquiry skills of observing, inferring, hypothesizing, isolating variables, and experimenting permits students to design and conduct tests of hypotheses. It takes considerable practice with less complex skills before children can effectively devise and evaluate tests of hypotheses. Evaluating hypotheses requires many other inquiry skills, which the strategies discussed earlier illustrate how to develop.

An excellent way to provide children with the opportunity to test and evaluate hypotheses is to use Type IV or Type V labs or field trips. As explained earlier, such activities place the burden of data processing on the students. They must process data while they design procedures to solve a particular problem, or in the case of a Type V lab or field trip, actually identify the problems themselves.

An important aspect of a scientist's work, involving the testing of hypotheses, is to construct simplified pictures of the world to help him to explain previously observed phenomena and predict new observations. These simplified pictures are called *models.* Model building is an excellent way to use Type IV laboratory activities and provide practice with most of the inquiry skills.

Scientists often build models to explain phenomena that cannot be directly observed. Models of the atom, or how the earth was formed, are put together from bits and pieces of experimental data. Such a model is usually first constructed to explain what has already been observed, and then used to predict an event that has not yet been observed. If the prediction is correct, the model is considered to be good, and new predictions are made. If the event predicted does not occur, the model is modified or discarded for a more acceptable one.

Model construction is more than a guessing game. Guessing is an inference with no factual basis, but model building, based on observations explains current information and predicts new observations. In order to illustrate this important activity in the classroom, a teaching strategy involving "mystery boxes" can be used. A mystery box allows the students to collect data actively and devise an explanation for the data in the form of a model. They also have the opportunity to predict new data based on the model that they have devised.

To use this strategy, the children could be presented with a mystery box. Their task is to develop a model of what they think the inside of the box is like, *without* opening the box. In order to do this, they must be able to supply evidence to support their model. Examples of different types of mystery boxes that can help provide children with practice on model building are shown in Figures 9-10 and 9-11.

If the students have all been given the same type of mystery box; that is, if the contents are all the same, then a discussion of the various models developed will be useful. You may want to use all of the class's data in order to construct a better model. Your first question, immediately after the students have observed

CHEMICAL MYSTERY BOX

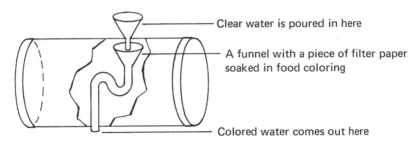

Clear water is poured in here

A funnel with a piece of filter paper soaked in food coloring

Colored water comes out here

OPTICAL MYSTERY BOXES

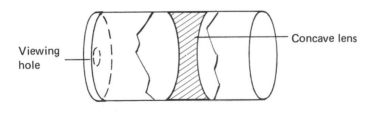

Viewing hole

Concave lens

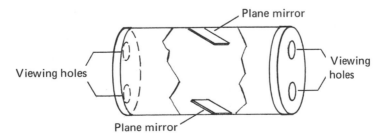

Plane mirror

Viewing holes

Viewing holes

Plane mirror

FIGURE 9-10
Some Examples of Various Types of Mystery Boxes.

MECHANICAL MYSTERY BOXES

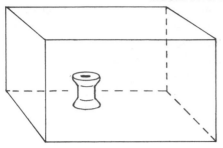 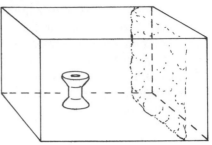

Any object such as a
marble, spool, pencil,
paper clip, or rubber
eraser

An object in a box that
has one wall covered with
cotton or rough sandpaper

STICK BOX

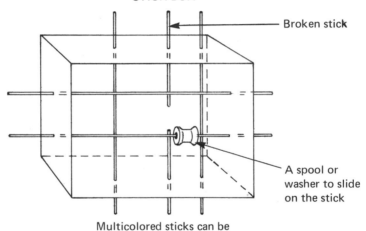

Broken stick

A spool or
washer to slide
on the stick

Multicolored sticks can be
removed

ROLLING BOXES

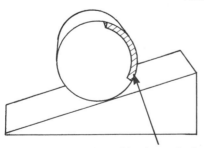

A bar of lead attached to
the wall of a cookie tin.
When released in this
position, it will roll uphill

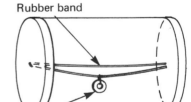

Rubber band

A weight attached
to the rubber band

When this cylindrical oat-
meal box is rolled away, it
will come back

FIGURE 9-11
Additional Examples of Various Types of Mystery Boxes.

the boxes, will be, "What did you observe?" By writing the class's observations on the board, you can help to focus their attention on what has been observed and help them to build a model based on evidence. After numerous observations have been given, you might then ask the class to develop a hypothesis concerning the inside of the box. After several hypotheses have been developed, you then direct the class to devise a way to verify each hypothesis. After completing their tests, students again share the data and revise the model, if necessary. This strategy is generalized in Figure 9-12.

Since both Type IV and Type V laboratory activities and field trips require the student to formulate his own procedure for solving a problem, and Type V laboratory activities and field trips have students formulate the problems as well, both should be included in strategies designed to provide practice for these inquiry skills. The complex inquiry skills of experimenting and isolating variables also require children to observe, predict, classify, and infer, so that Type IV and V laboratory activities achieve a two-fold purpose.

A generalized strategy for practicing the complex inquiry skills of isolating variables and experimenting is presented in Figure 9-13.

Before children can work efficiently and productively on a Type IV or Type V laboratory activity or field trip, they must have the necessary inquiry skills. You would find it difficult to have children work on a Type V lab or field trip if they have had little or no experience with Type III or Type IV labs or field trips. The laboratory activities and field trips, as described in Section II are organized into categories ranging from teacher directed to more student directed and student initiated, involve a greater number of the more complex inquiry skills. Watching your children work in the laboratory can give you an indication as to their readiness for student-initiated and student-directed experiences.

As a specific example, suppose you were conducting an investigation on the characteristics and properties of bacteria, such as Investigation V-6 from *Science Investigations for Elementary School Teachers.* Two of the instructional objectives for this investigation are that the student should be able to

1. Hypothesize methods of inhibiting the growth of bacteria.
2. Plan and conduct an experiment to determine the environmental conditions which will inhibit the growth of bacteria.

What does it indicate if your students are not basing their hypotheses on the data that they have been collecting? It might indicate that they are having difficulty justifying hypotheses with relevant data. Perhaps a short review of the skill of hypothesizing or inferring would be in order. During this review you could require students to find appropriate observations to support their hypotheses.

It is also helpful to discuss the importance of using all five senses and of being as quantitative as possible when making observations. If the children practice the skill of observing, you may find that much of their difficulty will disappear. A teacher should constantly be evaluating his students' inquiry skill proficiency, because often problems can be remedied quickly if the causes are determined early enough. Since inquiry skills vary in complexity, difficulty with a particular skill may really be caused by a problem with a more basic skill.

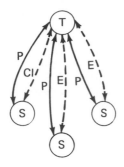

(a) "Without opening this box, how can we find out what the inside is like?"

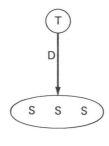

(b) Directions

Type IV laboratory activity

(c) Collect data

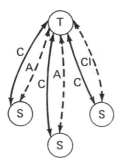

(d) "What did you observe about . . . ?" (Write observations on the board)

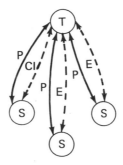

(e) "What would a model of the inside of this box be like?"

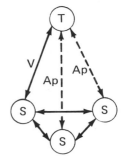

(f) "What could we do to find out if this model is correct?"

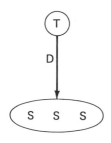

(g) Directions

(h) Type IV laboratory activity

Lab

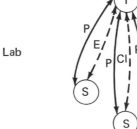

(i) "Based on the tests you have made, must we change our model?"

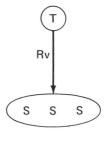

(j) Summarize

FIGURE 9-12
Paradigm Showing a Teaching Strategy Using Mystery Boxes.

Silent
demonstration

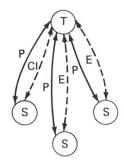

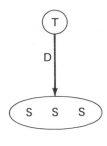

(a) A demonstration per-
formed without any
explanation

(b) "What problem was
presented?"

(c) "Devise a method to
solve the problem."

Lab

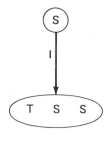

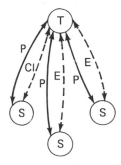

(d) Type IV
laboratory
activity

(e) A student describes a
procedure that he had
devised

(f) "What variables were
isolated in this pro-
cedure?"

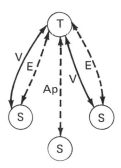

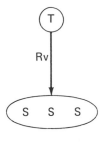

(g) The class discusses and
evaluates the merits of
all of the procedures
described

(h) The teacher reviews or
summarizes the main
points that were de-
veloped

FIGURE 9-13
Paradigm of a Teaching Strategy Emphasizing the Inquiry Skill of Isolation of Variables.

Inquiry skills can be practiced without the aid of laboratory activities. However, such practice is a highly language-oriented method, and therefore should be used with children in the upper elementary grades. Specific data processing skills can be the main focus of attention when using *quests*. In the teaching strategy to follow, the specific skills of comparing, inferring, and predicting are practiced.

Suppose that, in a unit on the environment, you felt it was important to investigate air pollution. To have students collect data on the kinds and amounts of pollutants in the air would be impractical, since the necessary equipment would be complicated. You could, however, collect this data from a book and present it to the children in the form of a table or chart. The students could then process the data in order to develop hypotheses or inferences concerning pollution. In this type of strategy, it is vitally important that you be sure the students understand the table of data before you ask them to make inferences or predictions from that data. Strategies using *quests* are good ways of providing specific practice with many of the inquiry skills.

In summary, several strategies for providing practice with inquiry skills have been developed and presented. Each has the ingredients of most teaching strategies—each gets students' interest and relates the lesson to their past experiences; each focuses the students' attention on a specific task; each extends the learning into new areas or reinforces the learning by having students actively participate in discussions; each strategy ends with some form of review that directs students' attention to the lesson's highlights. If your objectives in science are to help children develop the skills of inquiry, then your teaching strategies must include consistent and varied practice with these skills. Type IV and V laboratory activities and field trips, along with quests, give you a variety of activities from which to plan teaching strategies for developing inquiry skills.

Activities

1. Design a lesson as described in the objective on page 137.
2. Find any science experiment and reorganize it to incorporate at least two inquiry skills in the instructional objectives.
3. Teach the lesson that you have developed to a group of elementary school children.

Resource Material

Elementary Science Study (ESS) units available from Webster Division, McGraw-Hill Co., Manchester, Missouri, 63011.

George, Kenneth D. et al. *Science Investigations for Elementary School Teachers.* Lexington, Mass.: D. C. Heath, 1974.

Science: A Process Approach (SAPA). Available from Xerox Education Series, 555 Gotham Parkway, Carlstadt, N. J., 07072.

Science Curriculum Improvement Study (SCIS). Available from Rand McNally and Co., P.O. Box 7600, Chicago, Illinois, 60680.

Sund, Robert. *Elementary Science Discovery Lessons.* Boston, Mass.: Allyn and Bacon, 1970.

Psychomotor Objectives

Objective

To construct a lesson that includes the following:
(a) At least two psychomotor instructional objectives.
(b) Behavioral indicators of learning.
(c) A description of the procedure, including a Type I
     laboratory activity or field trip—the initiating, focusing,
     extending, and terminating tactics.

Psychomotor objectives emphasize the development of the manipulative skills necessary for safe and efficient laboratory work, besides the skills needed for the proper use of various measuring instruments. An effective way to develop these skills is to provide the students with the opportunity to practice them. After all, no one ever learned to play baseball *just* by reading about it. You have to go out and practice for hours at a time to develop the necessary skills. It is the same way with psychomotor skills in science—they must be practiced frequently. To avoid tedium, however, this repetition must be varied. For example, instead of weighing the same object again and again, students could weigh different objects; instead of measuring the length of the same object again and again, they could measure the length of different objects. The children need many opportunities to practice these new skills before they develop proficiency. Also, with younger children it might be more effective to use balances the children make themselves rather than laboratory equipment, since they are easier to operate and the children derive great satisfaction from constructing their own equipment. Also, the need for precision is probably not great enough to require the use of professional balances. Remember, the laboratory materials should *facilitate* the children's learning rather than posing any additional problems.

Students' physical development plays an important role in strategy building. Suppose you are teaching a fourth-grade class and you want to give your children some practice and experience weighing materials. Investigation II-2 from *Science Investigations for Elementary School Teachers*[11] is an example of a procedure you might want to follow. If, however, you were working with children in the first or second grade, you might want to begin with more basic activities, such as balancing. In planning a strategy for the development of a psychomotor skill, remember that the younger child must first work on the more basic skills, and he should have frequent practice.

One effective way of developing psychomotor skills is to include Type I laboratory activities or field trips in your strategies. They are more teacher directed than Type IV and V activities, but the Type I activities are *primarily* designed to provide students with the opportunity to practice and develop psychomotor skills. The Type IV and V activities are *primarily designed to develop the skills of data processing and evaluating.* It should be noted, however, that *all* of the different laboratory activities and field trips provide the students with the

---

[11] Kenneth D. George et al., *Science Investigations for Elementary School Teachers* (Lexington, Mass.: D. C. Heath, 1974).

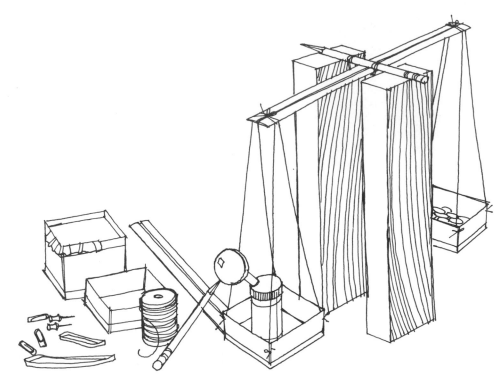

FIGURE 9-14
Example of a Simple "Homemade" Balance Suitable for Elementary Schoolchildren.

FIGURE 9-15
Children Working on a Field Trip. Outdoor Activities Are Valuable for
Developing Psychomotor Skills in a Way Children Find Enjoyable. (From
Thier, Teaching Elementary School Science, p. 117.)

opportunity to practice psychomotor skills. As long as the students are interacting directly with material, they are gaining valuable psychomotor practice and experiences.

The following is an example of a strategy in which your objective is to develop the skill of linear measurement for second-grade children. To begin the lesson, you might pose this problem to the children: "How long is your desk?" Not having much experience with rulers, they may try to indicate the length by spreading their hands apart. You might then ask: "How big is that?" Again, since their experience is very limited, they might not be able to answer. You can then indicate that the lesson for today is to learn a method for finding the size of things.

After showing the children, by way of a demonstration, how to measure length using a ruler, you would then hand out rulers similar to A in Figure 9-16. You explain the meaning of the lines and show that they are an equal distance apart. Note that only the major divisions are drawn on this ruler. You can make rulers like this from pieces of cardboard or posterboard.

Then hand out to each child a sheet that has lines on it, like those shown in Figure 9-16. Lines 1 through 4 are drawn to be exactly a multiple of 1 cm. Lines 5 through 8 are drawn to be a multiple of ½ cm. Lines 9 through 12 are drawn to any length. When each student has ruler A and paper, ask all of them to measure line 1. As they do this, you should circulate among the children to help those who have any problems. When they have finished measuring line 1, ask the

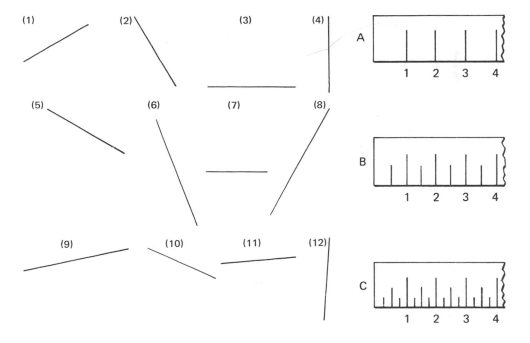

FIGURE 9-16
A Student Worksheet and Sample Rulers That Could Be Used in a Strategy to Provide the Students with Practice in the Skill of Measuring.

students for their results. Permit enough students to answer to assure you that most have measured the line correctly.

Repeat this procedure for lines 2 through 6. When students measure lines 5 and 6, they will have to estimate these lengths. This fact naturally shows the need for a more accurate method of measurement. When this need has been established, you can give out ruler B. After giving the students instructions on how to use this new ruler, have the students measure lines 5 through 10. Note that students will have to estimate lines 9 and 10, which in turn will show the need for still more accurate measuring tools. You can now give out ruler C. Note how this strategy provides a great deal of practice with the skill of linear measurement in different situations. It also moves from the simple (ruler A) to the complex (ruler C).

The application aspect of this strategy will come in future lessons, when the children use their rulers to measure other things, such as the height of plants or the length of insects. To spend several lessons measuring lines on paper would be quite boring, and the children would soon forget why linear measurement was important.

The proper use of measuring tools (rulers, thermometers, scales and balances, protractors,) is very important for young children to develop, since measuring instruments enable us to extend the use and the precision of our senses and make the collection of data more accurate.

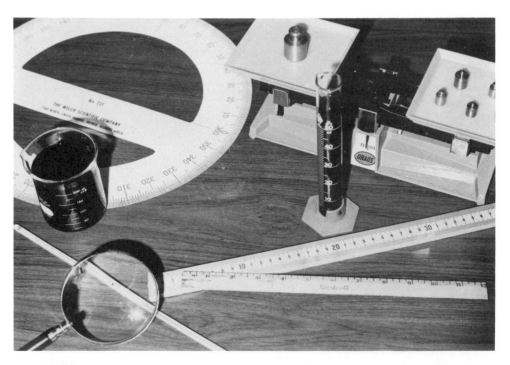

FIGURE 9-17
Some Examples of Common Laboratory Equipment Which Help Make Our Observations More Accurate and Precise. (Courtesy of Minaruth Galey, Temple University.)

These are other psychomotor skills which can be practiced using the strategy just described:

1. Measuring the length, width, and height of objects.
2. Determining the volume of a regularly or an irregularly shaped object.
3. Determining the weight of an object.
4. Demonstrating the proper methods of using such laboratory apparatus as
   (a) Balances, thermometers, and burners.
   (b) Beakers, flasks, and test tubes.
   (c) Microscopes and telescopes.
5. Constructing charts, graphs, or diagrams.

Young children can easily practice many of these psychomotor skills as they observe and compare the properties of objects. A teaching strategy stressing observing, comparing, and classifying is a very effective and important one for children in the early primary grades, since many of the psychomotor skills can be practiced. For example, children comparing the dimensions of objects and classifying them accordingly would need to measure the length, width, and height of various objects.

In general, when you are planning Type I laboratory activities or field trips, or any activity designed to help develop the students' psychomotor skills, there are several important points to keep in mind.

1. You should provide the students with many opportunities to practice the desired skills and tell them how well they have done.

FIGURE 9-18
Children Can Practice Making Their Observations More Accurate and Precise if They Have an Opportunity to Use Various Measuring Tools.

2. The children should be given a chance to practice the skills in a variety of different situations.
3. The relationship among many of the psychomotor skills must be emphasized so that the children can see how one may help others.
4. Directions for activities must be stated as clearly as possible, so that the children do not become confused.
5. The students should be carefully supervised, so that no equipment is abused and no accidents can occur.

A strategy employing a Type I laboratory activity or a field trip to develop psychomotor skills in children might be generalized as shown in Figure 9-19. It is interesting to note that the teacher in this specific example reacts to each of the data collecting responses with an *accepting* reaction. It would be very easy for you to reject an obviously incorrect observation, such as a wrong measurement. It would be much more useful, however, if the class were to develop the ability to decide whether the observation was erroneous or not.

Type I laboratory activities or field trips can be used *both* as *focusing* tactics or *extending* tactics in the development of psychomotor skills. They are *focusing* tactics if they are the main experience from which the students *collect* data as they practice their skills. They can, however, also be used as *extending* tactics, if the Type I lab or field trip provides the students with the opportunity to *apply* their skills to new situations. For example, if you were using the laboratory activity with the different rulers, just described, you would be using the Type I lab as a focusing tactic in which the children practiced psychomotor skills as they collected data by measuring various objects with the different kinds of rulers. After they had done this, they might go outside and use this skill by measuring the size of different objects around their school. This is an example of a Type I field trip used as an extending tactic.

Earlier, in our discussion of content objectives, a second-grade teacher was described presenting a lesson on the solar system. The concepts of *rotation* and *revolution* are difficult for young children to visualize. It was suggested that the teacher might help them understand these concepts by having them duplicate *rotation* and *revolution* in the classroom. One child could turn in place (rotation) while another could walk around the room, always facing the same point in the front of the room (revolution).

As a further step, you might have one child walk around the room, constantly keeping his face turned toward the center of the circle that he is making. This is analogous to the earth-moon orbit, in which the moon is rotating and revolving at the same rate. For that reason, we always see the same side of the moon's surface. These difficult concepts become more clear if the children have a chance to visualize them in a more concrete setting. Such role playing simultaneously gives the children a chance to practice and develop motor coordination, which is necessary for many of the more complex psychomotor skills. Children in the concrete operations stage of development benefit greatly from these direct experiences.

Activities

1. Design a lesson as described in the objective on page 151.

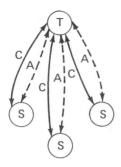

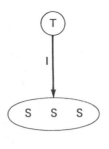

(a) Initiating tactics. (1) The children are asked data collecting questions involving measurement, and (2) the teacher informs them they will now be practicing some of these skills in lab

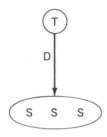

Type I lab or field trip

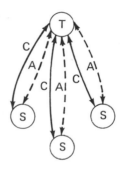

(b) Focusing tactics. (1) The students are given directions and (2) they begin working in the lab. (3) After the lab work is done, the data that was collected is shared and discussed

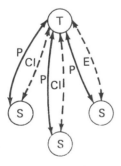

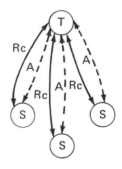

(c) Extending tactic. "How can we make our data collection even more accurate in the future?"

(d) Terminating tactic. A review of the main points of the lesson

FIGURE 9-19
A Paradigm Showing How a Type I Laboratory Activity or Field Trip Can Be Used in a Teaching Strategy to Provide Practice in Psychomotor Skills.

FIGURE 9-20
When Children "Act out" the Concepts of Rotation and Revolution the Ideas Become Easier to Understand.

2. Select at least two psychomotor skills that would be appropriate for second grade, and two for fifth grade, and design an instructional procedure to provide students with practice in these skills.
3. Teach the lesson that you have developed to a group of elementary school children.

Resource Material

George, Kenneth D. et al. *Science Investigations for Elementary School Teachers.* Lexington, Mass.: D. C. Heath, 1974.

Affective Objectives

Objective

To construct a lesson that includes
(a) One affective objective.
(b) Behavioral indicators of learning.
(c) A role-playing situation.
(d) A complete description of the initiating, focusing, extending, and terminating tactics.

Most teachers give very little conscious attention to achieving affective objectives. We are so concerned with covering the content that we fail to develop specific student attitudes, interests, or appreciations. While there is considerable debate on whether teachers *should* develop student attitudes or values, there are unquestionably certain attitudes that we are in a good position to help develop. We probably feel that it would be desirable to have our students like science more than they did before they were in our class, or appreciate the role that science plays in our modern and technological society. We rarely make any conscious effort to achieve these objectives. Not only that, how do you tell if a child *really* does "like science" or "appreciate the role of science in our society"? It is one thing to really like science, and quite another to tell a teacher, who is teaching you science, that you "like" science.

Many of us take a very indirect approach to the development of affective objectives. We often assume that children will like science, or appreciate the danger of drugs, or realize the importance of good health habits just because we talk about these things during class. Unfortunately, such is not the case! We are, however, very effective in unconsciously achieving other types of affective behaviors. For example, there probably isn't a child alive who was *born* afraid of snakes. This fear is something that they learned from their parents, from their friends, *and* from their teachers as they saw other people acting afraid of snakes. They begin to develop the attitude that snakes are something to regard with fear and revulsion, and they do so. We are very effective in transmitting our fears, beliefs, and prejudices to our students. One of the reasons why we are so successful in transmitting these feelings is that we are very *consistent* in our exhibition of these behaviors. If only we could be as effective in developing other types of behavioral changes!

None of us expects to turn out a class of children who will all become practicing scientists, but it is certainly desirable for them to develop a more positive attitude towards science. Before we talk about "liking" science in any more detail, it is important to decide, at least in some basic way, just what "liking science" means. A child can say that he "likes science," when he really doesn't. A child can write a 200-word essay on why he "likes science," when he actually hates it. A child can list science as his "favorite" subject, when he really can't stand it, if he thinks that *you* would like to have him feel this way. The question is: How can we differentiate between the child who says that he "likes" science, but doesn't, and child who says that he "likes" science, and really does? Also, how can we identify those children who like science but never really say anything at all?

A good guide to these judgments is the old proverb, "Actions speak louder than words." We have to ask ourselves, "What are the things that a child who *likes* science does, and that a child who *doesn't* like science does *not* do?" It is these behavioral indicators of "liking" science that we should look for. While they are obviously not always correct, these behavioral indicators seem to be a more valid test of a child's attitude towards science than the simple assumption that a child will develop a specific attitude because we aimed our teaching at this development. For example, a child who likes science might do the following:

1. Ask for more science classes during the course of the week.
2. Select books on science from the library during a reading period.
3. Ask to work on a science project during free period.
4. Bring in things from home related to science.
5. Volunteer to participate in a school science fair.
6. Select a trip to a science lab or a science museum, when given the choice.

It should be obvious that a student who really didn't like science would probably not *voluntarily* choose to do these things. However, if the above examples are done as a part of a school assignment, they are *not* indicative that a child actually likes science. If the behaviors are *voluntary* and *unsolicited,* they are much more reliable indicators. By being aware of behavioral indicators of this type, you can informally assess whether or not your children are developing a greater liking for science.

It is important to emphasize that the behaviors described above are voluntarily evidenced by the student. Too often we do not encourage a voluntary display of "liking science." We continually direct a child to do this or that. Perhaps this is the reason that voluntary behaviors are not often seen; we spend too much time having the students do work that we have assigned. If an environment were provided in which the child could, at least some of the time, choose what he wanted to do, rather than always doing what we want him to do, we would be able to observe more voluntary behaviors. Teaching strategies that incorporate Type IV and V laboratory activities and field trips will give most students some freedom of choice. In these activities the student is free to choose his own method of solving a problem, or even to identify his own problem to investigate.

In general, teaching science by an approach that encourages the active participation of the children and the direct interaction of the students with materials and each other is an effective way of developing more positive attitudes towards science. As was discussed in detail in Section I, students who are trying to solve *inconsistencies*—events that don't make sense to them—become naturally interested in trying to resolve them. Additionally, since the children are encouraged to discuss with each other their own ideas about the inconsistency, they are not competing against each other to get the "right" answer and the approval of the teacher. Each child is working more individually, and each one is contributing to the total data collected and processed by the class.

All of the above activities, if consistently used in a science classroom, will help encourage the children to like science. The section on *Individualizing Instruction* (p. 167) also gives other methods of providing students with the opportunity to make choices.

Research on how attitudes are changed is inconclusive, so it is not possible to present specific strategies. However, there are some general strategies for developing situations in which students can explore attitudes and values different from their own. Suppose you are planning a unit for your fifth-grade class on the problems of water pollution. You want your students to understand the problems from many different viewpoints—those of the industrial engineer as well as those of the conservationist. How best to do this? You could carefully explain the views of both sides and point out the differences of opinion. But would this really give the class a feeling for the different viewpoints? Probably not. There are more effective ways of familiarizing the class with the opinions and feelings of both sides—namely, role-playing situations.

Children naturally love to act. They enjoy playing the part of another person. By using role-playing situations, you can have children describe the different points of view as if they actually were the people involved. In addition to having two children playing the roles of the two antagonists, in this particular case the

FIGURE 9-21
Social Problems Involving Science and Technological Progress Can Be Interestingly and
Effectively Discussed Using a Role-Playing Strategy.

conservationist and the industrial engineer, you would have other children taking
part as mediators in an effort to reach a solution to the problem. As the children
research their roles, they will not only be exchanging information, but also gaining insights into the feelings and motivations that cause different groups of people
to act as they do. This active participation on the part of the children would be
very difficult, if not impossible, for you to duplicate if you tried to teach the
same topic by informing the children about the issues.

Quests in which the interactions between science and society are discussed
can be very effective ways for you to talk about today's current problems with
your class. Such topics as pollution, ecology, the impact of modern technology
on life, drugs, and the problems of man and machine can be effectively discussed
with these teaching tactics. Far too many of us tend to ignore or discuss very
briefly this humanistic aspect of science and its impact on our daily lives. We
sometimes tend to concentrate so heavily on the concepts of science that we
never take a close look at the much larger impact that science is having on all aspects of our lives. Quests of this type help to give the children a much wider
understanding of the total nature of science than does a program of instruction
that concentrates entirely on science concepts.

At this point an important distinction must be made. A major difference
exists between a student showing a temporary "liking" for science or indicating
that he has changed his attitude about some topic, and a student developing a
more permanent attitude change. All of us are aware that young children can become excited and "turned on" to a particular topic, only to have this enthusiasm
disappear with the passage of time. In order to develop more permanent attitude
changes, it is necessary to develop teaching strategies that extend over much
longer periods of time, These longer term strategies provide the basis for permanent changes in our students' attitudes.

Activities

1. Design a lesson as described in the objective on page 158.
2. Select a current problem facing science and society and show how it could be used to develop affective objectives with a group of elementary-school children.
3. Develop and teach a topic involving an affective objective to a group of elementary-school children. Include a quest as one of your teaching tactics.

Resource Material

Chesler, Mark, and Fox, Robert. *Role-Playing Methods in the Classroom.* Chicago: Science Research Associates, 1966.

Greer, Mary, and Rubinstein, Bonnie. *Will the Real Teacher Please Stand Up.* Pacific Palisades, California: Goodyear Publishing Co., 1972.

Long-Term Teaching Strategies 10

Unit Planning

Objectives

1. To state three strategies for organizing a science unit.
2. To construct a science unit that includes the instructional objectives and the experiences you would provide to help the students achieve the instructional objectives.
3. To describe two strategies for organizing an entire science program, lasting for one school year.

Science in the elementary school is sometimes taught as a semiweekly exercise, and often within that week the two lessons are unrelated. Science taught in this manner has little chance either for being remembered or being used. In order to overcome this problem, some unity must exist between lessons, and even across many lessons. In this discussion, we are concerned with those of you who have the time to plan a series of science lessons. We recognize that many of you have a tremendous task in planning lessons for four or five different subjects. For you, a commercially prepared curriculum guide might be of more immediate value. But for those of you who may teach in a team where your main responsibility is preparing the science experiences, or for those of you who are not yet teaching and want to organize a series of science experiences, we are going to illustrate several ways of doing this.

There are at least three ways of organizing science experiences for a long period of time. The first and most common strategy is to organize the experiences around a science concept or principle. Typical examples of science concepts are "heat," "birds," "forces," and "levers." An example of a science principle is, "green plants need water and air in order to grow." The second major strategy would be to construct experiences that answer a problem or question. "What are the variables affecting the swing of a pendulum?" "What animals live in our neighborhood?" The third and perhaps least-used strategy is to present science experiences with a historical approach. The theory of the evolution of our solar system is a good example. Beginning with observations about the motions of the stars and planets, an earth-centered theory of planetary motion can be developed. This theory is quite reasonable in terms of what we actually perceive. Then gradually presenting the evidence collected by Copernicus and Brahe in support of a sun-centered solar system will give the student an excellent historical view of science.

These three strategies for presenting science over a long period of time are certainly not the only ones, but they are the ones most frequently used. As with the short-term teaching strategies, variety in organization is essential. As you will soon see, each strategy can incorporate related subject matter from areas such as social studies, mathematics, language arts, and the fine arts.

Before deciding on a strategy, you must answer several questions. The first and perhaps most important is, What content, skills, attitudes, values, and interests do I want the students to acquire as a result of my instruction? As you think about these, remember that inquiry and psychomotor skills must be practiced again and again before the students gain facility with them. This means that they will not acquire such inquiry skills as inferring and experimenting as a result of a single unit of science instruction. The science content taught should emphasize the concepts and principles of science, for it is the concepts and principles of science that are more easily remembered. Specific facts should be acquired only if they are essential for developing the concepts and principles. All three strategies described previously should include the development of new concepts and the practicing of inquiry and psychomotor skills. These concepts, principles, and skills also form the basis for evaluating any learning that has taken place during your teaching.

The second question to be answered when developing a science unit is, "What direct experiences can be presented to the students to help them achieve the desired objectives?" We would even go so far as to say that if *no* direct experiences can be found, the concepts should not be taught. The younger the child or the fewer past experiences the child has had, the more important it is to include direct experiences. This is especially true of a child in the concrete operations stage of development. To help you answer this question, we have provided resource materials throughout this book. For organizing an effective unit, you must be thoroughly acquainted with the available resource material. This is one reason why we suggested that busy elementary school teachers consider using available science curricula in addition to developing their own.

A third question to be answered when constructing a unit is, "Why will the students be interested in this material?" Older students often ask this question themselves, and to say that they will need it later on is sidestepping the issue. A good strategy for organizing a series of science experiences is to begin with phenomena familiar to most students and then extend the learning into unknown areas. This helps the students to see how the experiences are related to them and, therefore, how they are relevant.

Now, using these three questions and strategies, we will illustrate with specific examples how to develop science units. Suppose you're a first-grade teacher and you want to teach a unit on the senses. The first thing you might do is develop the concept "senses." In a child's words, what does this mean? The five senses are seeing, hearing, touching, tasting, and smelling. One of your behavioral indicators might be that the students should be able to name the five senses—or to point out what part of the body they use for each sense.

Next, you might want to have the students use their senses in describing an object. At this age, the words associated with each sense would have to be acquired. Words needed to describe objects using the senses must be developed through practice. Notice how the behavioral indicator clearly specifies the experiences students need to have—practice in naming the senses, or in pointing to parts of the body used for that sense, and practice describing objects by using all of their senses. Type I laboratory experiences are quite appropriate. Additional experiences could be provided by reading stories to the students in which people use their senses. Indian stories, for instance, abound with examples of how others use their senses. Poems can also be used effectively.

The strategy emphasizing a problem or question can be illustrated in the following manner. Suppose near your school there is a lake, pond, or large puddle that never seems to dry up. Your fourth graders have often been seen lingering by this body of water. One day you approach them with the problem, "What kinds of animals live in that pond, and how do they stay alive?" Before posing this problem, however, you have carefully considered the approach to this problem. You might ask yourself, "If the students are going to work on this problem, what skills do they need?" They certainly will need to know where to look for the animals and how to collect them. If the pond is well established, surface animals, bottom dwellers, and animals that live in the mud could be collected—with a jelly jar for microscopic animals, and a net of some type for catching the larger animals. All of these methods require some instruction. Labelling the jars to describe where the contents were located is important. Once the animals have been captured, the skill of identification might be important. For your fourth graders, a hand-drawn picture of the animals observed may be all they need. If microscopic animals are to be observed with facility, a hand lens or microscope would be necessary.

To answer the question, "How do the animals stay alive?" careful observation and experimentation may be required. If snails have been captured, they might be placed in a jar with some plants and small microscopic animals. After several days of observation, the children could infer what the snails eat by observing what is missing. In identifying the skills that the children will need to be successful inquirers, you are beginning to determine what your instructional objectives would be. As you can see, we have developed the need for several psychomotor skills to be practiced and acquired—during the collecting of aquatic animals, during the use of microscopes and lenses, and so on. The inquiry skills of observing, inferring, and experimenting could easily be practiced during this unit.

The strategies just described are useful in planning for three to four weeks of instruction. You might ask, "What do I do for the entire year?" Again, we would answer that there are many ways to structure your entire science program. One successful strategy is to begin the year with structured activities—teacher demonstrations, Types I, II, and III laboratory activities or field trips, and quests. The main emphasis in this long-term strategy is to give the children content and skills needed to operate in a more unstructured situation. In working with your children you will soon see which children need the security of more structure and which can effectively work in an unstructured situation. As the year progresses, you would begin to provide students with the opportunity for more freedom. The gradual shift from teacher-centered to student-centered activities, such as Type IV and V laboratory activities or field trips, would provide the opportunity for student development and practice of the skills and attitudes developed in the more structured environments. Such a strategy provides the necessary content, skills, and attitudes to make inquiry more rewarding than frustrating. It helps the children to develop confidence in their ability to actively engage in inquiry.

The strategy just described is more effective for the younger child and for those lacking in the basic psychomotor and inquiry skills. For those who do have such skills as the ability to measure length, determine weight, observe, infer, and experiment, a different strategy would be more effective. You could permit the students to study in depth any problem of their choice that was related to the concepts they have already investigated. Such a strategy throughout the year would permit a sampling of the many aspects of science, while providing students with the opportunity to develop and practice the inquiry skills and attitudes acquired previously.

The strategies just described provide a balance between teacher-directed and student-directed activities. Both strategies allow students to make choices—a key ingredient of individualization. Both approaches give students the necessary content and practice with inquiry skills to make inquiry a rewarding experience.

Activities

1. Describe three strategies for organizing a science unit.
2. Using one of the following Elementary Science Study units as resource material, develop instructional objectives for a science unit. Include in your unit the concepts and principles to be developed, the inquiry skills to be practiced, and the psychomotor skills to be developed.

   > "Batteries and Bulbs" for sixth graders.
   > "Behavior of Mealworms" for fourth graders.
   > "Mobiles" for first graders.

   See the resource materials in Section II for the source of these manuals.
3. Using the following resource material, develop a unit on a science concept or principle of your choosing. Include in your unit the grade level; the instructional objectives, including content and skills; and the experiences you would provide for the children.

Resource Material

American Geological Institute. *Geology and Earth Sciences Sourcebook for Elementary and Secondary Schools.* New York: Holt, Rinehart and Winston, Inc., 1962.

Blough, Glenn O., and Schwartz, Julius. *Elementary School Science and How to Teach It.* 4th ed. New York: Holt, Rinehart and Winston, Inc., 1969.

Hone, Elizabeth et al. *A Source Book for the Physical Sciences.* 2nd ed. New York: Harcourt Brace Jovanovich, Inc., 1971.

Joseph, A. et al., *A Source Book for the Physical Sciences.* New York: Harcourt, Brace, and World, 1961.

Morholt, E., Brandwein, P., Joseph, A. *A Source Book for the Biological Sciences.* New York: Harcourt, Brace, and World, Inc., 1956.

Victor, Edward. *Science for the Elementary School.* 2nd ed. New York: The Macmillan Co., 1970.

Individualizing Instruction

Objectives

1. To state four methods for individualizing a science program.
2. To construct an individualized science unit.

The concept of individualized instruction is not new. Centuries ago, tutors were hired by the rich to teach their children. For present-day educational purposes, a one-to-one method of instruction is highly impractical, since in most classrooms there is one teacher for twenty to forty-five students. Yet this method is ideal for promoting individual growth. It is natural to ask if there is a way of implementing individualized instruction in present-day classrooms. We believe that there is. But before we present methods of individualizing instruction, it is important to define some terms.

Individualizing instruction is often thought of as "making the course relevant to the student." This phrase is quite popular, but there is much confusion as to its meaning. Some interpret it to mean that the student should be free to choose the subject matter he wants to study, since he is in the best position to know what is relevant. This position presents a paradox. Students want to choose what they study, but they usually choose those topics with which they already have some familiarity. How, then, will a child study something new? Will a child study topics in science if he has no experience with them? Probably not. Many topics in science, when only presented verbally, do sound boring; however, once encountered directly, they can be quite exciting. We will agree that individualizing instruction involves choices on the students' part, but absolute freedom to choose whatever he wants to study is not advisable until he has acquired a certain amount of background content and skills. How can a child freely study in depth a particular science principle without first having some background content? For example, if a student is investigating the properties of various materials, he may have to be able to use a laboratory balance. To allow the child to find out on his own how to weigh materials would be hard on the child, as well as on the equipment he may be using. This example indicates the importance of some preliminary skills before the child can freely select a topic to investigate.

A truly individualized science program provides a child with an opportunity to make choices within the bounds set by the teacher. The younger the child, the more clearly the bounds must be defined. In most science curricula, four types of choices are possible for the child: (1) the rate at which he will move through the material, (2) the objectives he will try to attain, (3) the activities he will pursue, and (4) the manner in which he will be evaluated. The more choices a student makes while studying science, the more individualized his studying becomes *and* the more carefully planned and organized you must become as his teacher. Let's examine each choice a student can make and then explore the implications of that choice for the science curriculum.

In the most common type of individualized instruction in most elementary schools, the teacher decides on the objectives, the instructional methods, and the evaluation tasks, while the child is permitted to work through the activities at his own rate. Students may complete the same lesson in different amounts of time. This form of individualized instruction, called *self-paced instruction,* is the easiest to develop and administer. The child engaged in this type of instruction has little freedom of choice. Each child achieves the same objectives; each completes the same activities; each is evaluated in the same way.

In a second type of individualized instruction, the teacher develops a list of objectives and related activities and evaluation tasks. The student is given the opportunity to choose the objectives he wishes to attain. Once he has chosen an objective, he then completes the prescribed activities and evaluation tasks. Each child choosing the same objectives has the same activities and evaluation tasks. This is different from the first individualized method in that there is more freedom of choice for the student. The child can not only work at his own rate, but is free to choose the instructional objectives he wishes to pursue.

We mentioned previously that students should be free to make choices within limits. This principle is especially true in the case of choosing instructional objectives. If one objective contains content or skills that are necessary for the attainment of another objective, then all students should work towards the attainment of the first objective. For example, *given any object, the student should be able to determine its size using a metric ruler* is a prerequisite for much that goes on in a science classroom. It should be required that *all* students be given the opportunity to achieve this objective. On the other hand, the objective "The student should be able to state three methods of detecting radioactivity" might not be so important that *all* must work towards it. For most topics taught there is probably a combination of objectives—usually basic content and skills—to be achieved by all students, and other objectives that may be achieved only by some students. Your understanding of the objectives of an elementary school science program will aid you in determining which objectives are important for *all* your students to attain. Here is an example of this type of individualization.

Directions: We are beginning a unit on the properties of matter. Each week I will give you a list of statements as your science objectives for the week. Those marked with a star (*), everyone must do. The number you do in addition to those with a star is up to you.

Objectives: By the end of the week, you should be able to
*1.   Measure the volume in metric units of any solid.
*2.   Measure the volume in metric units of any liquid.
*3.   Measure the weight in metric units of any solid.

4. Measure the weight of any solid while it is immersed in any liquid.
5. Measure the weight of any liquid.

In a third method of individualizing instruction, the child chooses the particular lessons he wishes to study from a list that you present. The child has no choice in the objectives he works to achieve, but for each objective you present to the child, there are variations in the activities that he can pursue. It has long been recognized that some students like to read better than others; some like to learn with more visual materials, such as films or film strips. Some like to perform experiments more than others. In this type of individualization, the child is free to choose the type of activity that he wishes to pursue. The main difference between this method of individualization and the two previously presented methods is the student's freedom of choice of the activities. The child is given an objective, and he is free to choose or design how he will achieve the objective.

In providing students with the freedom to choose activities, you should keep these reservations in mind. Some students may prefer to read their way through a science class, simply because they do not want to "dirty" their hands by performing experiments. Others may perform experiments primarily because they cannot or do not want to read. In situations like these, it is important that a teacher achieve a balance and variety in the activities. This can be done by requiring certain activities—some reading, some laboratory work—and then permitting students to have freedom of choice. It is still important to provide students with a list of possible activities from which to choose, because many students will not know what to do. Here is an example of this type of individualization.

Directions: During the next four weeks we will be investigating the properties of matter. All of us will be working towards the same objectives, but we will be approaching them from different directions. Some of us will be reading about the topics, in addition to performing experiments; others will only perform experiments related to the topics; and others may be interviewing people. After each of us has completed the activity, he will share his findings with the group. For each objective, everyone will choose those activities that he will do, and everyone choosing the same activity will work together. We will spend one week on each objective.

Objective: At the end of our unit, you should be able to tell how a town gets its drinking water.

Activities: 1. Reading.
     Text pp. 53-62, 127-132. Go to the library and find some books describing how drinking water is obtained. Summarize your findings by giving the class a ten-minute report.
2. Interview Mr. Jones, the Water Commissioner, and summarize what he said in a report to the class.

Objective: At the end of our unit, you should be able to tell how water is purified for drinking.

Activities: 1. Reading.
Text pp. 47-56, 133-145. Find an extra book in the library and summarize the reading in a report to the class.
2. Experiments.
Complete experiments 5, 6, 7, and 8 in the text and summarize your findings for the class.
3. Make a series of drawings that show the different ways in which water can be purified.
4. Look at the following films and summarize them for the class. Films 23, 28, 41.

Another method for individualizing science instruction is to permit the student to choose how he will be evaluated. Essentially, there are two choices to be made. The first is to permit the child to choose how he will be evaluated for each objective he pursues. The second is to permit the child to choose the grade he will earn if he attains the objectives.

It is quite difficult at times to conceive of more than one method of evaluation for an objective, but there are some alternatives that will be more thoroughly discussed later. The traditional method of evaluating a child is a paper-and-pencil test. It has long been recognized that some children perform better on pencil-and-paper tests than others, and that paper-and-pencil tests are limited in the achievement that they can measure. Since this is the case, a student's oral report, an oral examination, an evaluation of a product of instruction, such as a picture or a laboratory experiment—all these could be used to indicate how much a child had achieved as a result of instruction.

Having the child establish his own grade, or having him evaluate his own achievement, are two important methods of individualizing instruction. The first method is commonly called *contract learning.* After having established the criteria for different grades, you would then permit the student to choose the grade towards which he will work. This type of individualization is highly motivating for most children. In establishing the criteria for an "A," "B," or so on, you must

---

Contract

Grade	Requirements
C	All of the work we do in class. One reading from Chapter 12. Three experiments of your choice.
B	Requirements for a "C." One more experiment.
A	Requirements for a "B." An additional two experiments of your choice.

Notebooks will be collected on three dates. Each time you must have at least one-third of your work completed, since it will be graded at those times. The three dates to remember are
January 20th
February 3rd
February 11th

---

be sure that the higher grade indicates quality as well as quantity. Many teachers who employ this system of evaluation establish the amount of work done as the main criteria for an "A." The quality of the work is also an important factor to consider.

In the example on page 170, the teacher has decided that a "B" is more work than a "C," and an "A" more work than a "B."

Independent Contract

Here is a list of possible topics of interest to you:

Proving atoms exist.	Making solutions.
Observing different gases.	Studying the properties of water.
Growing crystals.	Separating mixtures.
Growing plants.	Raising guppies.

Any other topic of your choice.

If you choose to work independently:

1. Begin by reading about your topic—this may take several days or a week, using texts and the library.
2. Form questions you would like to answer—things *you* would like to find out. At this point, discuss your objectives and the grade you want to earn with me.
3. Find or develop your own experiments.
4. Record all of your work and results.
5. Summarize what you have learned with me and the rest of the class.

The work must be completed by February 11th.

You decide in advance, the grade you wish to earn, depending on the quality of work you are going to do. When you are finished with your work, try to do a self-evaluation. Ask yourself if you have reached all of your objectives and have answered all of your questions. Review what you have learned. Are you proud of your work? Plan on a conference with me.

Any classroom teacher will quickly detect that there are some students who can learn independently of the teacher. These students need less guidance. A single conference between the student and the teacher may be all that is needed to initiate learning. For them, the outline presented above could be used.

Other methods of individualizing instruction could combine certain aspects of the four methods just presented. A child may be free to choose his own objectives but required to follow a set of activities. Then, however, he could be evaluated with tasks of his own choosing. Another possibility is that every child works on the same objectives but is free to choose his own activities and evaluation tasks. The possibilities are numerous; it is up to you what combinations to use.

Which type of individualization should you develop in your classes? In order to answer this question, you must realize that the more freedom of choice available to the student, the better planned and organized *you* must be. As we mentioned before, it is quite easy to have thirty children doing the same thing at the same time, but it is much more difficult to have thirty children doing thirty different things. If you feel intimidated by the latter situation, individualization of instruction is probably not for you.

As mentioned several times in this book, the key to student achievement and interest is variety and clarity. A variety of objectives, activities, and evaluation tasks is a key ingredient. Permitting student choice in these areas is a key to successful individualization. The chart in Figure 10-1 summarizes the various methods of individualizing instruction.

Type	Objective	Instructional Methods	Evaluation
1	x		
2		x	
3			x
4	x	x	
5	x		x
6		x	x
7	x	x	x

FIGURE 10-1
Possible Types of Individualized Instruction. An *x* in a Particular Column Means That the Student Is Free to Make This Choice.

Activity

Using a science topic from any of the resource materials suggested in Sections II or III, individualize a unit with one of the methods suggested under this unit topic.

Resource Material

Triezenberg, Henry, ed. *Individualized Science—Like It Is.* Washington, D. C.: National Science Teachers Association, 1972.

Elementary School Science Curricula

Objectives

1. To state the similarities and differences in the new elementary school science programs.
2. To state some criteria to employ in selecting a developed science curriculum.
3. To apply the criteria you have developed to select a science curriculum for a specific school.

Since the early 1960s, a great many elementary school science curricula have been developed. Space does not permit an adequate description of them. Besides, others have adequately described them, and references to these sources are given in the resource material at the end of this topic. What we shall do is help you develop criteria for making a choice among the various alternatives. These criteria, plus your reading of the resource material and your perusal of the actual curricular material, should help you to decide which curriculum is best suited for the children that attend your school.

A brief description of how the various curricula are similar will help to limit the decisions you have to make. On most of the newer curricula scientists, teachers, and psychologists have worked hand-in-hand to develop a more cohesive science program. All of the newer elementary school science curricula emphasize the importance of direct experiences for the children. The laboratory approach is extensively used in developing the concepts and principles of science. Only one curriculum has developed what might be called a textbook in which students read about science. Yet, this one textbook is essential in developing the skills needed to work in the laboratory. All curricula have material in which students record observations and other pertinent data. All have extensive teacher's guides that provide useful background information on the topics presented, tell where to get materials and how much to get, give teaching suggestions, and list available supplementary material. But here the similarities end, and a teacher needs criteria that help distinguish among the various curricula.

"What approach to science have the developers used?" is a good first question to ask. Some emphasize the concepts and principles of science, while others emphasize the inquiry skills of science. Of course, there are several which strike a balance between these two extremes; which is most important depends on your view of science. We recommend strongly that a balance be maintained between the concepts and inquiry skills of science.

A second question to ask in developing selection criteria is about the developer's instructional objectives, and how they compare with your own. You will find, upon examining the numerous curricula, that some state explicit objectives, while others are a series of activities that could be fitted to almost any teachers' instructional objectives.

"Is there any flexibility in sequencing the units of instruction?" is another excellent question to ask. As you investigate in depth many of the newer science curricula, you will find that the sequencing of materials is quite important. For example, in some, the concepts and skills a child acquires in the second grade are applied again when working with the third-grade materials, thus making it difficult to use the curriculum at any other grade level. How important are these prerequisite skills for mastery of a more complex unit? Will they hinder the students' advancement? Both questions are important in deciding on a science curriculum. A similar question could be asked for the student. How free is the student to investigate topics of his own choosing? If he does investigate on his own, will this affect his future success in the curriculum?

An important consideration when adopting a curriculum is its evidence of success. What evidence exists that teachers like yourself, who work with students similar to yours, can succeed with the curriculum? The range of answers to this question makes it a good standard for discrimination among curricula.

Other factors, such as cost, ease in obtaining materials, special training programs for the teachers, and many more are important in deciding which curriculum to adopt. Only *you* can develop these criteria, because you know best the situation in which the curriculum will be used. The answers to the questions raised here provide you with some of the criteria to evaluate any commercially developed science curriculum. After you decide on the criteria, rank them from most important to least important in order to make a decision for adopting a curriculum.

Activities

1. List five ways in which the newer elementary school science curricula are similar. Different.
2. Develop six criteria you would use to select a science curriculum for your school.
3. Using the criteria developed in 2, apply them to the science programs called Science—A Process Approach (SAPA), Science Curriculum Improvement Study (SCIS), and the Elementary Science Study (ESS).

Resource Material

Hurd, Paul D., and Gallagher, James S. *New Curriculum Perspectives for Junior High School Science,* Belmont, California: Wadsworth Publishing Co., 1969.

Hurd, Paul D. *New Directions in Elementary Science Teaching.* Belmont, California: Wadsworth Publishing Co., 1969.

Lockard, David, ed. *Report of the International Clearinghouse on Science and Mathematics Curricular Developments.* American Association for the Advancement of Science and the Science Teaching Center, University of Maryland, 1972.

Evaluation is an integral part of the elementary school science program. Two processes are involved in evaluation: (1) finding out *what is*; and (2) *placing a value on what is.* Every teacher is an evaluator; as a teacher you are responsible for appraising your students' progress, the effectiveness of the school science program, and your own teaching.

Evaluation is the process of making judgments. Some of the judgments to make about the student are: How much does he know before instruction begins? How well did he learn the material presented? How well will he do in the future? Similar judgments can be made about a science program: How well will the science program meet the needs of the student? How well has the program met the students' needs? Judgments regarding your teaching ability could be: What are my weaknesses in teaching? How good has my teaching been?

In order to evaluate yourself, your students, or the science program, you must have some knowledge of the science content, the goals of education, and the terminal objectives of the elementary school science program. In the past, the definition of science as a body of facts served as a model for evaluation. Paper-and-pencil tests were used to determine how many facts a student could remember. This definition of science also led many teachers to teach by writing science words on the chalkboard, then having the students read about these words in a science textbook, write them in their notebook, and finally memorize them. This was an efficient method of instruction for transmitting a large body of facts in a short period of time. However, the material was also retained for a short amount of time. Consistent with this definition of science, the curriculum listed a set of principles that the teacher interpreted, and that students wrote down and subsequently gave back to the teacher on a test.

But we have rejected the definition of science as a body of facts. Therefore, we have also rejected the methods of instruction and evaluation associated with this definition. We have defined science as a body of content *and* the methods used to generate, organize, and evaluate that content. This definition should help you plan instructional objectives for the attainment of formal thought. Both your teaching tactics and strategies and the ways in which you evaluate will depend on these instructional objectives.

At some point in the learning process, student achievement is evaluated. Just as necessary, but less frequently practiced, is the evaluation of your teaching tactics and strategies and of the science program itself. The success of the tactics, strategies, and program can be inferred from student achievement.

The first step in evaluation is to find out *what is.* Hence, before beginning a set of lessons within the program, you evaluate your students to find out what they know. Either during or at the end of the lessons, you again attempt to discover what your students know. This information about students' knowledge allows you to infer something about the program and about your teaching strategies. Suppose, for example, many students demonstrate at the outset that they have *not* yet attained the objectives of particular lessons. You then teach those lessons, using many different materials and a variety of teaching tactics. You perhaps observe that some students are starting to understand the objectives, while other students are not. Such student reaction should prompt you to continue with the selected materials for one group but not for the other. Student reaction is thus a means to find out how appropriate the science program and your teaching tactics and strategies are.

The second process involved in evaluation is to *place a value* on what the student already knows. This can be done by testing the student's content and skills before, during, and after instruction. Testing at the beginning of the lesson (pretesting) will help you to identify those skills, concepts, and attitudes possessed by the child before instruction begins. With this information, the teaching tactics and strategies can be planned so that the child's previous knowledge will be used as much as possible to attain new concepts, principles, skills, interests, appreciation, and attitudes.

One purpose of testing is to find the best learning situation for each student. Such testing should continue during the entire learning process. Most teachers follow standard textbooks or curriculum guides for their lesson plans, and many of these teachers think that the printed word is completely free of error. Some may conclude that if the teachers' manual says to use a certain activity to accomplish the objectives of the lesson, this activity is the "best" way for children to learn. To avoid this error while doing the activities in the teachers' manual, observe how the directions and student responses from your class help to accomplish the objectives stated by the authors of the textbook or curriculum. In order to obtain the best learning situation, you must carefully choose both the type of question you ask while teaching and the type of activity in which you involve the students. Moreover, by changing the activities as needed to maintain student interest or by adjusting the teaching tactics and strategies as necessary to positively affect the learning of skills and content, you can help the student before learning difficulties are encountered.

A second purpose of testing is to help you predict future success of your students. While planning the instructional objectives of your lessons, you will probably identify certain skills that are necessary to attain these objectives. If you test the children to see how well they use these prerequisite skills, you may have some indication, before teaching the lesson, of how well the children will accomplish the lesson's objectives. In general, then, the major purpose of all evaluation activities is to promote and to improve learning. First you determine *what is* and then *place some value on what is.* Thus, evaluation will help predict student learning, ascertain student learning problems, and find the best learning situation for each student.

11 Evaluation Tasks and Performance Criteria

As an evaluator, your first challenge is to find out *what is.* You must answer "What is?" with respect to student learning, to your science program, and to your teaching. To do this, you can use some useful tools, *evaluation tasks.* These tasks can be *pencil-and-paper tests,* with multiple-choice, matching, true-false, or fill-in-the-blank items, or short or long essay questions. Such evaluation tasks are very useful when you are attempting to determine which students have some specific science content, skill, or attitude. Likewise, you can determine characteristics of the science program by using such tasks to identify student reactions to the program, or to keep an inventory of which activities help to accomplish the program's objectives. Today it is very common to use multiple-choice questionnaires of student opinion about "good" and "poor" teaching. A teaching characteristic, such as "friendliness and pleasantness in manner," is presented to students, and they are asked to circle a number, depending on whether they believe the teacher is (1) inferior, (2) poor, (3) average, (4) above average, and (5) superior on the characteristic. The essay format may also be used for the purpose of evaluating teaching; students are asked to list the characteristics of "good" teaching and the characteristics of "poor" teaching. They may also be given the chance to explain their comments.

However, if you wish to see if your students, the science program, or yourself as a teacher can do something, there is no better way to determine this than to do it. That is, there is a second type of evaluation task, *the performance task,* that can help determine which students can manipulate equipment, for example, or which teachers show a specific characteristic when they teach. Performance tasks can give you informal insight into the teaching-learning situation at any moment you care to observe. You observe the students as they work and interact with each other, or the materials you chose to accomplish the lesson objectives, or your own teaching strategies. Unfortunately, these informal observations are seldom recorded, and, it is difficult to take a systematic look at what is occurring in the classroom. More formal performance tasks can be planned and systematically used outside the teaching-learning situation. The checklist is one way to carry out such a systematic analysis.

178

Pencil-and-Paper Tasks

Objective

To construct paper-and-pencil evaluation tasks.

Different instructional objectives imply different methods of testing, as well as teaching. These objectives help you to determine how a test is constructed, written, and presented. Objective tests, especially the variations of the multiple-choice type (the true-false test, the matching test, and the fill-in-the-blank test), and the essay test are probably the most common paper-and-pencil tests. Objective test items and essay test questions may be constructed to measure inquiry skills, content, and attitudes.

Regardless of which type of paper-and-pencil task you select, you will need time beyond the instructional hours to determine how much learning has taken place. If a multiple-choice test is given, then you need time before the actual examination in order to construct the items. On the other hand, if the paper-and-pencil task asks for descriptions or explanations of an event, usually in an essay, you will need time to read and evaluate the individual student's responses. Although you will probably use some published, standardized tests during the school year, you will construct most of your own tests.

Let's examine more closely the multiple-choice evaluation task. Consider this item:

Using a pulley, a workman lifts a 200-gram weight 40 centimeters (cm) with about 50 grams of effort. What distance did he pull the rope?

(a) 10 cm   (b) 40 cm   (c) 80 cm   (d) 100 cm   (e) 160 cm

Such a question is composed of two parts: an initial statement and a set of five choices, one of which is the "correct" answer, and the rest of which, called distractors, are incorrect or inappropriate answers to the question. In the example above, the initial statement gives the reader some information and asks a particular question about this information. This initial statement is complete, in that the reader could answer the question without looking at the five choices.

These choices need special consideration, for there must be only one that is correct. You can be sure of this if you ask several other teachers to answer the question and to state why they believe their answer is correct. By collecting all their reasons, you have statements that defend your choice of the "correct" answer to the students who later take your test. This process also assures you that several people agree your answer is correct. Be careful that the ideas in the other choices, the distractors, are distinct from one another. You will also want to be sure that visual clues do not give away the correct answer. Keep each choice equal in length, and do not put the correct choice in the same position for several consecutive items.

What has just been said concerning the writing of multiple-choice questions is important to keep in mind when writing true-false, matching, and fill-in-the-blank questions. The true-false test, for example, can be considered a multiple-choice question with only two choices: true or false. The initial statement in this type of test should be written very clearly. Special attention should be given to the statements that are false. For example, avoid using two negatives in such a statement. The statement, "A pulley system is not inappropriate to lift a piano with little force," is better written, "A pulley system is appropriate . . ." Be sure you are testing science content, and not the student's knowledge of English grammar.

Matching tests have very short simple initial statements that can be matched with one out of many choices you suggest. Again, be careful not to overlap ideas among choices. The initial statement in this type of test item should also be distinct from the choices being offered. Directions to the students should be clear, however, so that there is no "trick" in the question, and you are indeed testing the student's science ability. Lastly, fill-in-the-blank test items ask the student to select the one correct choice out of all possible ideas he knows, rather than out of possible ideas that you present. This type of question is helpful in testing a student's recall of science content.

The advantages, most teachers say, to these multiple-choice tests are that they are fast to correct, they require very few directions for the class, and the students can find out their test scores quickly—they might even correct the test themselves. All these are true advantages only if a multiple-choice test is very well constructed. It takes time to construct good questions—that is, questions that find out what your students know or can do. When you teach a lesson, write several multiple-choice questions concerning the content or particular inquiry skill taught through this lesson. Keep these questions on file. Just before you wish to give a test, take out the questions and edit them. You will find that if you write the questions, put them away, reread them later, and even have a fellow teacher or friend read and try to answer them, you will have the start of a good set of multiple-choice questions.

Objective tests need not be constructed just with words. The use of diagrams and pictures helps evaluate the ability of children with poor verbal capacity. For

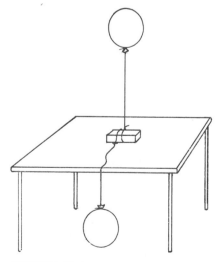

FIGURE 11-1
A Picture Problem with Two Identical Balloons.

example, you may wish to determine which of your students can recognize and state a problem. Write several ideas of situations that you believe the children will perceive as inconsistencies or problem situations. One such idea could involve two balloons of equal size, color, shape, and texture behaving quite differently. To construct the picture-test item, draw as much of the inconsistent event as you can. Be sure that such pictures or diagrams help the child to understand the question or the choice of answers rather than making it more complicated than when words alone are used, as in Figure 11-1.

Consider a second example. You have an instructional objective that states: "The student should be able to recognize that weights must be at specific distances from either side of the fulcrum to get the stick to balance." The behavioral indicator indicating to you that a child has accomplished the objective is that he can select the correct response on several multiple-choice items. One item could ask, "In which diagram will the stick be balanced?" Rather than write this in words, you could use pictures, as in Figure 11-2, to enable the child to demonstrate he has attained the objective of the lesson.

In some cases, a multiple-choice item can be used to evaluate inquiry skills, but such items are more helpful to determine the science content acquired by your students. To identify students who have acquired some inquiry skills or attitude, you can use the essay test. For example, the short essay is very helpful to determine if a student can compare several objects; you may ask him to write a short description comparing objects he has been given. Or, when you evaluate his ability to predict, you ask him to state and explain his prediction. The answer to an essay question will also indicate how well the student expresses himself and his ability to logically organize his thoughts.

When constructing an essay test, it is important that your question limit the answer so that there is one or very few acceptable answers. That is, an essay question for which any answer is the acceptable answer is a waste of time. Consider the following: "State what you think about the purity of the given water sample." Since this question asks the student what he thinks, such opposite answers as: "It is a pure sample" or "It is contaminated" are both acceptable—that may be what each student thinks. If every student in your class will get the correct answer, why take the time to give the test? However, the question can be revised so that there are only a few acceptable answers. The rewording could be "State the purity of the given water sample and specify the method used to determine this purity."

To make your essay questions readable and free from ambiguities, keep the

Circle the letter a, b, or c under that diagram
in which the stick would balance.

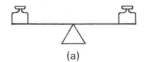
(a)
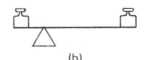
(b)
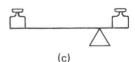
(c)

FIGURE 11-2
A Sample Item Using Diagrams.

wording simple. The question itself should also be simple; be sure that the acceptable answer is not too complex for the student to complete in a limited amount of time. One way to determine how long a correct answer will be is to answer the question yourself.

Essay questions and multiple-choice questions have been discussed here as paper-and-pencil tools to determine what students have learned. Throughout Section IV, there are additional suggestions for using various paper-and-pencil tests to determine *what is* with respect to the science program and to your teaching.

Activities

1. Construct three multiple-choice items, using only words. You may select any science content.
2. Construct three multiple-choice items, using pictures or diagrams, as well as words, and following steps (a) and (b):
    (a) Use the three multiple-choice items you wrote in the first activity.
    (b) Substitute, wherever possible, pictures and diagrams in place of words.
3. Construct an essay question. Write out the answer you would expect to this question. Designate the amount of time you expect it will take to answer this question.
4. Construct ten true-false questions based upon the science content you used for the first activity.

Resource Material

Gronlund, Norman E. *Constructing Achievement Tests.* Englewood Cliffs, New Jersey: Prentice-Hall, Inc., 1968.

Schwab, Joseph J. "What Do Scientists Do?" *Behavioral Science* 5 (1960): 1-27.

Travers, R. M. W. *How to Make Achievement Tests.* New York: The Odyssey Press, Inc., 1950.

Performance Tasks

Objective

To construct a performance task.

During a lesson, you will observe much student activity. Through these observations, you can informally determine the student's achievement or lack of achievement of science content, skills, and attitudes. Such student activity can be called a *performance task.* For example, if the student can place his ruler along a straight line and report the length of that line, you can usually assume the child has achieved one aspect of the skill of measuring. But performance tasks can also be more formal, such as a set of highly structured and planned activities apart from the classroom lessons. Here the student is specifically asked to do various tasks to demonstrate his achievement. Very often tasks that are done totally with pencil and paper, such as those described in the preceding topic, place some students at a disadvantage. The elementary schoolchild who is not as verbal as his peers, or the young child whose writing skills have not developed to the same level as his classmates', may really know the answers. Such a child could express them if the test were constructed in his favor; that is, so that he must do something rather than write something.

Performance tasks may be informal observations made during each activity, in which the teacher may note in a nonsystematic fashion the ability his students demonstrate. For example, your instructional objective for a lesson is, "The student is able to classify geometric shapes." You have specified these behavioral indicators: "Group and record all the shapes that have a selected characteristic in common; group and record all the shapes two additional times, based upon two different characteristics." The evaluation task you select is, "Cut triangles, circles, rectangles, and squares from colored paper and mark each shape with a different numeral. Place these shapes on the students' desk and ask them to arrange these shapes in groups that have something in common." Once the shapes have been grouped, tell the students to write on a piece of paper the numerals of the shapes in each group. The students have very few words to write; most of their answers consist of the numerals copied from each shape. You will probably wish to know why each student has grouped the shapes as he did. You can have him tell you the reason verbally, and then write it down yourself. Students who write with little difficulty can record their own reasons. Many evaluation tasks such as this one can happen each day in your classroom. In other words, you will have written evaluation tasks into your lessons.

It is also helpful to write a checklist for attainment of tasks that can be used during any lesson. After a few weeks of using this checklist, you will have a partial record of each student's successes. For example, a lesson could be planned around the instructional objective, "The student should be able to measure various straight lengths." One behavioral indicator is, "The child can use a ruler to measure the length of a straight line." During this lesson, you could place a check beside the child's name each time you observe him determine the correct length of any straight line. This may occur during the lesson on measuring as well as at other times throughout the school day.

Demonstrations are often used in the science classroom, but few teachers use these as informal tests. Since students are interested in a demonstration, you should take advantage of this interest, listening carefully to what students say during the demonstration. Suppose you wished to accomplish this instructional objective: "The student should be able to identify the variables involved when ice floats or sinks in liquids of different density." You decide that one behavioral indicator is, "The students can explain why two ice cubes react differently during a demonstration." So you place an ice cube in a glass of alcohol and an ice cube in a glass of water. The glasses are unmarked; students do not know what liquid is in each glass. You allow the students time to observe what happens in the two glasses, and then have the students write an explanation of their observations.

Before presenting this demonstration to the class, write down possible points of discussion the students may bring up. As each point is mentioned, you might write the initials of the person who discussed it. Thus, if you were using this demonstration at the beginning of the lesson, you would know how well students understood some of the science principles to be taught in the lesson.

Performance tasks can also be as formal as a set of highly structured and planned activities given apart from the classroom lessons. A student's responses on performance tests are usually recorded differently from responses on a paper-and-pencil test. During a performance task, you will probably have to do the recording, because the student is doing the task. For example, give the student a large water snail in a container and ask him to describe the object in the container. The objective of the lesson is to have the student "observe the characteristics of a snail." The behavioral indicator of this objective is, "When called upon, the student can describe three characteristics of a snail." While the student is performing the evaluation task, you can put a check in the column headed "acceptable" on a score sheet—if the student gives a description including three characteristics of the snail.

Attention has recently been given to performance tasks, rather than paper-and-pencil type tasks, since the former require fewer inferences by the teacher, in that performance is actually observed. However, performance tasks are usually given to only one student at a time. Otherwise, the actions of one student may be imitated by those around him. Whether the performance is "acceptable" or "not acceptable," the child may change his performance if those near him are doing something different.

Performance tasks require more personnel, space, and time than pencil-and-paper tasks. Therefore, you must consider all the advantages and disadvantages of these two methods of evaluation and then select the method most appropriate for your particular situation. Nevertheless, both paper-and-pencil and performance tasks can help you to evaluate your students prior to, during, or after instruction.

FIGURE 11-3
Some Students Show Attainment of Objectives Better with a Performance Test Rather than a Pencil-and-Paper Test. (Courtesy of the Science Teaching Center, University of Maryland.)

Activities

1. Examine a set of test questions at the end of a chapter in an elementary school science textbook. Change several pencil-and-paper questions into performance tasks.
2. Construct performance tasks that will help you to evaluate which students can use a scale to determine the weight of a large stone.

Resource Material

Science—A Process Approach (SAPA), available from Xerox Education Sciences, 555 Gotham Parkway, Carlstadt, New Jersey, 07072.

Wilson, John W., and Glennon, Vincent S. "Diagnostic-Prescriptive Teaching," Chapter 9 in *The Slow Learner in Mathematics,* ed. William C. Lowry. Washington, D. C.: National Council of Teachers of Mathematics, 1972.

Performance Criteria

Objective

To determine performance criteria in order to place a value upon what is known by the student, practiced by the teacher, and produced by the science program.

The student, the curriculum, and teaching strategies are usually appraised by a paper-and-pencil test, and in order to be acceptable, they must meet certain standards. These standards, called *performance criteria,* are statements specifying the number and the quality of the behavioral indicators used to determine whether a student, a curriculum, or a teaching tactic or strategy makes an acceptable performance. There are two types of standards in use today, those which are norm referenced and those which are criterion referenced.

Most teachers use class averages to determine acceptable performances for students; these averages are norm-referenced standards. Yet the use of this average as a standard against which to compare students automatically places 50 percent of the students below average or acceptable performance. For example, if your instructional objective was, "The student should recall what happens to two bar magnets when they are brought close together," you could have several behavioral indicators of learning. These indicators could be (1) State what will happen when like poles of two magnets are brought near each other; (2) State what will happen when unlike poles of two magnets are brought near each other; and (3) Make a list of the materials attracted to a magnet and a list of materials not attracted to a magnet. Next, you might construct an evaluation task directing your students to answer ten multiple-choice questions written to elicit these behavioral indicators. For the purposes of this example, assume that all ten questions are of equal importance and difficulty. Thus, you arbitrarily assign the value of ten points to a correct response. The scores of all your students would then be summed and divided by the total number of students in order to calculate the class average.

Using another method, you could observe where the middle score of all students is located. This score can be labeled "average," or the point above which one can identify students who have an understanding of the behavior of magnets. Again in the test on magnets, a student receiving the middle score (with 50 percent of the students above him) would be considered to have attained the instructional objectives.

Both of these methods of determining a standard for evaluating the students' knowledge about bar magnets reveal little difference. The student's success depends upon the scores his classmates receive, not solely upon his own achievements. However, another kind of standard, the *criteria-referenced standard,* can be used to judge a student's achievement on the basis of his work alone. As an example of a criteria-referenced standard, consider the instructional objective and behavioral indicators listed previously. Before the evaluation task is presented to each student, determine the *number* of behavioral indicators that each student classified as "understanding magnets" must do correctly. If a student falls below this number, he is classified as "not understanding."

After determining the number of indicators that the student must do correctly, determine the *quality* the response must have before you accept it as "correct." For example, among the behavioral indicators we just discussed, the student is expected to state what will happen when like poles of two magnets are brought near each other. At this point, you determine that the student's statement about the behavior of like poles must include a description of this behavior and an explanation of why they behave as they do. Similarly, with the third behavioral indicator, you must determine how many "materials" the student must list. The student is then given the evaluation task, and his responses are compared with the performance criteria specified prior to the test. If the student's responses reach or exceed this standard, he is judged to "understand," without any reference to or comparison with the response of other students.

Let us consider another example for determining which students can use a microscope, one of the psychomotor skills. As in the previous example with magnets, the objective and the behavioral indicators are identified. The evaluation task is then constructed. This task directs the students to (1) focus the microscope so that they can clearly see the impurities in a water sample, (2) draw a picture of what they see through the microscope, (3) increase the magnification of the water sample, and (4) draw what they now see in the microscope. Before the evaluation task is presented to each student, you must state that all behavioral indicators must be observed by the teacher if the student is to be classified as one who can use a microscope. If a student falls below this number, he is classified as "not able to use a microscope." You then determine the quality each student's drawing must show before it is an acceptable behavioral indicator of a student able to use the microscope. In the second and fourth indicators, for example, you would decide on the amount of detail expected in each drawing. After all these preliminary preparations, the student is given the evaluation task and his responses are compared with the criteria identified prior to the test. If the student's responses reach or exceed the minimum number determined as an acceptable performance, he is judged "able to use a microscope."

If you want to know just what skills the students possess, if you want to know if the curriculum you're using helps your students to learn, or if you wish to know which strategies help your students learn, then it is meaningless to compare students, or lessons, or teaching tactics and strategies with others in their respective group. This type of comparison never indicates which students have learned, nor what the curricula or teaching strategies actually contribute to student learning. Evaluation will help you or your students only if it helps you determine *what is* and the *value* of *what is.*

Activities

1. Determine the performance that will indicate to you that your students can use a microscope.
   (a) Stipulate the tasks a primary-grade student must perform to indicate that he can use a microscope.
   (b) Specify the additional performance you would expect of an upper elementary-grade student who can use a microscope.
2. Determine the quality of the performance to indicate that your students can classify a group of rocks.

Resource Material

Flynn, John T., and Garber, Herbert, eds. *Assessing Behavior: Readings in Educational and Psychological Measurements.* Reading, Mass.: Addison-Wesley, 1967.

Miller, B. W. "Skill Tests for Pedal Pushers." Chicago: *Safety Council Magazine,* National Safety Council, 1962.

12 Evaluation of Science Content, Skills, Attitudes, Interests, and Appreciations

Very often in elementary school science, it is your responsibility to select the content and skills that will help students attain formal thought. That is, you are responsible for determining at least the *instructional objectives* of your science program. However, curriculum guides, the science consultant, the principal, and in some cases the students themselves, will aid in your determination of a program's terminal and instructional objectives. With these objectives specifying the content and skills leading toward formal thought, you must then determine the behavioral indicators to evaluate the attainment of the objectives.

Evaluation requires that many inferences be made from student behaviors. Thus, it is extremely important that these inferences be valid. For example, suppose you identify as an instructional objective that the students should know "plants need light to grow." The word *know* can be demonstrated by many student behaviors, such as (1) identifying by circling this principle from a list of principles; (2) writing this principle in the student's own words; (3) stating verbally this principle; (4) applying this principle to a new situation; and (5) giving evidence supporting the validity of the principle.

Each of the above behaviors implies not only different teaching strategies, but also different *evaluation tasks*; that is, activities a student must do during the evaluation so that you can infer learning. The behavioral indicators used for evaluating the knowledge identified above are "to circle," "to write," "to state verbally," "to apply," and "to give evidence." The learning indicated could range from rote memorization to discovery by the student, depending upon his past experience. The evaluation tasks for the first behavioral indicator would probably be activities common to a multiple-choice test; the evaluation tasks for the second, third, fourth, and fifth behavioral indicators are activities common to an essay test.

Each of the above statements are observable behaviors, behavioral indicators, from which a knowledge of science can be inferred. Once you have selected the science content or skills the students are to develop, and have incorporated them into the *instructional objectives,* you must then identify specific *behavioral indicators.* Next you should determine the activities in which the specific behavior can be observed, the *evaluation task,* to be performed by the student. You should then state the *criterion-referenced standards* your students must meet in order to be judged "knowledgeable." When you use these standards, either a student meets them or he does not. The student is given the evaluation task, and his responses are compared with the criterion-referenced standard carefully specified prior to the test. If the student's responses reach or exceed the standard, he is judged to understand. This judgment is not dependent upon how other students have done on the test, as is the case in a norm-referenced standard.

As stated earlier, you will make two decisions before the actual science lesson begins: (1) the instructional objectives to be attained and (2) the teaching strategies to be used in attaining these objectives. After completion of the lesson, you must then ask, "How should I evaluate my students to know if the students learned what I intended to teach?"

Probably you will examine your students' performances, compare them to a predetermined, expected performance, and then interpret this performance cautiously. You should keep in mind what we have said earlier: the child's past experience and his stage of development will have an effect upon his skill performance and his knowledge of science content.

Evaluation of Science Content and Inquiry Skills

Objective

> To construct and administer tasks that evaluate the students'
> science content and inquiry skills.

We have stated throughout this book that in elementary schools today, science is not considered an unchangeable list of facts, concepts, and principles to be learned by memorizing. Science is a combination of learning both content and skills; that is, skills are directly involved in content learning. When you are constructing evaluation tasks to identify students who have a specific inquiry skill, we suggest that you first have in mind what a student with that skill can do. Secondly, you need some understanding of the science content that you are also evaluating. With this understanding, your next steps will be to (1) write the *instructional objectives* of your science lesson, after considering the science content and skills that will help your students to reach the terminal objectives; (2) design the observable behaviors, *behavioral indicators,* from which you can make inferences about your students' learning; (3) design a test, the *evaluation task,* that will give your students the opportunity to demonstrate specified observable behaviors; (4) establish standards by which you will judge whether your students have attained the instructional objectives; and (5) give the test, correct it, match each student's test performance with the prestated standards, and determine whether your students have attained the objective.

Following these steps, you can construct a task that will help evaluate the inquiry skill of *observation.* To write behavioral indicators for this skill, you must know the characteristics of a person who can observe. A person who has acquired this skill can "collect data through the use of the five senses and construct statements of observations in qualitative and quantitative terms." These characteristics should help you to determine the behavioral indicators to identify a person who can observe. These indicators might be (1) identify and name the physical properties of an object; (2) construct statements of observations in qualitative terms; and (3) construct statements of observations in quantitative terms.

In selecting the objects for a task to evaluate the skill of observing, you must be careful that one of the five senses is not favored more or less than another. For example, if you give the child a small piece of plastic to observe, and you have previously cautioned the child about putting objects into his mouth, you cannot expect that he will respond to that evaluation task with observations using all five senses.

Dimensionality of objects is important when choosing the materials to be used in this type of evaluation task. If the child has been working with three-dimensional objects and you now give him a two-dimensional picture of the object to observe, you will probably affect the number and kind of responses he gives. There is much evidence to show that the test directions also affect the various responses. You may select a set of objects and use these same objects in two different evaluation tasks—tasks which differ only in the directions given. If you ask the child, "Make observations using all five senses," you will get one set of responses; while if you say, "List those things that you can see about the objects, hear about the objects, feel about the objects . . .," you will receive a longer and more complete list of observations. These considerations just discussed should be kept in mind when writing evaluation tasks.

The following is a sample task that may help you to evaluate a student's ability to *observe*. Additional sample tasks are presented in Appendix B. These tasks are intended to help you evaluate each inquiry skill discussed in Section I. Since these skills cannot be evaluated without content, content is included in each sample. These samples also include an exercise for you to do to check your ability to evaluate each inquiry skill.

A Sample Task to Evaluate Observing Some Specific Events

Instructional Objective
The student should be able to observe and record what happens to iron filings sprinkled on a piece of paper placed on top of a magnet.

Behavioral Indicators
1. The student sketches the iron filings' patterns from the ends of the magnet outward at least twenty centimeters.
2. The student sketches the iron filings' patterns around the center of the magnet.

Evaluation Task
Have the students place a bar magnet under a piece of plain white paper and sprinkle some iron filings as evenly as possible on top of the paper. Instruct the students to sketch their observations of the iron filings.

Performance Criteria
Each student who has successfully attained the instructional objective must have

completed both behavioral indicators. Be sure that all sketches are observational and that the student has not included an inference.

Activities

1. Construct a task that helps you to evaluate a primary-grade child's ability to *observe and list the characteristics of mealworms.*
    (a) Reread the characteristics of a person who has acquired the skill of observation.
    (b) Specify the objects that you will give the child to observe.
    (c) State clearly the directions you will give the child as part of the test of observing.
    (d) State the behaviors that will indicate to you that the child can observe. These behaviors will then become the bases for establishing your performance criteria. Remember that these behaviors will be very much influenced by the objects and the directions in the test.
2. Construct a task that will help you to evaluate a middle-grade student's ability to *observe and list the changes that occur in an aquarium over a two-week period of time.*

Resource Material

Davis, F. B., French, E. G., and Lesser, G. S. "Identification of Classroom Behavior of Elementary School Children Gifted in Five Different Mental Characteristics." Mimeographed. New York: Hunter College, 1959.

Trueblood, C. R. "Promoting Problem-Solving Skills Through Non-Verbal Problems." *The Arithmetic Teacher* 16 (January 1969): 7-9.

Evaluation of Psychomotor Skills

Objective

To construct and administer tasks that help evaluate student psychomotor skills.

In general, the psychomotor skills used by students in your science classes involve the physical manipulation of equipment. These skills must be performed by the student in order to demonstrate that he has acquired them. Some of these skills include

Growing plants.
Setting up an aquarium.
Measuring distance with a meter stick; with a metric ruler.
Measuring volume of liquids with a graduated cylinder.
Measuring weight and mass with the appropriate balances.
Measuring temperature with a thermometer.
Measuring angles with a protractor.
Preparing seed crystals.
Preparing Euglena cultures.

When you write evaluation tasks for inquiry skills and attitudes, it is difficult to have the students demonstrate directly that they have been attained. You must infer from some overt behavior that the student has the skill or attitude. In other words, the skill or attitude are different from the behavior tested—they are not one and the same. But with the psychomotor skills, the action you ask him to do *is* the observable skill you hope he has acquired. You can ask a student to set up an aquarium, for example, or measure temperatures with a thermometer, and infer from his behavior whether or not he has attained the psychomotor skill.

To demonstrate any of the science psychomotor skills mentioned above, however, many less complex skills must be learned. As a primary-grade teacher, you may decide which simple skills the student must acquire. You will probably make this decision after considering the age and development of the student. Also, the appropriateness of the equipment you give the child for the evaluation task must be carefully considered. Scientific instruments have a certain amount of complexity to them. An upper elementary-grade student may be asked to use a standard metric ruler to measure a short distance, but a primary-grade student should probably be given a metric ruler with fewer markings on it. The latter student's answer will lack the accuracy of the former, but according to the performance criteria set up by each teacher, both students may be judged to have this particular psychomotor skill.

Likewise, you will have to decide whether a variety of equipment should be used by a student to show that he has a particular psychomotor skill. For example, you might require a student to use several spring balances, each with a different range of sensitivity, and, with each balance, arrive at an accurate measure of the object he weighs for the evaluation task. The child's ability to physically manipulate small delicate pieces of equipment, as well as living things, must also be considered when writing evaluations task. Finally, the directions given to the child while he is taking the test must be carefully determined. Will you say only, "Measure the given distance with the metric ruler?" or should you be very specific? That is, should you tell the student, "Place the zero mark of your metric ruler on the point marked 'A.' Now determine how far from point 'A' is the point marked 'B.' " Remember, the final acquisition of these skills may take a number of years.

The following sample evaluation task shows how you could evaluate students' psychomotor skills of *measuring*; that is, the ability to quantify observations with the aid of an appropriate frame of reference. Following this sample, there is a set of activities intended to give you some practice in writing tasks that will evaluate your students' psychomotor skills. As you try the activities, keep in mind that after completing your evaluation task, your students should have demonstrated that they can use equipment to measure accurately.

**A Sample Task to Evaluate
Psychomotor Skill**

Instructional Objective
The student should be able to measure and calculate the length, width, height, and volume of a solid, in metric units.

Behavioral Indicators

1. Given a metric ruler, a cube, and a rectangular-shaped solid, the student measures the length, width, and height of each object. He records these measurements.
2. Using the above data, he calculates the volume of the cube and of the rectangular solid.

Evaluation Task

Directions: Using your metric ruler, measure the length, width, and height (in centimeters) of the cube. Using metric units, calculate the volume of the cube. Record this information. Repeat these steps with the rectangular solid.

Performance Criteria

Each student must complete both behavioral indicators in order to have accomplished the instructional objective.

Activities

1. Evaluate the student's ability to measure temperature, in both Fahrenheit and Celsius units.
   (a) List the behaviors that indicate a child who can measure temperature in both Fahrenheit and Celsius units.
   (b) Describe an evaluation task that will allow your students to demonstrate each behavior you indicate.
   (c) State the performance criteria your students must meet to be judged able to measure temperature in both Fahrenheit and Celsius units.
2. Evaluate a primary-grade student's ability to prepare and grow plants.
   (a) List the behaviors that indicate a child can prepare and grow plants.
   (b) Describe an evaluation task that gives your students the opportunity to demonstrate each behavior you indicated above.
   (c) State the performance criteria that can be used to judge whether the objective has been accomplished.

Resource Material

DeRose, James. *Principles of Measurement.* Philadelphia: J. Weston Welch, 1966.

Lesser, G. S. et al. *Number Facility Scale.* Comparative Research Project No. 1835. Washington: Office of Education, U. S. Department of Health, Education and Welfare, U. S. Government Printing Office, 1964.

MacLatchy, Josephine H. "The Test of the Pre-School Child's Familiarity with Measurement." *Educational Research Bulletin* 29 (1950): 207-208.

Evaluation of Attitudes, Interests, and Appreciations

Objective

> To construct and administer tasks that help to evaluate the
> attitudes, interests, and appreciations of students.

In earlier chapters of this book, we identified some affective objectives that appear to help students act like scientists. In general, these objectives can be divided into categories that are usually called attitudes, interests, and appreciations. Some of the attitudes that seem to typify a student who acts like a scientist are curiousity, openness, precision, confidence, perserverence, satisfaction, and respect for another's ideas. Such a student also appreciates seeing ideas and arguments logically presented and knowing the consequences of actions or events. Among the interests of a student who acts like a scientist are a desire to search for data and their meaning and reluctance to make decisions until as much evidence as possible has been collected. If we believe that these characteristics should be taught, or at least encouraged in the science classroom, then we have the responsibility to determine which students have these qualities.

Although in the past few years attention has been focused on attitudes, interests, and appreciations, teachers who tried to evaluate these characteristics found it to be a difficult task. Let's consider again the steps necessary for evaluating a student. First, there is the task of stating an instructional objective—for example, "The student is curious about plants." This instructional objective includes the attitude of curiousity *and* the content that is affected by this attitude, for students are curious about specific things, such as plants and animals living in an aquarium, or electric light bulbs that light or do not light. In order to identify a curious student, we need some science content to capture his curiousity. Next we can ask, "What behaviors indicate a student who is curious about this content (some person, place, or thing)?" We then decide that such a student expresses, verbally or nonverbally, a desire to investigate the object of his curiousity, with no prompting by us. For instance, he may request more information about the object from you or from books. In addition, he tries to interact with the object and with things related to the object to gain some more information about it. Since students interact with objects in a variety of ways, you will probably need to devise ways to record nonverbal and verbal behaviors that indicate your student has acquired a specific affective objective. A student who is curious about some object may never say one word about it, but he may stare at it intently, or gently touch and poke it in various places, or come up and show it to you.

The major difficulty in evaluating the attainment of such affective objectives as "appreciation" is identifying the verbal and nonverbal actions characteristic of a person possessing this attribute. The actions you regard as characteristic is most important. In the past, teachers have expected very content-oriented behaviors from someone who "appreciates." For example, the teacher would identify as appreciating nature, students who could "name a plant or identify the elements in nature that keep a plant alive." However, these actions may not be appreciations at all! If we appreciate a plant, we may water it, "feed" it with fertilizers and soil nutrients, dust its leaves, and remove parasites and harmful insects from around the plant. In other words, we show our appreciation of the plant in many of the same ways that we show our appreciation of people and events.

The ideas suggested here are only intended as a starting point. As you become more familiar with your students, you will identify other actions that are characteristic of persons who possess these affective traits.

Finally, remember that the behavior you identify must be spontaneous. Even though you provide an environment likely to arouse the child's interest (by presenting him with persons, places, or things with which he is unfamiliar) *you should not actively draw the child's attention to it. The child's actions must be self-motivated.* (Rereading the discussion on pages 158-161 in Section III may be helpful.)

Activities

1. Review the affective objectives and behavioral indicators in Section I. Discuss whether you agree with the behaviors suggested for such traits as curiosity and openness. Samples of tasks that may be used to evaluate objectives are given in Appendix C.
2. Write an evaluation task that will help determine which students are tolerant about the differences in data collected by members of your class.
3. Select several teacher-made tests or tests found at the end of chapters in an elementary school science book. List the type(s) of test items and the objectives you believe these test items evaluate. Table 12-1 suggests that certain objectives can be evaluated with different types of test items. Using this table, determine what variety, if any, exists in the types of test items used to evaluate specific objectives in your selected tests.

TABLE 12-1
Types of Test Items That Can Be Used to Evaluate Objectives

	Types of Objectives			
Types of Test Items	**Content**	**Inquiry**	**Psychomotor**	**Affective**
Paper and Pencil				
Multichoice	√	√		
Matching	√			
True-false	√			
Fill-in-blanks	√			
Short essay		√	√	
Essay		√	√	√
Performance				
Observations	√	√	√	√
Checklists		√	√	√

The √ mark indicates the types of objectives in elementary school science that can be evaluated using various types of test items.

Resource Material

Maw, W. H., and Maw, E. W. *An Exploratory Study into the Measurement of Curiosity in Elementary School Children.* Washington, D. C.: U. S. Office of Education, 1964.

Penney, R. K., and McCann, B. "The Children's Reactive Curiosity Scale." *Psychological Reports* 15 (1964): 323-334.

Evaluation of the Science Program 13

You will probably make two kinds of evaluations concerning science programs: the evaluation of individual science lessons after you have planned them and the evaluation of a new science curriculum when your school develops it. Each kind of evaluation usually attempts to discover the effect of the curriculum or the lesson on student learning. For purposes of our discussion, we will call the first kind *lesson evaluation*: a systematic attempt to determine whether a set of specific activities is helping the students to attain the objectives of the lesson. We will call the second type *curriculum evaluation*: a systematic attempt to determine if a set of lessons is helping the students to attain the terminal objectives of the science program.

Evaluation of Lessons

Objective

> To construct tasks to evaluate the science lessons you have
> planned for your class.

Lesson evaluation will probably be your most usual involvement in program evaluation. When you begin teaching, you will probably be given a curriculum guide or a textbook. Science consultants may be employed by the school to help you use these materials as a guide for lesson planning. These guides usually state the terminal and instructional objectives for the science program. You will be expected to determine the materials, the behavioral indicators, and the teaching strategies that can best help your students attain these objectives. You will also be expected to develop the evaluation tasks to determine how well the students learn.

Let's assume that your curriculum guide states the terminal objective: "The student should be able to observe." You are likewise supplied with an instructional objective: "The student should be able to observe the physical properties of color, size, and texture for three given objects." You must then select the materials, behavioral indicators, and teaching tactics and strategies that will best accomplish this objective. Such materials could be a birthday candle, two pieces of peppermint candy (one piece wrapped, the other not wrapped), and a list of words describing the texture of objects. You have chosen these materials to aid the student to demonstrate the behavioral indicators from which you can infer that the objective has been accomplished. These behavioral indicators may be (1) The student states the color of the candle, the wick, the candy, and the candy wrapper; (2) he describes the size of each object, by comparing each object to the candle; and (3) he selects, from a given list of words, at least one word that describes the texture of the candle, the wick, the candy, and the candy wrapper. After giving each child the materials listed above, as well as a pencil and a piece of paper, you tell them, "Write on your paper the color and the size of the candle, the wick, the candy, and the candy wrapper." You have selected a teaching tactic that enables the child to handle the materials, explore ideas, and practice the skill of observing. That is, you have selected a Type III or IV laboratory activity as a focusing tactic.

Once your lesson has been completed, you will want to evaluate the students' behavior to determine whether or not you achieved the stated objective. You can do this by having students verbally summarize the lesson immediately after it is taught. You could also ask the students some questions directly related to the objective of the lesson to see if they can answer them.

In order to evaluate your lesson planning, be certain of the terminal and instructional objectives you wish your students to accomplish. Then select the materials, behavioral indicators, evaluation tasks, and teaching tactics and strategies that will best achieve your objectives. You will probably have a small variety of such tactics in any one science lesson. However, in the total science program there should be a variety of strategies. Finally, teach your planned lesson, and then evaluate the student's attainment of the objectives with the evaluation task.

Activity

Review and evaluate a lesson plan involving a Type IV lab activity as a focusing tactic.
- (a)   Reread the description of a Type IV lab activity in Section II.
- (b)   Use one of your own lesson plans involving this tactic and determine how well your plan meets this description.

Resource Material

Carin, Arthur A., and Sund, Robert B. *Developing Questioning Techniques.* Columbus, Ohio: Charles E. Merrill Publishing Co., 1971.

Evaluation of Curricula

Objective

To construct tasks to evaluate science curricula used in the elementary school.

If you are asked to serve on a curriculum-planning committee, your task could well be to develop and evaluate a science curriculum for middle elementary school grades. Your committee must first decide on the program's terminal objectives, which would involve the selection of the inquiry skills, conceptual schemes, psychomotor skills, and attitudes. Once these decisions have been made, you and your committee will probably determine the instructional objectives for the fourth-grade students, the fifth-grade students, and the sixth graders. Then identify the behavioral indicators that will show which students have attained the instructional objectives. You must then identify the materials and teaching strategies with which students can accomplish the objectives.

You are now ready to teach the lessons. Record student reactions to these lessons and compare these behaviors with the behavioral indicators identified by your committee. After these data have been examined, revise any portion of the new curriculum that seems deficient. At this point, other teachers can implement your committee's suggested curriculum and help to judge whether or not their children accomplish the curriculum's objectives through the materials and teaching strategies suggested.

The next step in curriculum evaluation is to establish a minimum performance expected of students accomplishing the instructional objectives. The committee generates a list of behavioral indicators for each objective. The classroom teachers observe and record behaviors of children who accomplished the instructional objectives. From these two lists, a suggested amount and kind of student performance can be identified. To what extent does the committee's list of the number and kind of behaviors indicating that the student has accomplished the objectives match the students' performances observed by the classroom teacher? What behaviors, if any, are missing from the committee's list, but observed in the classroom?

In addition to the committee and the teachers observing and checking the behavioral indicators for each objective, the students themselves should be asked to fill in a questionnaire on how they perceived themselves before, during, and after exposure to the new curriculum. Such a questionnaire could be similar to the sample evaluation form given here for a unit on plants.

Student Evaluation Form
for
a Unit on Plants

Please complete the form below. You do not need to sign your name. *Your* opinion will be appreciated, so don't ask a friend to help you, *please.*

Place an "X" in the appropriate blank.
1. Before you started the unit, did you like science?
    Yes_____   No_____
2. Do you like science now? Yes_____   No_____
3. Do you like investigating plants on your own, or would you rather have the teacher give you specific assignments?
    Own investigation_____   Teacher's assignment_____
4. What do you like best about the unit?

5. What do you dislike the most about the unit?

6. How could this unit be improved?

7. Rate this unit with a value of 1, 3, or 5. One (1) means you think it was poor; three (3) means you think this unit was good; and five (5) means that the unit was great. Your rating_____

This point in developing the curriculum may be a good time for the teacher to consider and reapportion, where appropriate, the content, skills, and attitudes intended for each grade level. The individual teacher's experiences using the curriculum in the classroom will be passed on to the committee, indicating the value of its planning, specifically the suitability of tactics and strategies. Thus, this process of evaluation leads to the adjustment of the original curriculum to a more workable program. As a new teacher, you may not be involved in writing a curriculum. However, you should be able to look at a science program already constructed, or look at several science curricula, and determine which would be the best curriculum to help your children accomplish the terminal objectives.

Activities

1. Evaluate at least one elementary school science curriculum developed after 1970 for your grade level of interest. You should be able to distinguish between the objectives and behavioral indicators of the program.
2. Evaluate at least one elementary school science textbook series.
   (a) Collect data from actual comparisons of materials, kits, articles, textbooks, and so forth.
   (b) Construct a set of criteria for selecting science textbooks for your grade level.
   (c) Apply these criteria to several possible texts.

Resource Material

Grobman, Hulda. *Evaluation Activities of Curriculum Projects.* AERA Monograph Series on Curriculum Evaluation, no. 2. Chicago: Rand McNally, 1968.

Schwab, Joseph J. "The Practical: A Language for Curriculum." *School Review* 78 (1969): 1-23.

Wolf, Richard. "A Model for Curriculum Evaluation." *Psychology in the Schools* 6 (1969): 107-108.

Evaluation of Teaching 14

Evaluation of your teaching can be done by you, by a fellow teacher, or by your students. Regardless of who does the evaluation, however, the same ideas are applicable. First, a model or standard for comparison must be developed. Second, evidence should be collected to determine what is. Finally, "what is" needs to be compared to the standard. If the two do not match, then remedial measures need to be employed to bring "what is" up to the standard. This same procedure can be followed for self-evaluation, colleague evaluation, or student evaluation of your teaching. Without evaluation of your teaching performance, it would be difficult to improve your teaching.

Self-Evaluation of Teaching

Objective

To select and try out various methods of evaluating your own teaching.

The learning environment includes the students, curriculum, text, materials, and—most important—the teacher, the person who diagnoses, plans, and executes learning-evaluation tasks. The way the teacher uses the curriculum produces certain student behaviors. Some of these behaviors may indicate that the student has attained the objective, others that he has not succeeded. When the student has not attained some objective, you must examine your teaching tactics and strategies as well as your planning. Some model of the teaching process will help you to make such an evaluation. We have stated that a good teacher of science uses a variety of tactics and strategies in order to achieve the stated objectives. As discussed in Sections II and III, a strategy is an over-all *plan* for achieving an objective, while a tactic is the *means* of achieving the objective. You must examine your teaching and judge it to be "good" or "poor" to the degree that your students learn science content and skills.

You may evaluate yourself, or you may have others, students or peers, evaluate you. For some, it is beneficial to start with self-evaluation of teaching tactics and strategies and then ask others to help in your evaluation. One self-evaluation device can be found in Table 14-1, where objectives are matched with teaching tactics. It appears that teachers use certain tactics to accomplish specific objectives. Using the checklist in Table 14-1, you can compare the objective selected for the lesson with the tactic you plan to use to attain this objective. This self-evaluation device may help you to select better teaching tactics for the objectives of the lesson.

TABLE 14-1
Lesson Objectives Matched with Teaching Tactics

Objective	Tactic
1. Present new information	1. Informing
2. Review assigned material, the previous	2. Reviewing or recall questioning
3. day's lesson, or chapter or unit	
3. Discuss the results of an experiment	3. Data collecting, data processing, or evaluating
4. Provide opportunity to practice a technique or skill	4. Type I laboratory or field trip
5. Verify a science concept or principle already known by the student	5. Type II laboratory or field trip
6. Discover relationships not previously known	6. Type III laboratory or field trip
7. Illustrate the value of certain methods of data collecting and processing in order to provide opportunity to integrate the se-selected inquiry skills already learned	7. Type IV or V laboratory or field trip

Another device to aid the process of self-evaluation is an audio-tape recording of segments of the class sessions. You can play back the recording later, focusing your attention on one aspect of the verbal interaction in your classroom. For example, you can listen to the questions you asked and determine the type of content or skill emphasized in these questions. You can listen to your reactions to student responses and see whether you adjust your behavior to meet the demands of each type of instructional situation.

At some point during the evaluation of your teaching, you should record your lessons on audio-visual tape if at all possible. This is currently a very popular method to help determine which points in your lesson contained the tactics and strategies that seemed to help students learn. Here both the audio and visual interactions of your classroom can be recorded on tape for analysis.

Still another method of recording classroom interactions is the anecdotal record, in which all or parts of what the teacher and the students say and do are written down. When you use anecdotal records, you must have another person observe you. This may be inconvenient, but it is well worth the effort; in the absence of an audio-visual recorder, you will have a record of the lesson to analyze.

Once you have compared your lesson with the checklist in Table 14-1 and prepared an anecdotal record, you are ready to take a critical look at the teaching techniques you used and the results they produced. You may also wish to note tactics and strategies actually used that were not planned. This analysis of your teaching can and should include more than just a matching of objectives with tactics. Your analysis should include the amount of time the teacher talks and the amount of time the students talk. You may wish to analyze this aspect by using randomly selected five-minute segments of the tape, or, if you have time, the whole tape. With this information, you can consider whether who was doing the talking had any effect on what was learned. Also, the type of questions that you ask your students during the lesson may have a direct effect on what they learned. When you examine your recorded lesson, you can group the questions asked into the categories in Section II of this book.

Activities

1. Analyze and discuss a taped lesson of your class.
    (a) Listen to a taped lesson.
    (b) Write a short report in which you identify the major strengths and weaknesses of the lesson.
    (c) Suggest a method of improving the weaknesses.
2. Devise your own model of a "good" teacher. Construct a list, in behavioral terms, of the characteristics of a good teacher.
3. Given the above list, construct an instrument that helps you to evaluate your own teaching.

Resource Material

Amidon, Edmund J., and Hough, John B. *Interaction Analysis.* Reading, Mass.: Addison-Wesley, 1969.

Bellack, Anno A., ed. *Theory and Research in Teaching.* New York: Columbia University Press, 1969.

Wallan, Norman E., and Wodtke, Kenneth H. "Relationships Between Teacher Characteristics and Student Behavior: Part One." Cooperative Research Project No. 1217. Salt Lake City: Department of Educational Psychology, University of Utah, 1963.

Evaluation of Teaching by Others

Objective

To select and try methods that can be used by others to evaluate your teaching.

There is another way to evaluate teacher performance besides self-evaluation. Your students, if old enough, can help you devise various methods of determining effective teaching. The students could be asked to list characteristics of "good" and of "poor" teaching. You could also do the same, and then compare these two lists. Your students could then evaluate your teaching, based on the characteristics identified in these lists. You may be surprised when you read the students' perceptions of your teaching.

As a teacher, you should be able to construct a model of what you consider good teaching and obtain comments from your peers as to how closely you exemplify this model. There are several models of teaching you might use; the tactics and strategies described in Sections II and III constitute such a teaching model. These tactics and strategies are based on the assumption that certain categories of interactions are more appropriate in one type of lesson than in another. A colleague, using a checklist of these strategies, can help you determine how closely you used them.

Likewise, ask your students to evaluate how closely you exemplify the various teaching models. If your students are in the middle grades, you can circulate several teacher evaluation forms to your class and summarize their results. This information will help you form a composite picture of your teaching. In addition to using questionnaires based on models of teaching developed by others, you should occasionally construct and administer a teacher evaluation form based on a model of your perceptions of good teaching.

The activities that follow, and additional ones in Appendix D, are intended to give you practice in developing a means of obtaining feedback from your students, in order to determine how they perceive you as a teacher.

Activities

1. At some time during your teaching experience, make copies of one of the teacher evaluation forms in the first part of Appendix D. Distribute the copies to your class and have the students complete the form.
2. At some time during your teaching experience, construct and administer to your students a teacher evaluation instrument, based on a model of what you consider good teaching.
3. Have a fellow teacher use checklists to help determine the quality of your teaching.
   (a) Reread the description of the various teaching tactics and strategies in Sections II and III.
   (b) Consider one tactic or strategy at a time. Ask a fellow teacher to sit in on one of your classes. This teacher can use the checklists in Appendix D to help you decide if the class presentation meets the criteria in the checklists.

Resource Material

Anderson, Gary J., and Walberg, Herbert J. "Classroom Climate and Group Learning." *International Journal of Educational Sciences* 2 (1968): 175-80.

Campbell, W. J. "Classroom Practices." *New Zealand Journal of Educational Studies* 3 (1968): 97-124.

Evans, Thomas P. "A Category System for Teacher Behavior." *American Biology Teacher* 31 (1969): 221-26.

Activity to Identify APPENDIX
Stages of Development

This task is designed to show you *how* a child attempts to solve a specific problem. The child is shown a test tube containing a clear liquid. When several drops of another clear liquid, labelled "G," are added to this test tube, a yellow color results. The child is told to reproduce this yellow color in *as many different ways* as he can, using five solutions that you will provide, labelled "1," "2," "3," "4," and "G." The solutions can be prepared as follows:

1. A solution containing one part of liquid household bleach and 100 parts of distilled water.
2. Distilled water.
3. Household vinegar.
4. A solution containing 75 grams of sodium thiosulfate—$Na_2S_2O_3$ (hypo)— in one liter of distilled water.
G. A solution containing 83 grams of potassium iodide (KI) in one liter of distilled water.

To perform the task, provide each child with a set of labelled bottles and an individual test tube. A plastic wash bottle will help to rinse the test tube after each trial. In order for the task to be effective, each child must work completely on his own and not be influenced by the work of anyone else.

Only combinations of 1 + G or 1 + 3 + G or 1 + 2 + 3 + G will produce the yellow color. If number 4 is present, the solution will not turn yellow, and a yellow solution will lose its color if number 4 is added to it. Remember, the primary purpose of this task is to observe the *method* that each child uses in solving the problem. It is not important whether or not the child is actually able to produce the yellow color.

As you observe different children performing the task, you will begin to notice similarities in the procedures each child uses. The child toward the end of the preoperational stage will use a random procedure. He will probably mix solutions haphazardly, without noting the specific liquids he is using. If he is able to produce the yellow color, he will probably not remember which solutions he used. Since he has no systematic approach to the problem, success or failure is largely a chance happening.

Children in the concrete operations stage will begin to use a more systematic approach to the problem. Toward the end of this stage they may begin taking notes and writing down the various combinations they try. They will attempt to avoid unnecessary duplications. In the beginning of the concrete operations stage, the child may try combinations of 1 + 2, 1 + 3, 1 + 4, 1 + G, 2 + 3, 2 + 4, and so on, and then stop. He has not realized that combinations of more than two bottles might also produce the yellow color.

It is not until the child is in the stage of formal thought that he will exhibit a completely systematic approach to the problem. The child carefully records all of the trials to avoid duplication. He will attempt combinations involving two, three, or more bottles, and he will not stop after one successful attempt. The child will write down possible combinations in advance in order to avoid duplication. He will also realize that the combination 1 + 2 + 3 may not produce the same results as 3 + 2 + 1; he realizes that the order might also be a factor. *All* of these variables will not be considered by a child who is still in the concrete operations stage of development. A child in the stage of formal thought will also attempt to investigate the precise role played by each solution in forming the yellow color. He might ask, for example: "Will adding more of number 3 affect the color, or will adding less of G have any effect?" A child in the concrete operations stage would not attempt to answer questions such as these.

Again, it must be emphasized that you are *primarily* observing the *method* that the child uses in solving the problem; you are not concerned with his success at producing the yellow color. It would be interesting to compare the results you obtain from this task with the results you obtained on the conservation tasks described in Section I. Is there a relationship between a child's method of solving this task and his ability, or lack of ability, to conserve?

> Construct evaluation tasks to evaluate the ability of
> your students to *compare* several objects, places, or
> events.

Comparing is the ability to recognize and state similarities and differences
among objects, events, and places. The behavioral indicators of this skill are

1. The student selects and records characteristics that a set of objects have
    in common.
2. The student selects and records characteristics that the set of objects do
    not have in common.

What was said in Section IV about the materials for an evaluation task on
observing must be kept in mind here. The two or more objects, events, or places
used in the evaluation task must have definite similarities and differences if you
expect the child to indicate these similarities and differences in his responses.
Also, you may find that the child can identify differences, but has a difficult
time listing the similarities among the materials. The complexity of the objects,
events, or places and the age and development of the child must be taken into
consideration.

You must be careful to be as specific as necessary when you write the directions for your test. Will you say, "Compare this set of objects with that set," or
will you say, "Describe the things you can see that make the objects in this set
different from the objects in that set"? It is not just a matter of being clear or
specific, but also a matter of deciding how many clues you will supply in the
directions. The following Sample Evaluation Task may help you write tasks to
evaluate the skill of comparing.

A Sample Task to Evaluate
Comparing Several Objects

Instructional Objective

The student should be able to compare lima beans, raisins, and prunes soaked in
water with those not soaked in water.

Behavioral Indicators

1. The student selects and records five characteristics the edibles have in common.
2. The student selects and records three characteristics the edibles *do not* have in common.
3. The student measures and records the volume and weight of each edible, in metric units.
4. Using the five common characteristics, the three unlike characteristics, and the volume and the weight, the student compares each edible with every other.

Evaluation Task

The teacher should soak enough lima beans, raisins, and prunes in water before the test so that each student will have one sample of each item. Give the soaked and unsoaked samples to the students and ask them to record their comparisons.

Performance Criteria

Each student who has successfully attained the instructional objective must have completed the four behavioral indicators.

Activities

1. Construct an evaluation task to evaluate a primary-grade child's ability to *compare the height of a plant against the number of hours of light and dark under which it grew.*
   (a) Reread the definition of comparing and the behavioral indicators of this skill.
   (b) Write an evaluation task in which the child does not have to do any reading in order to complete the task.
   (c) State the objects and the directions the child will be given for the tasks.
2. Construct an evaluation task that evaluates a middle-grade student's ability to *compare the weight in water of a metal, a wooden, a plastic, and an aluminum foil block.*
   (a) Follow steps (a) through (c) above.
   (b) State your performance criteria for judging which students can compare; attempt to keep your criteria realistic for the middle-grade student.

> Construct evaluation tasks to evaluate the ability of your students to *identify* objects, events, and places.

Again, let's begin by considering one possible descriptive definition of the inquiry skill of *identifying.* It can be considered the ability to (a) name objects, events, and places, (b) select from several alternates the designated object, event, place, or sequence, (c) devise a method to measure the properties of an object.

Parts (a) and (b) of this definition may suggest the following behavioral indicators of this skill.

1. Name the object by using its conventional name, where a name exists.
2. Name the object by creating a reasonable name where no name exists.
3. Select from a set of similar objects the object to be identified.
4. Collect sufficient data to substantiate your identification.

Part (c) of the preceding definition may involve another set of behaviors, directly related to the student's past experience. He would probably have to know several methods of measuring the properties of objects before he acquired this behavior. Following is a sample of a task that could evaluate a student's ability to identify an unknown solution.

A Sample Task to Evaluate
Identifying an Unknown Solution

Instructional Objective
The student should be able to identify an unknown solution.

Behavioral Indicators
1. The student records the conventional name of the solution; *or*
2. He records a descriptive name of the solution.
3. The student selects a sample of the solution to be identified from among several unlabeled solutions.
4. The student writes a description of the techniques used to identify the solution.

Evaluation Task
Give the students a small vial containing a sample of a solution. This solution can be made by combining two solutions that were used in the lesson. Thus, the students should recognize enough properties of the new solution to identify it, employing techniques previously used.

Performance Criteria
The student must have recorded accurately
1. The conventional *or* a descriptive name for the solution.
2. The one vial out of three that contains a sample of the solution.
3. All the steps of the technique used to identify the solution.

Activities
1. Construct an evaluation task to judge a middle-grade student's ability to *identify a procedure for determining the purity of a water sample.*
   (a) Reread the definition of *identifying* and the behavioral indicators of this skill.
   (b) Write an evaluation task in the form of a multiple-choice test.
2. Construct a task to evaluate a middle-grade student's ability to *identify*

a procedure to determine whether a substance is an acid. Follow steps
(a) and (b) in Activity 1.

Construct a task to evaluate the ability of your students
to *classify* a group of objects, events, or places.

One possible definition of *classifying* is the ability to formulate groups based
upon one or more observed common properties and to construct a graph from
a table of data. Possible behavioral indicators of this skill are

1. The student identifies and names the observable properties of objects in
    a set.
2. He divides all the objects in the set into two subsets: a subset of these
    objects with an observable property and a subset of objects without this
    same observable property.
3. Using other observable properties, he continues to divide the objects into
    subsets, until each object from the original set is the only element in
    a subset.
4. He identifies the dependent and independent variables from the table
    of data.
5. He constructs and labels the y axis for the dependent variable and the x
    axis for the independent variable.
6. He marks on the graph the values for the ordered pairs (x, y) from the
    data found in the table.

As these inquiry skills become more complex, it becomes more important that
your test directions are clear and concise. Be sure, for example, that young children understand your directions for classifying. You may find that the first three
behavioral indicators just listed can be accomplished by young children, but
graphing, the last three behavioral indicators, may be a more appropriate activity
for the upper elementary-age students.

A Sample Task To Evaluate Classifying

Instructional Objective
The student should be able to classify by physical characteristics all the students
in the classroom who can taste the chemical on a piece of PTC paper.

Behavioral Indicators
1. The student divides a list of students who can taste PTC paper into two
    groups: those who have some physical characteristic in common—for example,
    eye color—and those who do not.
2. The student divides each of the above groups of "tasters" into two smaller
    groups, using another common physical characteristic. He continues this
    subdividing until the name of each "taster" is the only name in each sub-
    group.

Evaluation Task
The names of students who can taste the chemical on a piece of PTC paper are supplied to the students taking the test. The students are then asked to group, or classify, the tasters with respect to their physical characteristics.

Performance Criteria
When the student has successfully completed the behavioral indicators above, he has attained the instructional objective.

Activities

1. Construct an evaluation task to evaluate a middle-grade student's ability to *classify all the students in his classroom who have "detached" earlobes.*
   (a) Reread the definition of classifying and the behavioral indicators of this skill.
   (b) Include in your evaluation task the stipulation that the student must construct a simple graph of the number of students who do and the number who do not have the pertinent characteristics.
2. Construct an evaluation task to determine which students can classify a set of rocks according to various observable characteristics.
   (a) Reread part (a) of the definition of classifying and the behavioral indicators of this skill.
   (b) Include in your evaluation task the stipulation that the student must form groups based upon one or more common observable properties of the rocks.

Construct a task to evaluate the ability of your students to *measure* a specific characteristic of an object.

The skill of *measuring* is the ability to quantify observations, using a frame of reference. Possible behavioral indicators of this skill are

1. Select and describe clearly the frame of reference in your method of measuring.
2. State all steps to be followed in the method.
3. Record the measurement of several objects, using your method.

The frame of reference used in measuring a quantity may be a standard one, such as a metric ruler, or it may be devised, such as a system of units invented by the child. For instance, such an invented system could be "paper clips." The length of the table, in this system, is the number of paper clips that can be placed end to end down the length of the table.

Upper elementary-grade students can be encouraged to use more complex frames of reference. They should have the opportunity to use several kinds of balances, microscopes, graduated cylinders, various time clocks, and other measuring devices that help the student record in very accurate units the particular characteristics of an object or event.

A Sample Task to Evaluate Measuring

Instructional Objective
The student should be able to measure, in metric units, the volume of an irregularly shaped object.

Behavioral Indicators
1. The student states clearly all steps he used to find the volume of the object.
2. The student states the volume of water, in milliliters, found in the cylinder before and after the object was placed into the cylinder.
3. The student states in writing the relationship between milliliters and cubic centimeters.
4. The student states the volume of the irregularly shaped object in cubic centimeters.

Evaluation Task
(To use this as a test question, the teacher must be certain the students understand how to measure volumes of regularly shaped objects and of liquids.) Tell the students to devise a method, using their previous knowledge, to measure the volume of an irregularly shaped object. Volume must be determined in metric units.

Performance Criteria
When a student has successfully completed the behavioral indicators above, he has attained the instructional objective.

Activity
Construct a task to evaluate a middle-grade student's ability to *measure the amount of mold on a slice of bread.*
  (a)   Reread the definition of measuring and the suggested behavioral indicators of a person who can measure.
  (b)   In your evaluation task, restrict the children from using a conventional method of measuring. They may use common instruments, such as a ruler, but there should be some degree of uniqueness in the way they measure the amount of bread mold.

> Construct a task to evaluate the ability of your students to *infer.*

Inferring is the ability to construct a judgment from a set of observations and comparisons and to interpret a table of data. The following behavioral indicators of this skill may help you to select performance criteria:

1. The student constructs several inferences from a set of observations.
2. The student constructs several inferences from a set of comparisons.
3. The student identifies observations that support an inference.

4. The student describes and demonstrates additional observations needed to test alternative inferences.
5. The student identifies inferences that should be accepted, rejected, or modified on the basis of additional observations.

Interpreting a table of data is one possible way of making inferences; numbers in a table are a set of observations. This type of data, however, is more understandable to an upper elementary-grade student than to a primary-grade child. The younger child may be able to make inferences about things he can see, hear, feel, and compare, but not about abstract numbers. The following sample evaluation task does not expect the student to graph data.

A Sample Task to Evaluate Inferring

Instructional Objective
The student should be able to infer an explanation of his observations of iron filings sprinkled on a piece of paper placed on top of a magnet.

Behavioral Indicators
1. The student writes one inference based on the position of the iron filings and one inference based on the motion of the iron filings.
2. The student describes the observations that support each inference.
3. The student records alternative inferences for each inference in item 1.
4. The student describes additional observations that would be needed to accept these alternative inferences.

Evaluation Task
(See the sample task on page 190 for testing the skill of observation.)
From the observations gathered during that previous evaluation task, have students infer an explanation of the position(s) of the iron filings.

Performance Criteria
The students must record accurately
1. One inference based on the position of the iron filings.
2. One inference based on the motion of the iron filings.
3. All observations supporting each inference.
4. Alternative inferences and supporting observations.

Activities
1. Construct a task to evaluate a primary-grade child's ability to infer the location(s) of growth in the leaf and stem of a plant.
   (a) List the behaviors that indicate a child can infer the location of growth.
   (b) Construct an evaluation task that uses only spoken directions and pictures.
   (c) State the performance criteria to be completed for an acceptable performance.

2.   Construct an evaluation task to evaluate a middle-grade child's ability to
     infer methods of preventing an infection caused by bacteria. Follow the
     steps (a) through (c) in Activity 1.

> Construct a task to evaluate the ability of your students
> to *predict* future events.

The definition of *predicting* used here is the ability to state a future occurrence from previous observations. Some behavioral indicators of this skill include
the following:

1.   The student is able to distinguish between a prediction and a guess.
2.   The student can make predictions by extrapolating beyond the range of
     observed events.

In order to write tasks to evaluate the skill of prediction, you must be clear
about the difference between a guess and a prediction. A guess is a statement
based upon no data or very limited data; a prediction is a statement based upon
several data, and these data are observations or science principles that have been
verified.

The task should include materials to manipulate and specific directions that
caution the student to write down his previous observations and any other information upon which he bases his predictions. You will then have some evidence
as to whether the student was guessing or predicting. To collect more evidence,
you may also want the student to rank his predictions from the one in which he
places the most confidence to the one in which he places the least confidence.
For example, a student may predict the time of sunrise three months from now
to be either 6:03 or 6:00, depending on which of two methods he uses to arrive
at these different predictions. The 6:03 prediction was made after consulting the
current almanac for times of sunrise over the months before and after the particular date he is investigating. The 6:00 prediction was made by finding that in
weather bureau records the time of sunrise on the particular date was 6:00, 5:50,
or 6:01 for ten consecutive years, and 6:00 for seven of these ten years. He may
be more confident in the 6:00 prediction, therefore, than the 6:03 prediction.

Predictions are closely related to inferences; for example, observe any two
points on the upper graph in Figure B-1. These pieces of data were graphed after
the heights of plants on several days had been observed and recorded. In the upper
graph, the points are not connected. In the lower graph, these same points are
connected. Since no additional data were available between the times the upper
and lower graphs were made, an inference was formulated that when more data
are collected, the points of the graph will form a straight line.

A Sample Task to Evaluate
the Skill of Predicting

Instructional Objective
The student should be able to predict the location(s) of growth on the stem of
a plant.

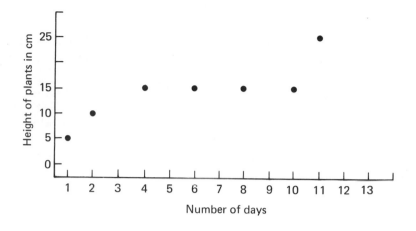

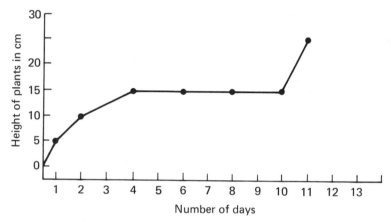

FIGURE B-1
Upper Graph Records the Collected Data; Lower Graph Records the Collected and Predicted Data.

Behavioral Indicators
1. The student marks all the places on the stem that will show growth.
2. The student explains the evidence supporting his prediction(s).
3. The student describes a test of his predictions of where growth will occur in a stem.

Evaluation Task
Give each student a small green plant. Have the student mark with India ink which sections of the stem will show growth. Students should also state the reasons why they mark particular sections.

Performance Criteria
The student must record accurately his predictions, the evidence supporting each prediction, and one way to test each prediction of the place(s) on a stem that will show growth.

Activities

1. Construct a task to evaluate the student's ability to predict the relative heating and cooling rates of equal weights of dry and wet sand, dry and wet dark sand, and water.
    (a) Require the students to graph the data that you supply.
    (b) Have the students arrange their predictions according to their confidence in them. Be sure they state observations upon which they made the predictions.
2. Construct a task to evaluate the students' ability to predict the effects of a carbon dioxide solution on marble and limestone. Follow only step (b) above.

> Construct a task to evaluate the ability of your students to *verify* predictions of future events.

Verifying is the ability to check or test the accuracy of a prediction. Some behavioral indicators of the skill of verifying are

1. The student describes the test(s) of his predictions.
2. The student performs the test(s) of his predictions.
3. The student compares the results of the test(s) with his original predictions.
4. The student accepts, rejects, or modifies his predictions according to the results of the tests.

The student makes predictions and devises tests to verify them. There are two possible ways of verifying the predictions: (1) wait and see if the event occurs as predicted or (2) observe some event that can only occur if the prediction is correct—for example, the student may say "the iodine will turn the white powder blue-black if starch is present in the powder." Tests of predictions, therefore, range from "wait and see" to the statement of an event that would occur if the prediction was correct. Once these tests have been conducted, predictions can be accepted, rejected, or modified based upon the test outcome.

**A Sample Task to Evaluate
Verifying Predictions**

Instructional Objective
The student should be able to verify his prediction about the location(s) of growth in the root of a plant.

Behavioral Indicators
1. The student describes one test to verify the predictions of location(s) of growth in a plant's root.
2. The student records all data and results while carrying out the test.
3. The student explains the similarities and differences between the test results and his predictions.

4. The student lists which predictions were correct and which were not.

Evaluation Task
(See preceding sample task for testing the skill of prediction.) After a week of allowing the roots of these plants to grow, return them to the students and ask them to verify the location(s) of growth in the root of a plant.

Performance Criteria
The student should record accurately
1. The test described; it must be a pertinent test for the predictions.
2. All the data and results.
3. Each prediction that was accepted, each that was rejected, and each that was modified.

Activities
1. Construct a task to evaluate the student's ability to verify his predictions of the similarities of plastic wrap, wax paper, and cellophane with dialysis tubing.
    (a) Reread the definition of verifying and the behavioral indicators of this skill.
    (b) Reread the task that you constructed to evaluate the student's ability to predict the similarities of plastic wrap, wax paper, and cellophane with dialysis tubing.
2. Construct a task to evaluate the student's ability to verify his predictions of what will happen when a sheet of aluminum foil and a ball of aluminum foil are placed on the surface of three different liquids. Repeat steps (a) and (b) above.

> Construct a task to evaluate the ability of your students to *hypothesize* an explanation for some specific event.

Hypothesizing is the ability to construct an answer to a problem. Behaviors indicating that a person can hypothesize include the following:

1. He recognizes a problem.
2. He constructs statements or hypotheses that answer the question posed in the problem.
3. He distinguishes between data that support a hypothesis and those that do not.
4. He constructs a test of the hypothesis.
5. He constructs a revision of the hypothesis based on data collected from the test of the hypothesis.

Hypothesizing may be a useful way of determining what problem a child recognizes in any given event. For example, consider Figure B-2. This picture may pose different problems or even *no* problem to a child. A child may recognize

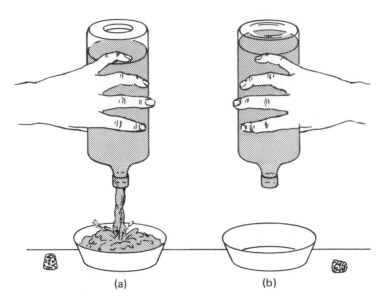

FIGURE B-2
This Pictured Situation Presents a Problem for Some Children.

that the water in the two bottles is behaving differently. However, one child may see no problem in the situation because he assumes that bottle b is stoppered in some way. A second child may see no problem in the situation because he knows the answer from previous experiences. Other children in the group may see several different problems.

Not only is the problem in the evaluation task important; as stated earlier, the directions given in the task are of equal importance. If you say, "Hypothesize an explanation for what you see happening in the situation," you must be clear about which problem each child is trying to answer. This particular ambiguity can be eliminated by being more specific in the test directions and by pointing out a specific problem the whole class must focus on while hypothesizing. The following sample task will illustrate these points.

A Sample Task to Evaluate Hypothesizing

Instructional Objective
The student should be able to formulate a hypothesis to explain the characteristics of the offspring resulting from the mating of selected fruit flies.

Behavioral Indicators
1. The student records at least one hypothesis to explain the characteristics of fruit fly offspring.
2. The student lists supportive data for his hypothesis.
3. The student describes and carries out a test of his hypothesis.
4. The student writes a revision of his hypothesis, if necessary, after the test is completed.

Evaluation Task
Supply the students with a list of the characteristics of the parent fruit flies. Give the students the offspring of these parents. Ask the students to formulate one hypothesis to explain the characteristics of the offspring.

Performance Criteria
The student should record
1. One hypothesis.
2. All data supporting his hypothesis.
3. The data and results of the test of his hypothesis.
4. One revision, if necessary, of his original hypothesis.

Activities

1. Construct a task to evaluate which students can formulate a hypothesis to explain the differences in the characteristics of plants grown in red, green, and blue light, sunlight, and darkness.
   (a) Reread the definition of hypothesizing and the suggested behavioral indicators of a person who can hypothesize.
   (b) Construct your evaluation task in such a way that students use plants to arrive at a hypothesis.
2. Construct a task to evaluate which students can formulate a hypothesis concerning the foods that mealworms prefer to eat.
   (a) Repeat step (a) above.
   (b) Construct an evaluation task with information and directions appropriate to a primary-grade child.

> Construct a task to evaluate the ability of your students to *isolate variables.*

Isolating variables is the ability to discriminate among factors which will, and will not, affect the outcome of an experiment, and to identify which factors are held constant and which factors are manipulated. Some behavioral indicators of this skill are

1. The student lists the independent variable(s) that will affect the event being studied.
2. The student specifies the manner and units in which the independent variable, the dependent variable, and all controlled variables will be measured.
3. The student designs and records all data and results to see the effect each variable has on the experiment.
4. The student identifies which variables from his list do affect the experiment, as suggested by the recorded data.

When planning your evaluation task, it is important to remember that the

FIGURE B-3
This Pictured Situation Presents a Problem for Some Children.

students being tested should identify as many of the variables as possible that will affect the outcome of an experiment. In order to do this, the student must have a clear understanding of what the experiment entails. Thus, when constructing an evaluation task for this particular inquiry skill, you will probably have to supply as complete a description as possible of the experiment or refer back to an experiment actually performed by the student.

To see if a primary-grade child has this skill, you will need to keep the experiment very simple. That is, it should be an experiment whose problem is stated and that comes directly from the experiences of the child. For example, you may present the child with the picture in Figure B-3 and then ask him to name the things in the picture that may explain why one set of boys can hold down the other set. Next, you can ask him to name the things he can *not* see, but can infer are present and affecting the pictured situation.

The second characteristic of a person who can isolate variables is the ability to quantify the independent and dependent variables. This is too difficult for a primary-grade child to do, but an upper elementary-grade student should be expected to quantify each variable.

The following definitions will help you to write your evaluation tasks.

The variables held constant are the *controlled variables.*
The variables manipulated are the *independent variables.*
The variables affected are the *dependent variables.*

A Sample Task to Evaluate Isolating Variables

Instructional Objective
The student should be able to isolate the variables that might affect the rate of motion of a pendulum.

Behavioral Indicators
1. The student predicts and lists the variables that will affect the rate of motion of a pendulum.
2. The student predicts and lists the variables that will not affect the rate of motion of a pendulum.
3. The student briefly describes the way he will measure and record these variables.
4. The student identifies the one variable he will manipulate and the variables he will hold constant for at least three tests.
5. The student records all data and all results of his tests.
6. The student identifies the variables that do affect the rate of motion of the pendulum.

Evaluation Task
Allow a pendulum, any weight or object suspended at the end of a string, to swing freely back and forth. With a stop watch, determine how quickly or slowly it is swinging. Ask the students to list the variables that affect the speed of the pendulum.

Performance Criteria
When the student has successfully performed the behavioral indicators above, he has attained the instructional objective.

Activities
1. Construct a task to evaluate the student's ability to isolate the variables that affect the growth of mold on bread.
    (a) Reread the definition of isolating variables and the behavioral indicators of a person who has this skill.
    (b) Construct your evaluation task so that the materials and directions are appropriate for a middle-grade child. Be sure that he specifies the manner and units in which the different variables will be measured.
2. Construct a task to evaluate the student's ability to isolate the variables affecting observed changes in an aquarium.

> Construct a task to evaluate the ability of your students to *construct an experiment.*

Experimenting is the ability to recognize and formulate a problem, plan and conduct a test of a hypothesis, and use the collected data to formulate possible answers to the problem. Behavioral indicators for this skill are the following:

1. The student states a problem containing an independent and a dependent variable.
2. The student identifies the variables that must be controlled and those that cannot be controlled.
3. The student performs the experiment.
4. The student makes conclusions based upon the collected data.

The ability to experiment encompasses many of the inquiry skills previously described. Since this skill is complex, the student may not possess it for many reasons. When constructing tasks to evaluate this skill, you must be careful to enumerate all the skills involved in experimenting and then keep each skill distinct from another. Thus, your test directions and materials will have to be detailed. The following sample task offers you some suggestions that can be used in developing an evaluation task for the skill of experimenting.

Evaluating this particular inquiry skill will probably take more time than the usual testing period. You should give your students more than just one day to demonstrate that they have acquired this skill.

A Sample Task to Evaluate Experimenting

Instructional Objective
The student should be able to plan and conduct an experiment regarding the rate of motion of a pendulum.

Behavioral Indicators
1. In one sentence, the student writes a problem regarding the rate of motion of a pendulum, including the independent and dependent variables.
2. The student lists the controlled and uncontrollable variables.
3. The student states his results and conclusions and identifies the data substantiating his conclusions.

Evaluation Task
This evaluation task can be part of the usual teaching situation. During one of the many opportunities that the students have to experiment, the teacher can collect the written report of the experiment and use this report to determine whether the student has (1) recognized and formulated a problem, (2) listed the controlled and uncontrolled variables, (3) stated his results and conclusions. He might also be asked to use the collected results to pose possible answers to the problem.

Performance Criteria
The student should record accurately the behaviors mentioned above.

Activity

Construct a task to evaluate the student's ability to plan and conduct an experiment regarding the behavior of *Euglena.*

(a) Reread the definition of experimenting and the behavioral indicators of a person who can experiment.

(b) Write your evaluation task so that your students would have about three or four weeks to demonstrate that they have the skill of experimenting.

APPENDIX C Evaluation Tasks for Affective Objectives

Instructional Objective
The student should demonstrate his *curiosity* about the contents of a sealed box.

Behavioral Indicators
Without direction from the teacher or from another student, the child should
1. Pick up the box and start to investigate what is in it.
2. Using his five senses, make observations regarding the contents of the box.
3. Ask the teacher if he can work with the box during free time.
4. Set up an identical box, with objects supplied by the teacher, in such a way that this second box has the same properties as the original box.

Evaluation Task
Several objects, including the sealed box, are placed on a table in the classroom. This sealed box contains various movable and unmovable objects known only to the teacher. The child can have, if he asks for it, a second cigar box and an assortment of objects. The child is told only that he can move around the room. The teacher then observes the child's behavior.

Performance Criteria
The child must be observed to have Behaviors 1, 2, 3, and 4.

Instructional Objective
The student should be open-minded about the variety of data collected by himself and by others while investigating the effect various weights have on a balanced meter stick.

Behavioral Indicators
1. The student accepts data from others that are contradictory to his own.
2. The student investigates the contradictory data as though they were his own.
3. The student accepts or rejects his own data after investigating the contradictory data.

Evaluation Task
Students can be given a meter stick, something upon which to balance the stick, and a variety of weights. Tell the students to balance the meter stick, then to place various weights on one side of the stick, and finally to rebalance the stick by placing weights on the other side of the stick. After students have had enough time to collect data, ask them to record their data on the chalkboard. Observe the students' reactions to the data.

Performance Criteria
1. The student expresses, verbally or nonverbally, an open-minded reaction to fellow students who have data contradictory to his own.
2. He plans and conducts an investigation using the data of his fellow student, accepting or rejecting his own data after the investigation.

PPENDIX D Evaluation of Teaching Tactics and Strategies

> Encourage your students to evaluate your teaching with a checklist and short essay.

Using questionnaires in the form of checklists and short essays can be an efficient way for your students to help you evaluate teaching. Students can give you useful information by describing how they view you as their teacher and how they perceive the atmosphere in the classroom. Since such questionnaires do ask for students' impressions and feelings, they should be interpreted carefully. On the following pages there are samples of questionnaires that fourth-, fifth-, or sixth-grade students might enjoy completing once or twice during the school year. Each sample has a short explanation at the top indicating how it is to be used. After you try samples such as these with your class, you may wish to devise a student evaluation questionnaire yourself.

Activities

1. With a checklist, determine how you and your students evaluate your teaching.
   (a) Have your students complete the first checklist.
   (b) Fill out the checklist yourself before you look at the student response.
   (c) Tally the number of responses that fall into each square on the checklist.
   (d) Compare the way you completed the checklist with the way your whole class completed it.
   (e) Make any appropriate inferences about your teaching from the tallies on the checklist.
2. Use a short essay questionnaire to determine how you and your students evaluate your teaching.
   (a) Repeat steps (a) through (e) above, but substitute the short essay questionnaire instead of the checklist.

(b) Compare your students' responses on the checklist with their responses on the short essay questions.

Date_____

My Teacher

Pretend that you could *change* your teacher in some way. For each number, check the box that *best tells how you would like your teacher to act. There are no right or wrong answers.*

	My teacher should do this.	My teacher does this now.	My teacher shouldn't do this.
1. Help me with my work.			
2. Yell at me.			
3. Make sure my work is done.			
4. Let me decide how I will work.			
5. Smile and laugh.			
6. Make me behave.			
7. Make me work hard.			

Clues About Classroom Life

To make life more interesting and important for everyone in class, you need to contribute your ideas of what should be improved. What things happen that shouldn't happen? What ought to happen but doesn't? Try to imagine you are a detective looking for clues to a "good day" and a "bad day" in this class. Jot down what you might look for or might see to answer these questions. *There are no right or wrong answers.*

What things happen that tell you you've had a good day in this class?
1. _____
2. _____
3. _____
4. _____
5. _____

What things happen that tell you the class is not going the way it should or the way you would like it to?

1. _____

2. _____

3. _____

4. _____

5. _____

What are some things that should happen a lot more than they do to make it a better class for learning and having fun?

1. _____

2. _____

3. _____

4. _____

5. _____

> With taping and observation by others, evaluate your teaching.

Checklists can help you to evaluate your teaching tactics and strategies.

Activities

1. Make a tape (audio-visual or audio) of science lessons. Evaluate your teaching with the help of a checklist.
    (a) Make a tape of at least two science lessons.
    (b) Select three checklists from those on the following pages and see how many characteristics on the checklists you can find in the recording of your teaching.
2. Ask another teacher to sit in on several science lessons and evaluate your teaching with the help of checklists.
    (a) Use the same three checklists you used in (b) in Activity 1.
    (b) Compare the results of the checks you made in Activity 1 with those made by your fellow teacher.

√ Checklist for Informing (Lecture Method)

> To present new information to students from several sources, excluding the test.

Place a √ in the left-hand column each time the teacher manifests the indicated behavior.

Verbal Behaviors

_____ Gets students' attention before beginning.
_____ Reviews previous day's material.
_____ Presents material in a logical sequence.
_____ Repeats important ideas several times.
_____ Relates new material to material previously studied.
_____ Relates new material to student experiences.
_____ Reviews day's important ideas.

Written Behaviors

_____ Writes important ideas on board and/or uses overhead projector.
_____ Writes clearly on the board.
_____ Writes material on the board in an orderly form.
_____ Supplements
   1. Diagrams.
   2. Handouts.
   3. Transparencies.
   4. Demonstrations.
   5. Models.
   6. Other (list).

Physical Movement

_____ Moves freely about the room.
_____ Looks directly at most students when talking or listening.
_____ Presents material spontaneously, not depending heavily on notes.

√ Checklist for a Review

To review assigned material, the day's lesson, a chapter, or a unit.

Place a √ in the left-hand column each time the teacher manifests the indicated behavior.

Types of Questions

_____ 1. Questions require students to recall information previously learned, or to recall ideas or events from experience.
_____ 2. Questions require students to describe observations about a demonstration or experiment just completed.
_____ 3. Questions require students to process data in a manner new to the student—that is, classify, infer, predict, hypothesize, and so on.
_____ 4. Questions require students to devise a test of a hypothesis or prediction just developed or presented in class.

Types of Reactions

———— 5. Prompts students when they cannot answer initial question.
———— 6. Rephrases questions not clear to student.
———— 7. Accepts student responses.
———— 8. Rejects student responses.
———— 9. Asks student to extend or rephrase a statement he just made.
———— 10. Asks student to give evidence to support statement he just made.
———— 11. Asks one student to evaluate the response of another student.

√ Checklist of Discussions

To discuss the results of an experiment or demonstration.

Place a √ in the left-hand column each time the teacher manifests the indicated behavior.

Types of Questions

———— 1. Questions require students to recall information previously learned, or to recall ideas or events from experience.
———— 2. Questions require students to describe observations about a demonstration or experiment just completed.
———— 3. Questions require students to process data in a manner new to the student—to classify, infer, predict, verify prediction, or experiment.
———— 4. Questions require students to devise a test of a hypothesis or prediction developed or presented in class.

Types of Reactions

———— 5. Prompts students when they cannot answer initial question.
———— 6. Rephrases questions not clear to student.
———— 7. Accepts student responses.
———— 8. Rejects student responses.
———— 9. Asks student to extend or rephrase a statement he just made.
———— 10. Asks student to give evidence to support a statement he just made.
———— 11. Asks one student to evaluate the response of another student.

√ Checklist for Type I
Laboratory Activity or Field Trip

To provide an opportunity to practice a psychomotor skill, such as operating a double-pan balance, measuring length, weight, and so on.

Place a √ in the left-hand column each time the teacher manifests the indicated behavior.

_____ Develops the need for such a skill.

_____ Provides adequate practice for the skill.

_____ Provides immediate feedback to the student about his individual development with the skill.

√ Checklist for Type II
Laboratory Activity or Field Trip

To verify a science concept or principle already known to the student.

Place a √ in the left-hand column each time the teacher manifests the indicated behavior.

_____ Relates the investigation to material currently being studied.

_____ Describes and/or clarifies the procedures for data collecting.

_____ Describes pitfalls and gives precautions.

_____ Guides students' data collecting procedures.

_____ Determines students' understanding of the objectives.

_____ Encourages students to continue on the task at hand.

_____ Collects data from students and arranges it so that the science concepts or principles can be verified.

_____ Shows how the verified concepts or principles can be applied.

_____ Shows how these concepts or principles relate to other principles and concepts.

√ Checklist for Type III
Laboratory Activity or Field Trip

To have the student discover a relationship not previously known.

Place a √ in the left-hand column each time the teacher manifests the indicated behavior.

_____ Relates investigation to material currently being studied.

_____ Describes and/or clarifies the procedures for data collecting.

_____ Describes pitfalls and gives precautions.

_____ Guides students' data collecting procedures.

_____ Determines students' understanding of the objectives.

_____ Encourages students to work.

_____ Collects data from students and arranges it in a manner suitable for discovering the concepts and principles.

_____ Probes and clarifies student responses regarding the discovered relation-ship.

_____ Shows how new relationship fits in with material currently being studied.

_____ Relates new relationship to concepts and/or principles previously studied.

√ Checklist for Type IV
Laboratory Activity or Field Trip

To practice skills of data collecting and processing.

Place a √ in the left-hand column each time the teacher manifests the indicated behavior.

_____ Relates the investigation to the material currently being studied.

_____ Describes some necessary precautions.

_____ Acts as a resource person for _guiding_ students.

_____ Guides students' evaluation of
    (a)   Data collected pertinent to the problem.
    (b)   Data processed to solve the problem.

√ Checklist for Type V
Laboratory Activity or Field Trip

To allow students to integrate the inquiry skills already learned, or to evaluate students' use of them, through a science investigation meaningful to students.

Place a √ in the left-hand column each time the teacher manifests the indicated behavior.

_____ Helps individual students clarify their chosen problem.

_____ Acts as a resource person, a patient and careful listener, and as a sounding board with which students can clarify their own ideas.

_____ Individually helps each student assess whether his conclusions are based on data collected.

_____ Individually helps each student extend his investigation.

√ Checklist for Demonstration

To illustrate a science concept or principle, a psycho-motor skill, or some inquiry skill.

Place a √ in the left-hand column each time the teacher manifests the indicated behavior.

_____ Has the equipment for the demonstration ready when needed.

_____ Makes sure that everyone in the class can see the equipment.
_____ Makes the demonstration a clear illustration of the concept or principle
to be taught.

√ Checklist for a Quest

To develop concepts or principles from data students
have *not* collected themselves.

Place a √ in the left hand column each time the teacher manifests the indicated
behavior.
_____ Presents background information before the quest.
_____ Presents data in one of the following forms:
    (a)   Chart or graph.
    (b)   A sequence of pictures.
    (c)   A table.
_____ The questioning sequence was
    (a)   Data collecting.
    (b)   Data processing.

Index

Index